T0373287

SAINT INNOCENT
APOSTLE TO AMERICA

T0373367

SAINT INNOCENT

Apostle to America

PAUL D. GARRETT

ST VLADIMIR'S SEMINARY PRESS
CRESTWOOD, NEW YORK

This book as been reprinted
in honor of the fortieth anniversary of
METROPOLITAN PHILIP SALIBA'S
archpastoral and apostolic labors in the
Antiochian Archdiocese of North America

LIBRARY OF CONGRESS CATALOGING-IN-PUBLICATION DATA

Garrett, Paul D, 1948-
    St. Innocent, apostle to America.
    Includes bibliographical references.
    1. Innokentii, Saint, Metropolitan of Moscow, 1797-1879. 2. Christian
saints—Russia—Biography.
    I. Title.

BX597.I55G37   281.9'092'4 [B]   79-19634
ISBN 0-913836-60-5

copyright © 1979 by
ST VLADIMIR'S SEMINARY PRESS
575 Scarsdale Road, Crestwood, New York 10707
1-800-204-2665
www.svspress.com

First printed 1979, reprinted 2006

ISBN 0-913836-60-5
ISBN 978-0-913836-60-6

PRINTED IN THE UNITED STATES OF AMERICA

TO JUDY, TANIA, MICHELE AND MATTHEW

TABLE OF CONTENTS

FOREWORD

It is a privilege to contribute the foreword to this book on the life of our holy father and hierarch, Innocent, the first bishop of Alaska, the enlightener of the Aleuts and apostle to America. The ministry of St. Innocent has a personal significance for me, for it was in his first diocese that I began my own archpastoral ministry, a ministry which provided me with both a vision of the past and a vision of the future of the life of Orthodoxy in America.

Upon arriving in Sitka, I was immediately confronted with the reality of a past that was still very much alive. The cathedral church built by Innocent had recently been destroyed by fire and one of my first tasks was to assume leadership in the search for funds to build the replica church which now stands on the original site. The entire Alaskan community rallied behind the project, for it was truly felt that an essential part not only of their history but of their present life was lacking as long as this church no longer stood in the center of Sitka, the former capital of the state.

The connection with the past was not limited to the cathedral building. As I entered my first episcopal residence in Sitka, I was surrounded by the relics of Innocent's life. The building itself was the 1842 Mission House, established by Bishop Innocent as the first Orthodox Ecclesiastical Seminary on this continent. In it was his chapel, containing his mitre and the precious vessels from the cathedral that many persons had risked their lives to save. The small bishop's apartment held some of the fine furniture handcrafted by Innocent, a mantel clock and a wooden calendar which he devised to help the native peoples to count the passage of time and identify the days of the church feasts. These were some of the physical artifacts that stood as constant reminders of his life and presence in the place that was my first home in Alaska.

As a result of my pastoral visitations and personal study of the archives and published books on the life of Bishop Innocent, I began to realize the breadth and depth of this unique pastor and missionary. Although he was a person of humble beginnings with only a lower seminary education, Innocent proved in his life to be a highly talented, knowledgeable leader—something in fact, of a "renaissance man." As this book notes, he was to reveal and utilize many and varied talents during his pastoral ministry, serving as carpenter, watchmaker, inventor, linguist and original translator, naturalist and noted ethnographer, sociologist, missionary, teacher and scholar, as well as pastor and shepherd of his flock. His physical exploits alone, in traveling throughout the territories of his diocese by dog-sled across great expanses or in a one-man kayak through rough freezing waters, reveal something of his faith, courage and inner stamina.

It was with great joy, therefore, that the Orthodox Church in America assisted in the preparation of the documents which led to the official recognition and canonization of St. Innocent on October 6, 1977, by the Holy Synod of the Church of Russia. We are grateful to all those persons, past and present, who have contributed to the documentation and research of the life and works of St. Innocent, to St. Vladimir's Seminary Press for the publication of this important work, and especially to Mr. Paul Garrett, who has prepared this excellent account of our first archpastor and teacher in America. It is my hope that all who read this work will be drawn to the personality and power of this man who truly earned the title of "enlightener and apostle of America."

> † *Theodosius*
> *Archbishop of New York*
> *Metropolitan of All-America and Canada*

INTRODUCTION

Work on this book began soon after word was received from Moscow that the name of the first[1] Ruling Bishop of what was destined to become the Orthodox Church in America had been added to the calendar of the saints. Initially the book was to haved been a condensed[2] translation of *Innokentii, Mitropolit Moskovskii i Kolomenskii po ego sochineniiam pis'mam i razskazam sovremennikov* [Innocent, Metropolitan of Moscow and Kolomna, According to His Writings, Letters, and the Stories of His Contemporaries] by Ivan Barsukov (Moscow: 1883). Soon, however, it became clear that this would be inadequate. Barsukov all but admits that this would be so in his preface, where he writes (p. vii):

> Four years have passed since this worker for the Faith of Christ fell asleep in God, and it seems to us that the time has come to survey his life and works. Inasmuch as we were able, we have collected into one book the scattered data concerning him, which we hope will simplify the work of a future biographer.

Indeed, Barsukov himself was not content to stop there, but continued for the next twenty years collecting materials on this great hierarch which he eventually published in six volumes.[3] Turning to these, we found them often superior in

[1] Or second, if Bp. Joasaph, who died before reaching his See in Kodiak, be counted.

[2] Condensed because of its length (769 pages plus appendices).

[3] *Tvoreniia* [Works] in three volumes (Moscow: 1886-1888), including his "Autobiographical Notes," a large number of sermons, speeches and writings, including *An Indication of the Pathway Into the Kingdom of Heaven* and *Notes on the Islands of the Unalaska Region*; and *Pis'ma* [Letters] in three volumes (St. Petersburg: 1897-1901).

11

content, style and clarity to those included in the early biography. (For instance, the "Asian Years" were clarified and
augmented from materials furnished Barsukov by Bp. Dionysius of Yakutsk [Dmitrii Khitrov] only in 1885.) When
subsequently another source, Innocent's *Bumagi* [Papers] in
three volumes,[4] apparently unknown to Barsukov and hence
never published, was found to augment the narrative of the
saint's crucial early years in America (1821-1840), it was
decided to work directly from the primary sources rather than
be bound to Barsukov's rather limited initial collection.

The Thus freed from the translator's duty to render insofar
as possible both the word and the spirit of the original intact—
which in the case of Barsukov's extremely florid style would
have made for difficult reading in twentieth-century English—
it became possible to attempt to clarify those points in
St. Innocent's life which Barsukov, writing for his contemporaries in nineteenth-century Russia, quite naturally took for
granted. To this end secondary literature[5] on the period, and

[4] Obtained in microfilm copy from the Library of Congress, made from
original manuscripts once held by the Alaska Historical Library and Museum,
Juneau, and now preserved at St. Herman's Orthodox Theological Seminary,
Kodiak.

[5] Select bibliography: (1) General-interest literature on Alaska: H.
Chevigny, *Lord of Alaska* (Portland: 1951) and *Russian America* (New
York: 1965). (2) General history of Alaska: H. Bancroft, *History of Alaska*
(New York: Hafner, 1970). (3) Descriptions of travels, explorations etc. in
Alaska and Siberia: I. Barsukov, *Graf Nikolai Nikolaevich Murav'ev-Amurskii*
(2 v. in 3, Moscow: 1891) G. Keenan, *Siberia and the Exile System* (2 v. in
1, New York: Praeger, 1970); O. Kotzebue, *A Voyage of Discovery Into the
South Sea and Beering's* [sic] *Straits* (2 v., New York: Da Capo, 1967) and
A New Voyage Round the World in the Years 1823-1826 (2 v., New York:
Da Capo, 1967); A. Kruzenstern, *Voyage Round the World in the Years
1803, 1804, 1805, and 1806* (2 v., New York: Da Capo, 1968); F. Lütke,
*Voyage autour du monde, exécuté par ordre de Sa Majesté Nicolas Ier, sur la
corvette La Séniavine dans les années 1826-1829* (3 v., New York: Da Capo,
1971); H. Michael, ed., *Lieutenant Zagoskin's Travels in Russian America,
1842-1844* (Toronto: University of Toronto Press, 1967), and G. Sarychev,
*Account of a Voyage of Discovery to the Northeast of Siberia, the Frozen
Ocean, and the Northeast Sea* (New York: Da Capo, 1969). (4) Historical
studies of Russian America: S. Federova, *The Russian Population in Alaska and
California, Late 18th Century-1867* (Kingston, Ont.: Limestone Press, 1973);
J. Gibson, *Feeding the Russian Fur Trade* (Madison: University of Wisconsin
Press, 1969) and *Imperial Russia in Frontier America* (New York: Oxford,
1976); F. Hatch, *The Russian Advance into California* (San Francisco: R & E
Research Associates, 1971); R. Makarova, *Russians on the Pacific, 1743-1799*

on Russian America in particular, was consulted in an effort to make clear how this man's life was typical and normal in its day and how it was unique. (Without a doubt the comforts of modern America certainly distort our perspective on the "rigors" of the past, falsely over-emphasizing and discounting them simultaneously.) This is particularly important if we are to perceive in this man — truly unique in terms of the enormity of the things he accomplished and endured—an example perhaps more apt and accessible for us today than any other figure from traditional Orthodox societies of the past.

To accomplish this we have broken with what is apparently scholarly "canon" by keeping to a minimum the use of elements which for English readers would make St. Innocent appear unncessarily "foreign." We have avoided the use of technical terms (e.g., *promyshlenniki* or *baidarka*) usually found in literature on early nineteenth-century Russian America. Place and given names are likewise given in what was considered to be their most familiar English form ("Alaska" rather than *Aliaska*, "Innocent" rather than *Innokentii*); measurements are in the American system (miles rather than *versts*). This "unscholarly" decision made, it likewise followed that footnotes and citations be held to a minimum; only where the ultimate source is not one of Barsukov's seven volumes is mention made of this.

Guided by this same desire to make our portrait of St. Innocent as clear and well-rounded as possible, a second decision was made: to divide the work into two volumes. The first volume is a biography strictly speaking; therefore, only those quotations from the hierarch's writings which could be included without destroying the continuity of the chronology found inclusion here. Those which by reason of

(Kingston, Ont.: Limestone Press, 1975), and P. Tikhmenev, *A History of the Russian-American Company* (Seattle: University of Washington Press, 1978). (5) Works of relevant church history: G. Freeze, *The Russian Levites* (Cambridge: Harvard University Press, 1977); Bp. Gregory (Afonsky) of Alaska, *A History of the Orthodox Church in Alaska (1794-1917)* (Kodiak: St. Herman's Theological Seminary, 1977), and N. Sokolov and B. Pivovarov, "A Short History of the Diocese of Irkutsk," *Journal of the Moscow Patriarchate* (1977:12, pp. 58-69). Additional sources actually quoted will be found in footnotes to the text.

length or subject matter could not be conveniently fitted into the narrative will be found in the second volume of "Selected Writings."

Having discussed why methodologically it was necessary for us to abandon Ivan Barsukov's earliest attempt at a biography of St. Innocent, we must nevertheless acknowledge our tremendous debt to him. Undiscouraged by the hierarch's warning that most of his papers had probably already perished at sea or in an accidental fire which struck his cell in Yakutsk on February 23, 1858 (a loss which hardly disturbed St. Innocent, who declared, "they would have burned up at any rate with the earth in the apocalypse!")—Barsukov persevered, contacting Innocent's surviving children and known correspondents in order to recover the impressive 2843 pages of published material that we now possess. (One must note, however, that with rare exceptions the correspondence *to* Innocent is entirely lost.)

This said, it should be clear that any work on this great hierarch of both the American and the Russian Churches must in large measure stand as a monument to the humble and devoted man who in his preface (pp. vi-viii) makes his own the words of Epiphanius the Wise, biographer of St. Stephen of Perm, himself one of Russia's greatest missionaries:

> I, a poor, unworthy, and wretched man, seized by desire and moved with love, wished to write... in recollection and in memory of the good and marvelous life of our bishop... [and] sought out and collected [things] here and there, putting down about his life things heard abroad and seen by his disciples... And there are some things which my own eyes have seen; others which I have obtained from having spoken with him, and have grown accustomed to. The rest I asked of old men, as the Holy Scriptures say, "Ask your father and he will tell you..."

PART ONE

THE PREPARATION

CHAPTER 1

CHILDHOOD

"The Lord guides a man safely in
the way he should go."
—Ps. 37:23

Already towards the end of August, light snows begin to
dust the hill country north of Lake Baykal. The spongy earth
of the forests takes on a firmer step, and with the demise of
the delicate wildflowers which for three short months bring
it life and color, the landscape returns to its more characteristic
hue. In each of the multitude of tiny far-flung villages which
dot this region of Siberia, the just-ripened hay and garden
vegetables are feverishly laid in as the people face once again
the rigors of winter.

In the year 1797 one such village paused in its autumnal
preparations for a celebration of life and joy, as on August 26,[1]
a son was born to the parish sacristan in Anga. In strict
accordance with the ancient custom of commending newborns
to the protection of one of the saints commemorated on the
eighth day after birth, Eusebius and Thekla Popov named
their first-born son John, in honor of John the Faster, Patriarch
of Constantinople. At his baptism John's sponsors were Savva
Chubashev, a peasant, and Justiniana Tiurkova, the wife of
a Cossack.

Belonging to a clerical family, the young boy was by the
facts of ecclesiastical life at the turn of the nineteenth century

[1] This account, provided decades later by St. Innocent himself, differs
from the official parish records which state that he was born on September 11,
1797. (Note that here and throughout this work dates are given according to
the Julian [or "Old"] Calendar then in force in the Russian Empire.)

virtually sure to follow a life of service to the Church. He would possibly—even probably—serve in the same Church of the Holy Prophet Elijah in which he had been baptized and in which his father and uncle Dmitrii, the parish deacon, both served.

To do so he not only would have to learn to chant the services, but would need to become one of those rare people in the Siberian backcountry who could read and write. And so, even before he reached the age of five, John's education was begun at home. Eusebius had been ill for some time, and was forced increasingly to take to bed for long periods of time. Whenever his son was not busy tending to the garden or doing his other chores, he would call him over to his bedside, open a large old Psalter or other liturgical book, and listen attentively as the young boy pronounced the ancient sacred words. John's studies progressed well for about a year, until one day in late August of 1803, as the parish records state, Eusebius Popov, having "confessed his sins, received Holy Communion, was anointed with oil, and died at the age of forty."

The light snow which covered Eusebius' fresh grave heralded the coming hardships. John later recalled that the pressures of harvest time had not allowed them to indulge their grief. Beyond that, the widow was suddenly alone with two daughters and a son to care for in addition to the baby she was still expecting. A small measure of relief came when her brother-in-law, Deacon Dmitrii Popov, offered to care for his nephew and took him into his own home. There John once again took up the heavy old tomes, and by the age of seven (or perhaps, he himself says modestly, eight) he had progressed sufficiently to be allowed to read the epistle at Christmas Day Liturgy in his parish church. The little boy in rough homemade clothes touched the parishioners' hearts with his clear and intelligent reading of the text, and inspired in his mother the hope that her eldest son might be confirmed by the bishop in his father's position, and thus provide the family with some income. John, however, was still far too young for this to be allowed, and stricter regulations by this time required that even sacristans receive some formal seminary training before being appointed to a parish. Therefore John went on studying with his uncle, who—as a watchmaker and self-trained mechanic as well as a deacon—directed his nephew's education into new, fascinating, and practical fields.

In 1806, after repeated denials of her requests to have her son appointed sacristan in Anga, Thekla obtained his appointment on a rare (but miserly) stipend to the diocesan seminary in Irkutsk. And so, at the age of nine and a half, John Popov left his tiny native village for the first time, bound for the largest industrial and commercial city in the region. It happened, however, that John was not to be left alone in this new world of his, for at the same time his aunt died, and the widowed Deacon Dmitrii took monastic vows with the name David, and was likewise transferred to Irkutsk. There, ordained to the holy priesthood and assigned to the Bishop's Residence, he was able to continue looking after his beloved nephew.

His presence must have brought no small comfort to the young boy, for adjustment to seminary life at the time was liable to be traumatic. Peter the Great's *Ecclesiastical Regulation* of 1721, which still governed clerical life and training, candidly admitted that "such a way of life appears to young people to be irksome, even prisonlike, but for those who become accustomed to living in this way—be it only for a single year— it will prove most agreeable." In spirit it was monastic; in regimen, military: times were assigned to the seminarians for everything they did—when to sleep and when to rise; when to pray, when to study, when to go to the refectory, when to relax (and how)—and so forth. The upperclassmen, or "Commanders" as they were termed, were assigned to police the conduct of their juniors, and punishment was most exacting for misconduct in church or tardiness in arriving—even if this meant trudging through –60°F weather to reach the cathedral in time for matins at 4 A.M.! Academic mediocrity was routinely forgiven in hopes that with time the young men might improve, but misconduct in church was unforgivable. Classes met in the same crowded rooms in which the boys lived, ate and slept.

From the time it opened in 1780 the Irkutsk Seminary had followed the standard of the Latin grammar school which

Peter had imported to Russia from the West. Its chief intent
was to mold the seminarians into a cultural elite within Russian society. Therefore, after several years of preparatory
training in reading and writing Church Slavonic, in singing
and in basic catechism, the young men turned most of their
attention to the thankless task of learning classical Latin, a
course of study requiring—in theory—six years but often in
practice many more. The niceties of Latin grammar, rhetoric
and composition behind them, they spent their last two years
of formal education studying some very scholastic and im-
practical philosophy and theology. By the time John entered
the seminary some welcome changes had been introduced
into the curriculum: there was a greater emphasis on Russian
(and even a bit of Greek) somewhat simpler textbooks were
put in use, and purely religious instruction had been woven
throughout the course. Nevertheless the studies remained a
heavy yoke upon the students' necks. While the teachers were
for the most part sincere, teaching (as John was later to
recall) less by what they said than by what they did: by their
example of sincere piety, regular church attendance, fasting
and general decorum in public, they were often themselves
but recent seminary graduates awaiting choice appointments
or ordinary parish priests in need of additional income, and
the quality of instruction frequently suffered for this reason.
Untrained to utilize any other teaching method, they often
resorted simply to reading aloud, in Latin or Greek, entire
volumes to their bewildered pupils, expecting that they
memorize these word-for-word. No written examinations
were given. Instead, monthly "convocations" were held, when
all of the students were gathered before the administration
to have their knowledge and behavior scrutinized. A general
atmosphere of fear pervaded these sessions, heightened
doubtless by the presence in the doorway of a particularly mean
and ugly fellow nicknamed "Larva" by the students, who
brandished a menacing thatchet of rods.

Under such conditions it is scarcely surprising that many—
indeed most—of the young men sought their freedom as soon
as possible. Many simply fled, knowing full well the severe
punishment which awaited them if—and when—they were

apprehended and returned. Others took advantage of the desperate shortage of sacristans in the rural parishes of the diocese. Accepting the lifelong prospect of drastically reduced salaries and other inconveniences which accompanied such positions, they abandoned the seminary legally and in droves. Others, hoping at least to relieve the poverty in which they existed, accepted part-time assignments in urban parishes near enough the seminary to enable them to continue their education. Still others married during their final year and obtained positions in the city as deacons or priests. Students coming to class in the clerical cassock were by no means an uncommon sight. Only a tiny minority of the seminarians actually graduated, but it was for them that the choicest assignments in the diocese were reserved.

John Popov was ill-prepared to enter such an environment. His character reflected his simple upbringing and the disruption of family life which marked his early years. His clothing, a bizarre mismatch of formal and informal, inadvertently set him apart from his fellow students, and this, coupled with his extreme aloofness, forced him to endure their taunts and insults for many years, until his natural abilities began to win them over. In spite of all, John was an excellent student, and after each monthly convocation he received the marks *"eleganter," "egregie," "eximie"* ("very good," "superior," "excellent").

In 1814 the Irkutsk Seminary received a new rector. Archimandrite Paul (Nekrasov) was a pleasant man, intelligent and well-educated, who soon perceived the dire need to improve the dismal state of the institution. He made friends with the Governor of Irkutsk, Nicholas Treskin, and mentioned once in passing how insufficient was the annual funding (some 2000 rubles) that he received from the Holy Synod, especially since there was no trained economist on the staff. "If you'd like," offered the Governor, "I could put at your disposal a young, active, keen-witted Cossack, Poluektov, who I hope should be able to straighten out the seminary's finances to your satisfaction—and the students' as well." Fr. Paul eagerly accepted the proposal and assigned John Popov to assist Poluektov with the paper work. Soon their work brought perceptible improvement in the material and spiritual life of the seminary, although as John himself was later to recall, "I studied well but never even tasted fresh rye bread (without the chaff) until I graduated from seminary."

Another of Fr. Paul's decisions had a direct effect on John. The rector found that there were simply too many "John Popovs" and similarly common names[2] in his school. Some way of differentiating them all had to be found. Setting his mind to the task, the priest eventually found one excuse or another for having to change the last name of nearly every one of his students, either in order to alleviate confusion in the class rolls, or to eliminate names which he found particularly unsavory. At first he simply added to each of the "Popovs" an indication of where he came from. Thus our John became "John Popov-Anginskii,"—as distinct from "John Popov-Tunkinskii," "John Popov-Taiturskii," and all the rest. But the rector enjoyed too high a reputation for ingenuity for there to be much likelihood of this solution remaining final. And indeed, it did not. From the very day of his arrival in Irkutsk, Fr. Paul had been hearing stories about the late Bp. Benjamin,[3] whose impressive outward appearance and enlightened mind had left a profound mark upon his flock, and he was decided that it would be most appropriate if this hierarch's memory were preserved by assigning his name to one of the students. John Popov-Anginskii was judged to be the student most deserving this honor, and so from that time forward he was known as John Veniaminov, from *Veniamin*, the Russian form of Benjamin.

John matured into a formidable, athletically-built young man, eventually standing about six foot three inches in boots— quiet and pensive, yet filled with energy, utterly incapable of sitting idle for any length of time. Little by little he trained himself to become an assiduous worker, diligent in every undertaking, sober-minded yet clever, exacting and thorough— traits owed in large measure to his early training in mechanics. The uncle who imparted to young John his technical abilities

[2] Popov, meaning "Priestly," would have been in the seminary milieu about as common as "John Smith" is in American society at large.

[3] Died July 8, 1814.

also stamped upon his very nature a passion for working with machines, as can be seen from the following incident.

Michael II, the new Bishop of Irkutsk, decided to have a large clock installed in the cathedral bell-tower, and invited a master watchmaker named Klim to do the work. Klim was given quarters near the bishop's own residence—near enough, in fact for it to be observed that one of the seminarians was paying frequent visits to the watchmaker (and probably thereby neglecting his studies). The seminary administration was duly informed and the matter came under investigation. When it was discovered, however, that the visitor was John Veniaminov, one of the best and hardest-working students, the bishop did nothing to interfere with the visits. For his part, Klim was more than pleased at having such a gifted apprentice, and assigned him to carve the gears and cogwheels. Thus, young Veniaminov was able to satisfy his natural curiosity while mastering a trade which would serve him well in later life.

Between classes and visits to Klim's workshop, John indulged in one of his favorite activities: reading. Bp. Benjamin had bequeathed his library to the seminary, and among its many titles John found a Russian translation of *Continuing Magic; or, The Wizardry of Nature Used For Profit and Amusement* by Johann Samuel Halle. He read it eagerly and put into practice the things he learned. Using a discarded knife and an awl found in the trash, John set about shaping mountings, wheels and hands from scraps and splinters of wood until one day, much to the delight of his fellow seminarians, there appeared in one of the rooms a water clock—in those days quite a rarity in Eastern Siberia! Its face was a piece of writing paper; its "ticking" was produced by water dripping from a hollowed-out birch root into a tin pan suspended below. On the hour a bell chimed. This invention was quickly followed by a pocket-sized sun-dial so simple in construction that many of his companions soon proudly owned one. In this way John's fellows ceased to make fun of him and unwittingly began to admire—and even like—him.

CHAPTER 2

DECISION

Irkutsk stands on the right bank of the Angar River at the junction of its tributary, the Ushakov, some forty miles north of Lake Baykal. Just over three miles away across the river stands the picturesque Monastery of the Lord's Ascension, where Fr. Paul maintained his residence.

It was the rector's custom early every morning to cross the Angar on a pendulum-like ferry boat, spend the day at work at the seminary, and return home late in the evening. Normally the river cooperated with his plans. A tranquil waterway, yet swift enough that December temperatures plunging to −35°F often left its center still free from ice, it utterly changed its temperament in springtime when, fed by snows melting in the hill country where water cannot penetrate the permafrost just below the earth's surface, its course swells, sending large chunks of ice hurtling downstream and making it only prudent for travelers to avoid taking to the water for a season. Fr. Paul, being such a prudent man, contented himself with life within the monastery wall's until all danger was past.

In the year 1817, just when it appeared as though the ice hazard was nearly past, the temperatures suddenly and quite unexpectedly plummeted again, causing the jagged chunks of free ice to re-pack and rendering impossible all but the most heroic of passages. And so it happened that particular spring that all communications between monastery and seminary were interrupted for an extraordinarily long period of time—precisely at the time when John Veniaminov made up his mind to marry. Physically unable to discuss the matter with the rector, he proceeded without the latter's knowledge to obtain the required ecclesiastical permission and began the task of finding himself a bride. According to the practices of the day, a match was quickly arranged. A local priest's daughter named Catherine was found for him, and on April 29, 1817, the two were married. By May 13 he was already Deacon John Veniaminov, ordained by Bp. Michael and assigned to serve in the Annunciation Church in Irkutsk while completing his final year of studies.

Deacon John remained an excellent student and graduated in 1818 at the top of his class, having studied, as his records show,

> ... Russian grammar, sight-reading of music, natural history, geography, Latin and Russian versification, rhetoric, philosophy and theology, German and Greek.

He had completed his eleven years of schooling none the worse for the spartan conditions under which they had been passed. He was knowledgeable and healthy both in body and in spirit, and was soon assigned, in addition to his deaconal ministry, to teach music in the parish school while awaiting an opening for a priest. Teaching he found little easier than studying. Supplies were few, and he was forced to compile his own textbooks. For lack of paper he adopted the novel approach of using charcoal to mark musical staffs on the walls of his classroom. Finally a vacancy occurred, and John Veniaminov was ordained to the holy priesthood on May 18, 1821. His assignment was as second priest in the Church of the Annunciation.

Fr. John soon proved to be as excellent a pastor as he had been a student, earning the respect not only of his own parishioners but of the entire community as well through his intelligence, his upright life, his obedience and the care he took in celebrating the services. More than by anything else, perhaps, people were impressed by his zealous pastoral work, for he did such then-unheard-of things as organizing catechetical classes for both boys and girls in church before Sunday

Liturgy. The educated and uneducated alike were drawn to him, as were those students still preparing themselves for the priesthood who found in Fr. John—in the reverent and solemn way in which he served—a fine example for their own future ministry. He provided for his family's material needs by making clocks, a skill he had by this time mastered, and by fashioning little barrel-organs which played church hymns.

Fr. John Veniaminov thus fell into the perfectly "normal" pattern of clerical life in early nineteenth-century Russia. In time he could look forward to becoming an archpriest, to seeing his new-born son Innocent off to seminary to serve the Church in his own footsteps; his daughters—should he be blessed with any—would marry seminarians, and the whole family would eventually be forgotten by history in that most obscure province of the vast Russian Empire.

But this was not the path which lay before him. Certainly Fr. Paul had entertained different plans for him. The rector's mind had been made up. With his perceptive mind and excellent behavior, John Veniaminov was an obvious candidate for advanced work at the Moscow Theological Academy whenever an opportunity to appoint him should arise. One did in June of 1818, but John was no longer eligible for appointment, being by then a married man and a deacon at that. What had thwarted the rector's plans? Veniaminov himself perceived that on the surface the decisive factor had been that peculiar cold snap the spring before. He would later write: "Had this situation [with the ice] not occurred, the rector would certainly not have allowed me to petition to be married, and then I should have gone to the Academy rather than to America." Had that been the case, he would have fallen into a second "normal" pattern of Russian ecclesiastical life; monastic tonsure and ordination to the priesthood, appointment first as instructor in and than as rector of a seminary; elevation to archimandrite, and perhaps in time consecration to the episcopacy and assignment as vicar to a series of large archdioceses in European Russia.

But the weather *had* been unpredictable in the spring of 1817, and it is not at all difficult, again with Fr. Veniaminov himself, to perceive beneath the surface of these events the very special plan which God Himself had prepared for him. In 1823 this plan began moving rapidly towards its realization, as Bp. Michael of Irkutsk received instructions from the Holy Synod in St. Petersburg to provide a priest to service the Russian-American Company's colony on the Island of Unalaska in America.

Missionary work was, as it were, the founding principle of the diocese of Irkutsk when it was separated from Tobolsk in 1727 to constitute an independent see. The imperial ukase instructed that there be sent "to Siberia a bishop suitably educated to convert the indigenous peoples to Christianity." By the zeal of its first bishop, St. Innocent (Kulchitskii) and his successors, mission became firmly established at the very center of the Church's life. Over the years, following the secular advance into new territories, its diocesan boundaries expanded eastward to include Yakutia, the Kamchatka Peninsula, and Okhotia. Finally, when Russia crossed the ocean to America, Irkutsk was at the center of the drive.

Years later, in 1839, Fr. John Veniaminov penned the following brief account of this advance. It provides the necessary background for the remainder of our narrative. "The Christian faith," he writes,

> came to the shores of America along with the first Russians to arrive and settle those parts. Captain Bering, the first to discover the Aleutian Islands during his second voyage (from Kamchatka eastword) and to point out to the Russians a route to America, brought back with him several valuable furs, and awakened the active and courageous Siberians to a new enterprise hitherto unknown to them. The desire for enormous profits sent many a Russian off into unknown lands, inducing them to undertake difficult voyages attended by incredible toils and dangers. But of the first men to lead these fortune-hunters to occupy new, hitherto unknown places in America (and thereby lay the foundations for a new industry for Russia and prosperity for themselves),

there were a few who also laid the foundations of Christianity among the savages with whom they settled. Thus, for instance, the Cossack Andrean Tolstykh, who around 1743 discovered the *Andreanof Islands*, was probably also the first to baptize their inhabitants. The seafarer John Glotov, who in 1759 discovered the *Fox Islands*, first baptized the young son of a native Fox-Aleut chieftain and took him along to Kamchatka. There this first-born of the Unalaskan Church lived for several years learning Russian (including how to read and write it) before returning to his native land empowered as head *toion* (or chieftain) by the Governor of Kamchatka. His example did much to spread Christianity. On Kodiak the Christian faith appeared only during the time of G[regory] Shelekhov, who established the present American Company and is the first founder of the American Church.

There are no details concerning the further spread of Christianity, except that as the number of Russian arrivals in the Aleutian Islands increased, thereby decreasing and subdividing the mutual profits, the Aleuts themselves also came to be divided up (their numbers having already been decreased by more than half by the "suppression"). Hence the number of hunters was lessened. This caused certain of the Russians to adopt other means of increasing their own quota of hunters and workers—namely, by convincing the Aleuts to accept Holy Baptism, whereby they could make more adherents for themselves since baptized Aleuts honor their sponsors as fathers and will serve them exclusively and diligently: no other Russian can lure away another's "godchildren."

Thus, the Russian's desire for larger profits served as a means of spreading the beginnings of Christianity among the Aleuts, and eased the work of the missionaries who followed.

Shelekhov's primary intention in his many plans for the good of the American region was to spread Christianity and build churches. To this end, after returning from Kodiak in 1787, he immediately submitted a report to the Government asking that a Spiritual Mission be appointed, which he and his friend Golikov would transport and maintain at their own expense. Through his intercessions and by Royal Command, there was subsequently formed in St. Petersburg a mission consisting of eight monastic clerics headed by Archimandrite Joasaph in order to *preach the Word of God to peoples under Russian dominion* (as Mr. Khlebnikov says in his *Life of Baranov*, p. 13).[4] With very adequate outfitting by Messrs. Shelekhov and Golikov and additional well-wishing donors as well, the mission left St. Petersburg in 1793 and arrived in Kodiak next autumn. They set to work immediately. Hieromonks Macarius and Juvenal spent two months that same fall traveling all the way around Kodiak Island, baptizing all its inhabitants. Next year, 1795, Hieromonk Macarius was sent to the Aleutian region where he, beginning from the Shumagin Island and on out to the Island of the Four Mountains, baptized all Aleuts who had previously not been. Next year he departed for Irkutsk. That same year (1795) Hieromonk Juvenal left Kodiak for Chugich, where he baptised over 700 Chugaches before going on to the Kenai Gulf, where he baptized all the local inhabitants. Next year, 1796, he went to Alaska, to Lake Iliamna (or Shelekhov) where he ended his apostolic ministry along with his life, having served the Church more than all his brothers. The savages killed him. His murder—so people say—was caused partly by the fact that from the very beginning he had commanded any savages who accepted Holy Baptism to forsake polygamy, and partly by the fact that Fr. Juvenal convinced the local chieftains and

---

[4] Cited here according to the pagination in Colin Beame's English translation, in *Baranov: Chief Manager of the Russian Colonies in America* (Kingston, Ont.: Limestone Press, 1973).

notables to give him their children to be educated
in Kodiak. Fr. Juvenal was leaving with them when
the savages changed their minds and ran after them.
They caught up with him and attacked. It is said that
when the savages attacked, Fr. Juvenal took no
thought at all of defending himself or of running
(which he could surely have done successfully,
especially as he had firearms along), but surrendered
to them with no resistance whatsoever, asking only
that they show mercy to his companions—which they
did. A long time later the Americans themselves [i.e.,
the natives] told how after he had been killed,
Fr. Juvenal arose and followed his murderers, saying
something to them. The savages, thinking him still
to be alive, fell upon him once again and beat him,
but as soon as they left he rose again and followed.
This was repeated several times. Finally, in order to
be finished with him once and for all, the savages
slashed him to pieces. Only then did this zealous
Preacher—and one might say, Martyr for the Word
of God—fall silent. But the power of his Word was
not silent: from where the Preacher's remains lay—
they say——there immediately arose a column of
smoke reaching up to heaven.

The other members of the mission remained im-
mobile and limited their activities to the normal
ministry in church and a bit of instruction to the
children in school. The monk Herman,[5] almost from
his arrival and right up until his death, lived on an
isolated island (Spruce Is.), praying and farming.
After a few years—and especially towards the end—
he taught several boys and girls—Aleut orphans—
to read and write as well as the basics of Christianity
and needlework. His little institution was very well
supported, especially after the visits of Baron von
Wrangell, the former Colonial Governor. Although
Fr. Herman was not a priest, he was not found to be
without a word of advice or instruction for the sur-

[5] Glorified by the Orthodox Church in America in 1970.

rounding Aleuts who came to question him. This I heard myself from certain Aleuts who studied with him. With Fr. Herman's death (1837) the Kodiak Mission ended. One ought also to add here that Hieromonk Gideon, who stayed in Kodiak from 1805 to 1806 aboard the ship *Neva* until its departure for St. Petersburg via Okhotsk, translated the Lord's Prayer into Kodiak (with authorization from the Holy Synod). In his day and for some time thereafter it was sung in Church and taught in school, but later fell into disuse and has been completely lost.

Shelekhov's zeal for spreading the Word of God among the Americans was not limited, however, simply to having a mission established there. He proposed opening a diocese in America ruled by its own bishop whose residence would be in Kodiak. He supposed it to have up to 50,000 inhabitants. Honoring his proposal and in view of such a large number of inhabitants, it was decided to open a diocese in America. Joasaph, archimandrite of the Kodiak Mission, was subsequently summoned to Irkutsk, and in March of 1799 was consecrated to the episcopacy by Bp. Benjamin of Irkutsk. But that same year, the newly elected Bishop of Kodiak (Kamchatka) and America, while returning to Kodiak aboard the *Phoenix* (a ship belonging to the Russian-American Company) perished at sea together with his entire retinue and rich vestry. Judging by the items belonging to the mission which washed up on shore and were found all along the Alaskan coastline, it can be surmised that the *Phoenix* went down not far from the shores of Kodiak and Unalaska.

Soon after this tragic event, Shelekhov himself died, and with this ceased all attempts both at opening an American diocese and at spreading and establishing the Word of God through priests. Thus, since the days when Hieromonks Macarius and Juvenal baptized the Aleuts, Kodiaks and other savages, the condition of the American Church remained static so to speak, until 1816; in all of America there was but a single priest, Hieromonk Athanasius in Kodiak, and he ministered to and served only the chief settlement of Kodiak, travelling virtually nowhere to teach the savages who had been baptized . . .

Thus by the year 1821 there existed the distinct possibility that whatever Christianity the Aleuts had absorbed might soon be lost forever. That very year, however, the tsar renewed the privileges of the Russian-American Company, and one new provision helped avert just such a tragedy. According to the new charter, the Company was duty-bound "to have a sufficient number of clergy in the colonies." Thus the Administration of the Company initiated the request which led to the 1823 ukase of the Holy Synod.

Faced with the requirement of finding a candidate to be sent to America, Bp. Michael issued the following orders to the Irkutsk Consistory:

Handle in the normal manner the three ukases which accompany this [letter]. To fulfill the *first* of these (No. 1462), read it in the presence of all the priests and deacons in the city of Irkutsk in order to see if any of them would like to go to America to occupy such a lucrative priestly position on the Island of Unalaska. Inquire as to the reasons both of those who wish to go and of those who do not. This is to be noted on the reverse of this paper and be told to me . . .

To a man the clergy declined. Fr. John recalls:

When all the clergymen in the diocese were asked by order of the late Bp. Michael if they would like to go to Unalaska—and if *not*, then why?—I like all the the others stated that I did *not* wish to accept the position because it was too far away. I wrote this in all sincerity, reasoning that if our widows even now are destitute living just six or seven miles from the authorities (social security was as yet unknown in those days), then what would become of them 6,000 miles away? That's what I told my companions.

Irkutsk was not only the spiritual center of the mission to America. It was the hub of all commercial activities in Eastern Siberia as well. There food supplies and equipment from Russia and Western Siberia were collected and packed for trans-shipment to the Pacific seaboard and beyond, while an opposite current of furs collected in the American colonies flowed westward into the city for routing to their final destinations. Most of them went to near-by Kiakhta, Russia's only authorized border crossing into China, the prime market for the Russian-American Company's only real export commodity. Thus, with its strategic location astride the trans-Siberian trade route, it was not at all rare to find in Irkutsk men returning from tours of duty in America. And, because travel throughout Siberia is necessarily seasonal (springtime being, as we have already glimpsed, completely impassible), neither was it rare for these adventurers to spend several months in the city before continuing their westward trek.

One such adventurer, an old man named John Kriukov, had spent the extraordinarily long period of forty years among the Aleuts before returning home to Russia, leaving his grown children behind. Fr. John became his spiritual father during his stay in Irkutsk, and over the months enjoyed many an occasion to hear the fascinating stories which he told about that distant place. But, as Fr. John would later write:

No matter what stories he told me about America in general or about the Aleuts in particular, no matter how he tried to persuade me to go to Unalaska, I remained deaf; none of his persuasion even touched me. Indeed, how could I—*why* should I (humanly speaking)—have travelled God-knows-where when I had one of the best parishes in the city, when I enjoyed the love of my parishioners and the good graces of the authorities, when I already owned my own home and had a larger income than the salary being offered to whomever was assigned to Unalaska?

In mid-February Kriukov prepared to resume his westward trek, and as he and Fr. John bade one another farewell, he made one last, futile attempt to convince the young priest to go to America. Again, Fr. John recalls what transpired:

Later that same day we met again in the bishop's residence; Kriukov had come to say good-bye to him as well. I happened to be there by coincidence (indeed, it was the first time that I had ever been in the bishop's drawing room), and Kriukov again began to tell me of the Aleuts' zeal in prayer and hearing the Word of God (I doubtless had heard these same things from him many times before), when suddenly *Blessed be the Name of the Lord!*—I began to burn with desire to go to such a people! Even today I recall vividly the tortures I endured while waiting impatiently to inform the bishop of my wish. He was truly amazed and said simply: "We shall see."

The surprise of suddenly having a volunteer did nothing, however, to convince the bishop to abandon his own plan for selecting a candidate to go to Unalaska. Over the months he had received and considered each cleric's written explanation of why he did not wish to accept this mission, and had spoken personally with each of them in turn, trying to persuade them to change their minds. Four of those who came before him, he found, "gave no honorable reasons—simply an unwillingness which I dismiss as impudent stubbornness," and these he therefore ordered summoned on February 5, 1823, for a solemn casting of lots whereby the decision would be made. This, he reasoned, would be both fair and traditional, as his instructions for how the gathering was to be organized make clear.

The Holy Gospel and the Cross lay on a table in the center of the room. The Consistory, like an apostolic company, gathered around it. Fr. Veniaminov joined the four officially summoned candidates as the "ground-rules" were announced. All were obliged *in advance* to accept the outcome: the "winner" would go to America. All agreed. The text of Acts 1:19-26 was read with due solemnity, down to the words, ". . . and they cast lots for them, and the lot fell on Matthias; and he was enrolled with the eleven apostles." The same was then done in Irkutsk, and it fell upon Fr. John's companion from seminary days and good friend, Deacon Athanasius Malinin of the cathedral staff. "I'd rather join the army than go to America!" replied the stunned cleric. Fr. John himself describes the aftermath of this decision. Malinin offered

> various excuses—his *"sacred"* responsibility to his aged parents, and so forth, but primarily his wife's poor health. I must say, she was destined to outlive him . . . He died in 1839, in Krasnoiarsk, a soldier filled with bitter remorse over his stubbornness.

With Malinin's refusal, Bp. Michael finally accepted Fr. John's plea that "the Lord had determined that no one but myself should go to America at that time," and gave his blessing to this new ministry. Fr. John hurried home through the snow. Entering the house he scooped up his infant son Innocent, kissed him and announced, "Kenia, Kenia! Guess where your feet are going to walk!" The meaning of these words was hidden from no one. The whole family begged him to reconsider. They too had heard their share of stories about those distant lands—and not just about the piety of the Aleuts, but about extraordinary hardships and great cruelty. Their tears, however, fell in vain. Fr. John's mind was firmly made up. They would go to America.

A week later the bishop circulated a letter to all members of the Consistory:

> By their answers they have revealed their shameful coldness towards the holy work of their heavenly calling, and their lack of pure Christian love and faith—a lack of true, guileless, and burning zeal for

the salvation of the souls entrusted to their care,
souls purchased by the Blood of the Savior of the
whole world. They have forgotten the fear of God
and my pastoral admonition sent to all of them in
1821 in a printed letter. Of the many who were
called, only one, a Son of Obedience, has been—to
my spiritual joy—found chosen, the priest of the
local Church of the Annunciation, John Veniaminov-
Popov. He eagerly agreed to my summons to be
sent on this most important mission . . .

And as a concrete sign of his appreciation, Bp. Michael
awarded the young priest the unusual right of wearing the
nabedrennik "like an archpriest" during divine services. All
of this archpastoral enthusiasm, however, contrasts starkly
with the new missionary's own evaluation of his decision:

May my own example serve as a new proof of the
truth that the "Lord guides a man safely in the way
he should go," and that each of us servants of His
Church is no more than an instrument in His hands.
He saw fit to establish my field of ministry in America—and that despite my opposition.

"After this," he concludes, "how can I in fairness regard my
going to America as meritorious, as some sort of a great feat?"
Haste now became essential. A ship was even then being
outfitted in Okhotsk for departure to America that spring,
and should they miss it there would be at least a year's wait
for another. Bp. Michael personally pressed the Company to
provide for all of Fr. John's needs. He saw to his salary (which
would equal that of the priest in the colonial capital of Sitka);
he listed a substantial inventory of sacred vessels, vestments
and liturgical books which would be needed to convert the
existing chapel on Unalaska into a functioning parish church.
He blessed Fr. John to build an altar and iconostasis for the
church and to consecrate it accordingly. More importantly,
he entrusted to the priest two antimensia, one to be placed
on the altar of the church on Unalaska, and a second, "perso-

nal" one for Fr. John to take with him wherever he traveled. With this he would be able to celebrate the Divine Liturgy and offer Holy Communion to the faithful in all the places which had no church. He would thus enjoy far greater freedom than any missionary to America before him.

One final request by Fr. John created some difficulty. He asked that a good cantor be sent along with him to Unalaska, someone who "besides helping to serve and sing in church would be able to learn the Aleut language." The Company balked. They had already decided that the "best, most moral" and literate of the creoles* in America could fulfill this function very well with but a little training by him in practical liturgics. Clearly their chief concern was financial: "The colony there is not yet in a position to accept superfluous Russian personnel—especially a cantor (who is doubtless married)— when we already have in the colonies a class of people capable of being of service to the Company as well . . ."

Their protest arrived too late, however, for Bp. Michael agreed to the proposal, and blessed a volunteer who stepped forward to go on this mission. The volunteer was Fr. John's nineteen-year-old unmarried brother Stephen, currently assigned as sacristan in the cemetery church in Irkutsk. He was accordingly blessed to wear the sticharion.

By noon on May 7, 1823, all preparations were completed, all farewells had been said. The danger of spring floods was past, and the summer route lay open. Joining Fr. John, his wife, son and brother, was his widowed mother Thekla. The path before them was an arduous one. The natural route from Irkutsk directly to the sea—across Lake Baykal and down the Amur River—was closed to Russia by the Chinese, and so, like all travelers to the Pacific seaboard and America, the Veniaminovs were forced to make an awesome, 2200-mile circuitous trek through some of the most forbidding terrain in Siberia. The first leg of their journey, however, was blessedly short—a dusty cart ride to the village of Anga, where in the Church of the Holy Prophet Elijah they prayed for a safe journey to the New World and a new life. After venerating the icons they set off, bound for Yakutsk.

* Offspring of Russian settlers and native women.

This part of their trip was one of the longest (some 1500 miles), but one of the easiest as well, once they reached the headwaters of the Lena River at Kachuga landing, some 150 miles to the north. There for the first time they realized the magnitude of the eastward movement of men, animals and material which they were about to join. By May this small town would have been in utter turmoil as merchants vied to see their goods off before as much of the competition as possible. The Veniaminovs watched their possessions being carefully wrapped and weighed by Buriat workmen before being loaded on covered flat-bottom barges. This done, they too stepped aboard and the voyage was begun.

The Lena is one of Siberia's chief waterways, a placid giant almost totally free of turns or rapids. Floating along its gentle currents by barge through stands of cedar forest with but an occasional bluff to break the monotony, Fr. John later recalled as "nothing but rest from our previous trip. Indeed, traveling down the Lena is just pure enjoyment of nature." Human beings in those parts were a great rarity. In such conditions Fr. John had plenty of time to contemplate the enormity of the task which lay before him. He grew troubled as he thought of how he would deal with complete illiterates—how he would teach them, how he would root out their bad habits, how he would prevent their backsliding. Such concerns he registered in the first of many letters he wrote to Bp. Michael and mailed home when they reached Yakutsk.

In Yakutsk all idleness and pretense of comfort were cast aside like excess baggage, as the travellers exchanged barges for sturdy little Yakut pack horses and lumbered off towards the coast along narrow, vaguely-traced paths through dense forests and mosquito-infested swamps, over swollen streams and snow-bound peaks rising thousands of feet into the air— for a dangerous and seemingly endless 700 miles. One of Fr. John's friends from seminary days, Procopius Gromov, who later took this route himself describes it in these vivid terms:

It can be said that for our sins we suffered on the Okhotsk Road ten tortures similar to those of Egypt:

rabid horses; quagmires where land turned to water
for us; nocturnal darkness, often overtaking us en
route amidst thick woods; branches threatening us
with blindness; hunger; cold; mosquitos; gadflies—
truly *biting* flies; dangerous river crossings and sores
[anthrax] on the horses—the tenth punishment! [7]

What relief must surely have filled the hearts of these
weary travelers as their ears caught the first faint sounds of
waves breaking against a not-too-distant shore. Slowly it grew
into a roar, and they savored their first few breaths of fresh
salt air as the masts of Russian sailing vessels moored in the
harbor provided their first glimpse of Okhotsk.

Neat, clean, and regular, a rather pleasant town of some
1500 residents, Okhotsk was by comparison with other settlements along the fringes of the Russian Empire a comfortable
place to rest from the long journey past. And as visitors did
so, wandering about awaiting their ships, they were treated
to a glimpse of what awaited them on the equally long trip
ahead. Over the years Okhotsk had served not only as Russia's
chief Pacific coast port, but as its major supplier of ships as
well, and a good number of these, grown so derelict that they
could no longer venture out to sea, now served officially as
storage facilities, but unofficially as (in one traveller's words [8])
"a complete *museum* of vessels, presenting curious specimens
of antique ship building, from the commencement of the enterprises of the first Russian traders to the northwest coast of
America, down to modern times." Such a sight doubtless
provoked much general curiosity, but in those as mechanically
inclined as the Veniaminov brothers, close inspection of this
fleet would surely have turned curiosity into apprehension as
they pondered the fact that still over a third of the vessels

[7] "Put' iz Iakutska" [The Route from Yakutsk] in *Pribavleniia k
Irkutskim eparkhial'nym vedomostiam* [Supplements to the Irkutsk Diocesan
Messenger] 1896, n. 17-18, p. 217.

[8] Peter Dobell, *Travels in Kamchatka and Siberia* (London: 1830)
I:297-298, cited in J. R. Gibson, *Feeding the Russian Fur Trade* (Madison:
University of Wisconsin Press, 1969) p. 137, to which much of the background
material in this chapter is indebted.

putting out thence ended up as had the *Phoenix* two years after Fr. John's birth.

On August 30, 1823, time came for the travelers to depart again. With the tide in and the winds just right, the sloop *Constantine* safely cleared the treacherous sandbars at the mouth of the Okhota River and put to sea, bound for the Kuril Islands. Fog and ever-shifting winds always make travel hazardous in the waters of the North Pacific, but on October 20, 1823, they arrived safely in the colonial capital of New Archangel (or Sitka) after weathering a final night of heavy storms at sea while already—frustratingly—in sight of land.

CHAPTER 3

LAYOVER

Since winter was by this time quickly setting in, making it unsafe to continue on to Unalaska for several months, the Veniaminovs settled down in Sitka, and Fr. John met with the General Manager of the Russian-American Company to discuss what he might do constructively "while living here such a long time idly."

His first suggestion—that he offer catechetical instruction to the city's children on a regular basis—was quickly and enthusiastically accepted by Matthew Muravev. Mindful of the need to bring some civility to the rowdy population, he had seen to it that rudimentary religious training be included in the school's curriculum, but no comprehensive training had ever been undertaken. On October 26 Fr. John began offering twice a week—to boys for two hours on Wednesdays, and to girls for two hours on Fridays—the kind of lessons which had proven so successful and popular in Irkutsk. A bit later he arranged for another hour-long session every Sunday before Divine Liturgy, set for that hour because with "everyone free from work, not only the students but everyone who wishes to, will be able to be present and hear the Word of God." His method was simple: read the Gospel to the people in Slavonic, then re-tell it in his own words, simply and straightforwardly. Finally he would draw from it some moral which all could apply to their lives and ask questions of his hearers to be sure that they had understood him correctly. In the first few weeks he came to understand how desperately his work was needed, and how difficult it would be—even if he were to remain in Sitka permanently—just to introduce some civility into the people's crude speech.

A second concern which Fr. Veniaminov placed before the Chief Manager was his desire to obtain an Aleut tutor in order to begin learning "at least a few of the words . . . which I must surely know in order to convert and exhort the inhabitants there." Again, Muravev honored his request, and Fr. John's first lesson took place on Saturday, October 27.

The months passed. On November 15 he celebrated a service of thanksgiving to mark his son Innocent's birthday, and the next day he was presented with a daughter, his first, named Catherine, in honor of her mother. Except for his teaching and own language studies, Fr. John had few real duties, and so he indulged himself in exploration of the Company's rather rich library, which throughout his stay in America would remain a source of entertainment and learning. Each month he read several books (Thomas à Kempis' *Imitation of Christ*, Karamzin's *History of Russia*, some Plutarch, and other titles in philosophy, theology, history, travel, etc.), and made arrangements to have new volumes sent out to him on Unalaska.

The time for such concerns was clearly at hand. Spring was approaching, Fr. John grew anxious to depart for his assignment in the islands. He had been treated most kindly in Sitka, and was rewarded for his own efforts by a voluntary gift from the inhabitants of 675 rubles' worth of colonial currency. All of these things he dutifully reported to his bishop, along with his greatest concern, that with communications between Russia and the chief settlement in the colonies being so poor (Fr. Sokolov in Sitka had not even been made aware of the full *name* of the diocese in which he served until Fr. John informed him) he be not totally forgotten out on Unalaska, but might receive all ukases and other news from home regularly.

Finally, before departing, Fr. John sought to clarify his position relative to the Russian-American Company. He asked the Chief Manager how he should administer his parish and was told to do exactly as he would in any parish in Russia, but "guided by what is practical." Muravev promised to send written instructions to the Unalaskan office to supply him with whatever things he might need and which could be

provided locally without disrupting Company business; everything else should be reported to him personally both by the
local office manager and by Fr. Veniaminov for necessary
action.

One specific question which bothered Fr. John was his
right to accept furs as voluntary gifts from his parishioners.
Muravev informed him that according to the terms of the
Company's imperial charter it enjoyed the exclusive right to
receive and own furs; however, he vowed, any promises which
had been made to Fr. John by ecclesiastical authorities in
Russia would be honored; he would have only to report each
year the amount of profit he made to the local office.

The priest's reply surprised the Chief Manager and
delighted all who read its noble message for it boded well
for the future of the mission to Unalaska:

> *...hoping that according to the promises of the
> Chief Management of the R.-A. Company I will be
> satisfied with my financial support,*[*] I renounce all
> such contributions allowed me as priest on Unalaska.
> That is, for as long as I shall remain there I will
> not accept any offerings from the Aleuts—neither
> furs nor currency nor anything else—either for per-
> forming services or as gifts:
>
> 1. Because such offerings (beyond the false-
> hoods you foresee and the fact that (going counter
> to the general [rules] they could destroy the cus-
> tomary order under which everyone serving the
> Company exists) could in some way weaken the
> power and sanctity of many decrees in the eyes of
> the local islanders and prove to be a pretext for much
> unpleasantness and dissatisfaction between myself
> and the local authorities;
>
> 2. In order to avoid the correspondence inevit-
> able in such a case between my higher authority and

* The passages in italics were, in the original manuscript, bracketed by a
hand other than St. Innocent's. Note that throughout this book any abbrevia-
tions used in the original are retained in translation without the continual use of
sic to indicate this fact.

the Chief Management of the R.-A. Company—which could be disadvantageous to me;

3. Since (in my opinion) a simple, sincere, and altruistic teaching and preaching of the faith *as befits a servant of the Gospel* can have a greater and freer impact on the souls and hearts of newly-converted savages than can an equally sincere and eloquent teaching which is, nevertheless, accompanied by remunerations through such offerings, etc. . . . .

Finally the day of their departure from Sitka arrived, and at 7 A.M. on July 1, the Veniaminovs boarded the brig *Rurik* and slid quietly out of the sound and into the waters of the North Pacific once more.

PART TWO

"ENLIGHTENER OF THE ALEUTS"

CHAPTER 1

AUNALAKHSKHA

> On frequent journeys, in danger
> from rivers, danger from robbers,
> danger from my own people, danger
> from the Gentiles, danger in the
> wilderness, danger at sea, danger
> from false brethren; in toil and
> hardship, through many a sleepless
> night, in hunger and thirst, often
> without food, in cold and ex-
> posure. And, apart from other
> things, there is the daily pressure
> upon me of my anxiety for all the
> Churches.   (2 Cor. 11:26-28)

Long before they had drawn near enough for their eyes
to verify the fact, all hands aboard the *Rurik* were informed
that their destination was at hand by a rising chorus of seabird
voices piercing the thick fog. *Aunalakhskha*—"This is Alaska,"
proclaims the Aleut name for the second largest island of
the Aleutian archipelago, a veritable "kingdom of eternal
autumn" as Fr. John declared. The mists' first grudging re-
velations of the approaching eastern coastline were little
more inviting than the weather: a wall of rock rising starkly
from the waters. But as the *Rurik* pressed on through Akutan
Pass and rounded the northernmost point of the island, its
features gradually grew more distinct, and became—in some
measure—a bit less awesome as well. First a small, elongated
volcanic island could be seen distinguished from the rest of
the mountainous terrain; as they passed along its shore into
harbor a beach and some rolling foothills could be seen sepa-

rating the inland mountain ridges from the sea. Closer still—
indeed, at anchor close-in to shore—the Veniaminovs were
able to survey their new home.

Harbor Village,[1] *Illiuliuk* in Aleut, and nicknamed
"Harmony Village" by its unharmonious founder, was the
chief settlement on this island—and, indeed, in the region as
a whole. In 1824 it consisted of a tattered-looking wooden
chapel, several nearby sod houses, and a dozen or so earthen
mounds, the "yurts" or native dug-out dwellings scattered
down the beach to the right. Fr. John provides the following
description of the location:

> The village is completely surrounded by mountains.
> Only to the NNE can the sea's horizon be seen. The
> mountains, beginning at the cape overlooking Ka-
> lekhta straits, run in a chain almost straight-line SW
> beyond the top of Captain's Bay, in places rising, then
> falling, then rising again. From the top of this bay,
> about 4.6 miles away, they join the first group of
> mountains which from here run due N without break
> to Amakhinak, and then at right angles turn inland
> across the island, being divided by Nateekin depres-
> sion from the rest of the northern mountains. Thence
> begin two ridges lying along the island whose one
> end is set against Makushin Volcano and the other
> ends in Captain's Harbor beyond Amakhak cliffs.
> They form a great valley or *wide* depression. Directly
> in from of the village to the N is tall Amaknak
> Island which slopes to the south and is pleasant to
> the eyes. Right beside the village on the SSW side
> and shielding it from the southwest stands a low
> mountain completely separate from the second group
> of mountains. In the distance to the NW can be seen
> a small waterfall. To the S from the village there
> stretches a large plain jutting into the interior of the
> second group of mountains. In its center there stands
> a rather large, deep lake from which issues a stream,

[1] Its modern name is "Dutch Harbor."

and along whose shores on the hills and mountains
there grow a variety of berries.

There was little time to take in the scant scenery. A call
came out from shore. The wife of a Russian hunter lay in bed
for a month now suffering from tuberculosis, and Fr. John
scarcely had time to reach shore, hear her confession and
administer to her Holy Communion before she died. "It
seemed as though she had just been waiting for this," Fr. John
recorded in his diary.

The Veniaminov's third day on Unalaska marked the
official beginning of his ministry there, and it was destined
to be etched in the memories of the people for years to come.
It was August 1, the Feast of the "Procession of the Precious
Wood of the Life-Giving Cross of the Lord"—a day on which
the Church sings:

Today the Cross is lifted up, and the world is
        freed from deceit.
Today Christ's resurrection is renewed, and
        the ends of the earth rejoice!

And indeed, on that day one of the most remote corners of
the world venerated the cross, and the Divine Liturgy was
celebrated on Unalaska, as Fr. John records exhuberantly in
his diary, "for the first time since the birth of Christ—in fact,
from the creation of the world!"

A procession then formed and made its way to the stream
which separates the spit of land upon which Harbor Village
stands from the main body of the island. There the waters
were blessed and sanctified as they had been centuries before
in Constantinople to put to an end a deadly plague, when this
particular celebration was first instituted. After encircling the
entire village the procession returned to the chapel, and a
tradition had been firmly planted on the island. Fr. John then
had portions of his official orders from the Irkutsk Consistory
read, and addressed his parishioners formally for the first time.
His words (unfortunately unpreserved) contained both greetings and exhortation. The day's celebrations ended with a

service of thanksgiving for the Veniaminovs' safe arrival, and a solemn proclamation of *Many Years* to all.

It was then the Unalaskans' turn to welcome their new priest. The General Manager of the Russian-American Company for the entire Unalaskan region, Rodion Petrovskii, stepped forward and read a carefully prepared text:

> You stand with fear before that furnace, the altar, O Pastor and Teacher of the spiritual flock of Christ our God, and will enlighten the people to praise the Lord—
>
> O merciful Pastor, Father John!
>
> Through the Providence of our Creator Most-High, this region is made glad by the arrival of Your Blessing to teach in these parts the Orthodox Christian faith. After short periods of time spent here by reverend individuals preaching the Word of God— beginning with the arrival of our venerable Father Macarius in 1795; then by Fr. Gideon, hieromonk of the Trinity Lavra's Cathedral, who visited in 1809; and then in 1820-21 by the Priest Michael— *you* are established here as a *permanent* presence to convert through your assignment and lawful ministry our earthly chapel into a Church of God and to set us by active sacramental and liturgical ministrations and soul-saving exhortations on the true path of the Orthodox religion.
>
> Therefore, to you, our Pastor, we declare the gratitude and esteem aroused in us, your spiritual children—both Russians settled here for the time being and inhabitants whose roots run very deep. To this end we have circulated once throughout the local colony a sign-up sheet for everyone—each according to his zeal and abilities—to offer you a monetary sum in colonial currency placed in your name in the local store for the purchase of any items you might need.
>
> Most humbly we ask you to bless us by accepting this freely-offered sum from our society as a token of our devotion . . .

The list he presented contained 203 names—over one-fifth of the local population— and altogether the Veniaminovs received 885 rubles to ease their adjustment to their new home. The largest single contributor (at thirty rubles) was Petrovskii. Symeon Petelin, the Company's clerk on Unalaska gave half that amount, as did Stephen Kriukov, the native chieftan on Umnak Island to the east. (It was his father whose stories convinced Fr. John to abandon the comforts of Irkutsk and to come to minister here.)

One other name on the list soon came to offer Fr. John far more than even his rather generous donation of eleven rubles. This was John Pankov, the 46-year-old chieftain of near-by Tigalda Island. Bilingual and literate, Pankov was already well-known throughout the region for his Christian zeal as witnessed by his self-appointed efforts to fill the void as a lay preacher for many years. Now that a priest had come he quickly befriended him and became his new language teacher as well as a constant and valuable companion, interpreter and guide throughout the islands of his parish.

As Fr. Veniaminov saw it, three tasks faced him at the outset of his ministry here: first, to visit all of his parishioners; second, to establish a center where they could gather to hear the Word of God; and finally, to learn their language well enough to preach this Word to them. Clearly, none of these would be simple, but without Pankov, they would have proved immensely more difficult than they were.[2]

The secular authorities made available to Fr. John a detailed village-by-village census of those unbaptized, unchrismated and unmarried, together with an indication of how far each village lay from Harbor Village. Some of these distances were considerable, for of the three "parishes" in America,[3] the "Unalaskan" one was by far the largest, stretching from the mid-point of the Alaskan Peninsula all the way out

[2] For more detailed information concerning John Pankov see Lydia T. Black, "Ivan Pan'kov: an Architect of Aleut Literacy," *Orthodox Alaska* 7:4 (Oct. 1978) 1-28 with "Epilogue" 29-33; the main article first appeared in *Arctic Anthropology* 14:1 (1977) 94-107.

[3] The others being Sitka (second largest, stretching from Mt. St. Elias southeast to Fort Ross, California) and Kodiak (stretching west from Mt. St. Elias to the middle of the Alaskan Peninsula).

(in theory) to the Kuril Islands—but in practice "only" out to Atka (farthest point from Unalaska, some 360 nautical miles). It encompassed the Fox, Krenitsyn, Shumagin, Rat and Near Island groups. In addition, Fr. John was responsible for the Pribilof Islands lying some 290 miles northwest of Unalaska. A first visitation of any of these outlying regions would become possible only after the passing of winter, and fortunately there was plenty of work to be done at home.

In Harbor Village virtually the entire population had been baptized, but by laymen, and would still have to be chrismated by a priest. Most couples would need to have their civil marriages sacramentally blessed; and everyone would have to have his confession heard and receive Holy Communion. Fr. John spent the winter months preparing them to receive these sacraments. It had always been his practice never to administer a sacrament without preaching about it first: the people simply had to know what they were doing and why. And here, under conditions of general ignorance, more than ever this was necessary. Through an interpreter, Fr. John began to speak in simple terms about God, who and what He is, and about fallen man and his need to repent and confess his sins in order to return to God. Daily he offered spiritual nourishment and knowledge to those who gathered in the chapel, and gradually the people were prepared for a deeper participation in the life of the Church.

One of the hallmarks of his pastoral work had always been catechetical instructions for the young, and Fr. John wanted to introduce them here as well. He found, however, that

to my dismay I simply cannot undertake this integral part of my duties here, for there is no school (nor has there ever been), and few even of the adults know Russian. To those who do, however, I give—and plan to keep on giving—certain lessons for their salvation every Sunday and on great feastdays (whenever the winds allow). By all means I plan and hope (with the help of the local clerk, a well-intentioned man) to build a school soon . . .

Lack of a building alone need not have hindered Fr. John's teaching; he could always find some other suitable place to begin his work, such as the chapel. But soon he found that here too there was a problem, as he reports to his bishop. The chapel,

> which is supposed to become a full church, cannot be consecrated, for although constructed like a church and decorated with a (rather decent) iconostasis ... it is already quite ancient and near falling down —which is to be feared because of the fierce winds here during the winter ...

When approached about this matter, the Chief Manager in Sitka promised to send lumber and "good carpenters, ... very capable in their work" aboard the next available ship. This, however, would certainly not be before the following spring, and although with the help of the local population the Veniaminov brothers could certainly have had a church well on its way to completion given the needed supplies, they were assured that there grows on Unalaska nothing larger than the rose willow, whose strongest trunks are fit for nothing more substantial than framing the shells of kayaks.[4] Hence, there was nothing to do but wait for wood and go on serving in the rickety old chapel—winds permitting.

The third task facing Fr. Veniaminov was to learn the Fox-Aleut language. He arrived on Unalaska knowing over two hundred words, acquired mostly through his own careful observation of the pronunciation and intonation of the Aleuts living in Sitka (his tutor had proven of little worth), and now, under John Pankov's skilled tutelage, he continued to listen and transcribe these sounds so completely foreign to the European ear and to strive painfully to articulate them properly. The process had begun slowly and continued on so, and while it is apparent from his writings that Fr. John never felt confident enough to preach without an interpreter, it is

---

[4] Because it is a more familiar term to English readers, we shall uniformly favor the Eskimo term *kayak* for the skin-boat referred to in Russo-Aleut as *baidarka.*

just as clear (as we shall see) that he in fact mastered the language. Perhaps even more important, his long hours of study and observation gave him ample opportunity to learn firsthand the way of life, the customs and the traditions of the Aleuts.

CHAPTER 2

THE ALEUTS

Filthy and tattered, unperturbed by hours spent in practiced indolence; sluggish, awkward and, when at long last moved to action, utterly without zeal for their work—at first glance, Fr. John's flock seemed to present no admirable picture. Worst of all, perhaps, were their faces, always peaceful yet tinged with sadness, and showing no real emotion, no expression which would offer a key to penetrating into their souls. And yet, in those first autumn months, as he came to know them—and they him—he began to notice that increasingly their terse communications with him included the word "*aug*," with a special intonation of voice which signaled "you are our friend." Increasingly, too, he began to catch a glimpse of joy in their eyes, a subtle hint of true love and affection which they could not bring themselves to show in public. He discovered that the Aleuts express their feelings more in deeds than in words, and that with them silence means no more than that they have nothing of real importance to say. As trusting as children, they could not abide excessive frankness or even the mildest undeserved rebuke. They never lost their temper, never dared to argue. "I don't know," they would say when challenged. "You know. You Russian."

The real key to their character, Fr. John in time perceived, their finest and strongest trait, was patience—patience, he records, "to the point of insensitivity; it would seem impossible to invent a difficulty, a condition so unbearable as to move an Aleut or cause him to complain." True, they were lazy ("that must be said, plainly and directly"), but this surely was a product of their almost innate lack of concern for tomorrow. Born in poverty and hunger in a cold and filthy yurt and seeing their devoted elders accept this and yearn for nothing more, the young Aleuts too sought no more luxury than a serviceable kayak, weapons for the hunt and a change of clothing when soaked to the skin. And more often than not they had to settle for far less than even this. They ate heartily when food was plentiful, and endured silently for as long as necessary in time of need. Unable to plan ahead or ration a winter's provisions, they found hunger a general rule and yet managed to be supremely generous. This Fr. John experienced from the very day of his arrival on Unalaska. Whenever a newcomer arrived, the entire village, from the oldest to the youngest and even those who were ill, would come out to greet him, would vie for the honor of receiving him in their humble dwellings, and would share with him the last morsel of their meager food supply.

Fr. John found that despite their innate laziness, when moved by dire necessity the Aleuts were capable of working very well and of imitating the most sophisticated of foreign trades. Their work would never be termed rapid, but once they began they never flagged until the task was done, and then, although they usually collapsed with fatigue, not a single complaint was heard even though they had labored against their will.

Over the months spent in Harbor Village Fr. John began to understand his flock well enough to become a real pastor to them. Lying, stealing, envy and other sins of "civilized" man he was pleased to see were foreign to their very nature, but he yearned to gain still greater insights into that nature in order better to understand and minister to their spiritual needs. With an astuteness that would bring credit to the trained anthropologist of today he observes:

> ... There is nothing amazing or unforgivable in the fact that the Aleuts even today are superstitious ... I think that anyone who describes a people should pay if not more, then at least an equal amount of attention to their superstitions as to their character, for these can provide evidence and ex-

planation for their degree of learning, their mental capabilities, their customs etc.—and even for their character itself. But to my disappointment, I was unable to learn about the Aleuts' superstitions and prejudices, for considering many of the old superstitions amusing and hollow, the present-day Aleuts have either forgotten them or are embarrassed to tell about them, not wishing to be mocked because of their current superstitions.

The Aleuts, he already knew, never lied or made up idle tales. They believed all they were told and expected equal credence from those to whom they spoke. When in time they perceived such openness in Fr. John, they began to reveal to him some of their former traditions.

Their former faith, the priest began to learn was like the shamanism dominant throughout Siberia and Kamchatka. The Aleuts believed in a supreme Creator of all things visible and invisible, but ascribed to him no providential activities at all and, hence, offered him no worship. Instead they worshipped any power stronger than themselves. Light, a rare commodity in the far North, was therefore one of those things most worshipped, and the Aleuts were still afraid of offending the sun, moon or stars.

They had had no temples or idols, but offered furs in remote cliffside caves as they besought success in the hunt or victory in war. Central to their life was the shaman, someone seized against his will by spirits to serve as their intermediary with men to foretell the future and to heal the sick. The Aleuts told Fr. John about one such revelation which came to them shortly before the Russians' arrival—how white men would come from beyond the sea with new ways for the Aleuts to adopt. After the Russians' arrival a second vision came—of bright light above the eastern horizon filled with a multitude of strange new faces, while below in deepening darkness stood but a few remaining people . . .

"Are these, indeed," muses Fr. John, "the words of the shamans, or inventions by the elders? I leave that to each person's judgment; I, however, if not wholly, then at least in

part, tend towards the former, for the Aleuts all accepted the
Christian faith suddenly and without the slightest pressure."

The moral precepts of their former life Fr. John found
of particular interest. The positive commandments included
caring in old age for the parents who had cared for them as
babies, helping relatives in the hunt or battle, learning from
the old in order to live long as they had, aiding the poor (for
no one remains stable throughout his life; therefore the rich—
not knowing when their wealth will fail—must be generous
and share, while the poor—not knowing when their fortunes
will change—must bear their condition obediently), hospitality, help for newcomers (for all were strangers once),
refraining from excessive speech (which brings strife), and
teaching the young tenderness, valor and the need to achieve
glory in life.

Conversely, the Aleuts were strictly forbidden to offend
or strike anyone (except enemies in war), to steal (a particularly shameful act), to inform on others or otherwise lie, to
become impatient with nature—the winds, the clouds, the
tides (this for them was "blasphemy"), to bear illegitimate
children (a lone capital offense) or to marry a twin. With
the exception of these latter two conditions, their sexual
mores were rather lax. Polygamy and concubinage with slaves
were both accepted in principle, but fortunately were little
practiced, having become economically unfeasible. The
attitude, however, remained a major problem.

Again, we read a shrewd observation on the priest's
part:

> Since all the Aleut's rules and opinions which I
> gathered come after almost a century of acquaintance
> with the Russians, and as most of them are acquainted
> with the precepts of the Christian faith, are these
> really their own ideas? Nevertheless, it is pleasing
> to see in them the ability to adopt . . .

And so, in such studies,[5] the Veniaminovs' first winter

[5] These observations were not, of course, written up in final form until
years later. Cf. below p. 117.

on Unalaska passed, a cold winter if compared with the previous one in Sitka, but far less severe than those they had endured at home in Siberia. And although he was told that the final traces would not be gone before May (or perhaps even into June), Fr. John began in March preparing for the work of summer.

CHAPTER 3

KISAGUNAK

March—*Kisagunak* in Aleut—"we have things to eat." By March the people have eaten their larders clean, and hunger makes them look forward fondly to the hunt. Soon whales will again be found in the northern waters, salmon will return to their streams, lobsters and fish will fill the coastal waters. Until their stomachs are once more filled and a few days' provisions have been laid in, the men will work unceasingly. Then, with less avidity (more, really, in the spirit of sport than in fulfillment of their obligations) they will put out to sea in kayaks to hunt seals and other fur-bearing animals for the Russian-American Company.

For Fr. John too, March of 1825 brought a growing feeling of enthusiasm and anticipation as well. Great Lent was well along, and Pascha was on its way, but on the morning of March 24, it seemed as though even the Feast of Feasts had been passed by as twenty-two village children, having just received Holy Communion, filed solemnly out of chapel two-by-two singing the Troparion of Pentecost:

You are most blessed, O Christ our God,
Who showed the fishermen to be most wise
By sending down upon them the Holy Spirit.
Through them You drew the world into Your net,
O Lover of mankind, glory to You!

The occasion for such celebration was the long-awaited founding of a school in Harbor Village.

The procession made its way through a narrow doorway

and down a few steps into the cramped native hut which until
better quarters could be secured would serve them as a school-
house. Like all of the houses on the island at that date (including the Veniaminovs), over a dirt floor recessed several feet
into the ground to conserve heat rose a latticework of willow
trunks and smaller branches over which were piled sod matting
and dried grass. A gut window with an icon hung above gave
the yurt its only light. Inside, Fr. John stooped to remove his
vestments and then began to teach the children the beginning
letters of the Russian alphabet. A great number of villagers
had accompanied the procession, and the priest next turned
to them to stress the great value of learning—for the children
and for themselves. After congratulations had been offered
all around, the day's activities concluded with the Lord's
Prayer and a solemn recession. From that day onward classes
met regularly except on Sundays, feastdays and throughout
Holy Week. Stephen Veniaminov joined his brother in teaching.

The break for Holy Week was soon upon them, however, and on March 29 Fr. John celebrated his first Paschal
Liturgy on Unalaska. In the morning he went from yurt to
yurt bringing to each family individually the glad news that
"Christ is risen!" He found everyone in noticeably good
spirits—far better, in fact, than could be accounted for by their
first exposure to this central Christian mystery (especially as
it had been celebrated in Slavonic). And in turn, from them
he caught the native spirit of *"Kisagunak."*

At first merely with attention, but later with true admira-
tion, he watched the Aleuts check and grease their sleek, skin-
covered craft, light enough for a child to carry and yet "so
perfect in its type," he writes, "that even a mathematician
could scarcely (if at all) add anything to the perfection of
its sailing qualities." He saw his filthy, tattered flock preparing for the hunt, becoming, as it were, transfigured, until the
Aleut appeared

> quite unlike any other [people] on earth. It seems
> then as though he was created for the kayak—or that
> the kayak was invented just for him, to show him

from his best side. Several times I have seen Russians seated in kayaks, yet none of them—even the most dignified and stately-looking of them—had the appearance of even the most ordinary of Aleuts.

This being the case, it was perhaps with some trepidation that Fr. John himself prepared to squeeze into one of these frail boats to begin his first visitation of the western part of his parish. The Russian-American Company provided him with all the equipment and supplies he would need to accomplish his journey, including a two-seat kayak (called *"uliukhtak"* in Aleut), a tent and native traveling clothes. He found for himself that in wet and cold the Russian frieze, a ponderous, shaggy-piled woolen coat, could not compete with the lighter native garb, and so he happily adopted them. These consisted first of the parka, a long shirt sewn from the skins of 40-60 birds (preferably woodpeckers from Sitka). With its narrow sleeves and standing collar, it provided excellent protection against wind and frost and in addition served the Aleuts as clothing, bedding, blanket and home while on the road. In the rain a second long shirt, the *kamleika* was worn. This garment, made from the intestines of larger mammals (sea lions, bears, walruses, sometimes even whales), kept its wearer warm and comfortable even in the worst of storms. The *kamleika* had to be frequently rubbed down liberally with rancid animal fat in order to extend its usefulness; this process at the same time made wearing it less than appealing to the novice.

On the afternoon of April 13, 1825, a favorable wind coming up, Fr. John completed his detailed instructions to his brother on what to do in his absence in case of emergency, and set off in the company of several other kayaks. (A cardinal rule of travel in these parts—even for seasoned veterans—was to travel in groups for safety.) Scarcely had they rounded the northern point of the island heading west than the afternoon's light breezes turned into a violent headwind, and his companions' sharp senses warned them to seek safety quickly on shore. The storm built up and raged on for three days. As they sat idly waiting for the winds to calm, Fr. John drew new first-hand insights into the Aleuts' prime virtue—patience.

On the fourth day the party succeeded in putting out once again to sea, but managed to row a scant 23 miles before being forced ashore again. As they rowed in through the crashing surf, Fr. John's hopes for a time rose, for this time his guides had at least found a village for them to visit. Instead, he learned a second lesson about life in the Aleutians: Most of the many villages throughout the islands are only seasonally inhabited. During the summer when the hunters live as nomads these may, as need arises, see a small band step ashore, but they soon leave again, and for most of the year the yurts stand deserted. Once again the order of the day was patience.

By Sunday evening, however, when the winds had not yet abated and supplies were running low, Fr. John's patience could hold no longer. If they could not put out to sea, they would cross the mountainous interior of the island to pay a visit earlier than expected to the village of Makushin. By mid-morning, with the weather still threatening, the supplies which Fr. John would need to conduct his ministry were divided up among the Aleuts, and off the party set on foot.

There were, of course, no roads, just steep hills not yet free of slushy snow, and as if things were not bad enough with this, about midway squalls blew in to further slow their progress. The Russians, though unencumbered by the heavy packs their companions bore, grew tired quickly, much to the amusement of the Aleuts for whom such treks were commonplace. In fact, the usual roles were completely reversed on this trip, for the Aleuts, who normally found themselves the butt of derisive Russian laughter over their crooked little stubby legs encased in ridiculous seal-flipper bootlets, now had the satisfaction of watching the foreigners fight at every step to keep their footing on the mossy rocks, while they nimbly and confidently hopped forward. By 8:30 that evening the party reached its destination.

For the next four days Fr. John taught the pitiful handful of people he found inhabiting Makushin, a lonely sand spit at the mouth of a bay deeply incised into the island's interior. He chrismated those too young ever to have seen a priest, performed the Sacrament of Matrimony for all the married couples, heard confessions and gave Communion to

all. On their fifth day in Makushin, before dawn, they began
the trek back to where they had left their kayaks, hoping
thence to resume their voyage to the next village down the
coast, Kashega.

The wind, though fully as erratic as Fr. John had come
to expect in this region, did indeed now allow the company
to cast off, and before dusk they had set up the tent which
would serve as a chapel throughout their stay in Kashega.
That evening Fr. John chrismated twenty-three people, and
he spent the following day preaching about repentance and
hearing the confessions of all. On his second evening he
served vigil, and on the third morning he celebrated Liturgy,
distributed Communion, served a general funeral in the cemetery, performed six weddings, struck the tent and brought his
ministrations in Kashega to an end. With calm winds behind
them they set out for Chernofski.

From Chernofski they entered for the first time the normally treacherous pass separating Unalaska from the south
shore of Umnak Island. Fresh winds, however, moving with
the currents assured that their passage would be safe from
the whirlpools which terrified even the Aleuts, and in fact
even allowed them to hoist their sails—a Russian "improvement" upon the kayak—and to rest their arms from rowing.

As they traveled down its rocky shore Umnak appeared
as lifeless as Unalaska. Crowned by twin volcanic peaks, it
numbered but two villages, and it was for the larger of these
that they were heading, Nikolski on the northwest shore. Just
past the westernmost peak the island flattens out and nar-
rows, and on the beach there the party abandoned its kayaks
to proceed on foot across a level valley floor blanketed with
grass and soft moss. Summer's flowers had not yet bloomed,
but Fr. John was all the same elated. "A beautiful location!"
he exclaimed, "Completely unlike our hilly, rocky Unalaska!"

As the company approached Nikolski shots rang out—
a welcoming volley, Fr. John was told, as the village turned
out in typical Aleut fashion to meet the approaching strangers.
This was a prosperous village, judging by the buildings there,
for besides the usual native yurts there stood a very ancient
chapel—the oldest, in fact, in the islands, built in 1806 from

driftwood by the inhabitants under the direction of none other than Fr. John's old friend, John Kriukov.

As he had on Unalaska, and at no less demanding a pace, Fr. John began a regular cycle of services, interspersed with instructions carefully aimed at various ages and groups of people in the village. He prepared everyone to receive chrismation, and as they grew ready each day another group would receive this sacrament. Those old enough intelligently to do so confessed their sins before him. Everyone received Holy Communion. Wedding after wedding was performed, and by Saturday, May 19, all ministrations were completed in this, the westernmost village he would reach on this first trip. After Liturgy that morning Fr. John paid a visit to each family in its yurt and in the dead of night left Nikolski, almost the entire population of the village accompanying him and his retinue back across the isthmus to the south shore where their kayaks awaited them. It was after midnight when they arrived, but as Fr. John hoped very much to be home in time for Pentecost, they put out to sea immediately.

Many a time this goal appeared impossible. Contrary winds blew almost constantly. Great swells in open water and whirlpools in the straits struck fear in the travelers and slowed their progress. Fr. John pressed on, however, feeling justified in saving some time once he realized that most of the people in the nearer villages had visited Harbor Village during the Lent just past. Against all hope and probabilities the party arrived in Captain's Harbor safely at 9:00 P.M. on May 16, the very eve of Pentecost. The vigil service began immediately and it was only after noon the next day, following a lengthy festal celebration of Liturgy, Vespers with the kneeling prayers, and a prayer-service of thanksgiving for the safe completion of this first trip to the western parts of his parish, that a weary missionary priest finally found time to rest.

After such a journey the next few weeks should surely have seemed anticlimactic for him, for according to the rhythm of life in the colonies the single scheduled ship from Russia would soon arrive, and a year's worth of reports and letters had to be prepared in the meantime for shipment home. But

in one of these, addressed to Bp. Michael, we sense the exhila-
ration which still filled Fr. Veniaminov:

> With spiritual joy I have the honor of informing
> YOUR GRACE, my ARCHPASTOR, that my doctrine
> (which is not my own, but of Him Who sent me)
> was received everywhere with evident joy, zeal, and
> respect. Strengthened by this reception on many such
> occasions, I plan next year to visit the entire eastern
> region of my parish, although it is quite distant—to
> the very borders of the Kodiak Church . . .

CHAPTER 4

BUILDINGS

As expected, on June 6 the ship *Constantine* from Sitka slipped into Captain's Harbor, and while it remained at anchor Fr. John hurried to prepare answers to all the official mail it had just brought from Russia. As he worked a second craft unexpectedly joined the *Constantine* in harbor. The brig *Buldakov*, it seems, had been dispatched from Sitka in fulfilment of a promise made by Matthew Muravev. The lumber for their church was here! Fr. John interrupted his paper work long enough to get the project under way.

July 2 began with the Hours read in the old chapel. Then a procession of villagers bearing icons and the cross made its way solemnly to the building site. At the very end walked Fr. John, vested and carrying a hand cross. A prayer-service was chanted; the ground, the workers and the building materials were sprinkled with Holy Water; and Fr. John unvested to begin personally the job of sawing up the lumber. Ceremonial demanded that the real work not begin until each of the Company officials and local notables had taken his turn, but when it finally did get under way in earnest, the priest signalled this by lifting the cross high into the air, and the three ships offshore joined the shore batteries in firing a salute to the occasion.

Floorplans for the building—but none of the other needed drawings—had been sent from Sitka, and so from the beginning Fr. John was compelled to take a more active part in the project than he would (perhaps) have wanted. As the preliminary work moved successfully forward he returned to his paper work, however, and it was not until the *Constantine*

departed that he was free to turn his attention to the church—
and to such diversions as reading four-year-old journals freshly
received from Russia.

One of the letters Fr. John sent home dealt with another
building project he had in mind, and it demonstrates so clearly
the depth of his commitment to bettering the condition of his
flock that we quote it at length. "The income of this church
is very great," he informs his bishop,

> and although last year I requested that the Chief
> Management prepare and send everything necessary
> for the church and charge it against our savings,
> these savings have not, as you can see, diminished.
> There will, therefore, be sufficient money to cover all
> expenses and still have something left over to use
> elsewhere—unless the R.-A. Company forbids this
> (which is scarcely to be anticipated).
>
> Therefore, would it not please YOUR GRACE to
> allow the priest in Unalaska to make use of a por-
> tion of these funds—which belong undisputably to
> the Church—to aid either the school or some poor
> and ailing Aleuts? (It goes without saying that I
> shall give a most detailed accounting to whomever
> I am told) . . .*

By August 1 the lumber had all been cut, and work on
the first floor of the church was completed. The two remaining ships were preparing to follow the *Constantine* home to
winter port in Sitka when the carpenter demanded to be taken
along. Full responsibility for completing the project thus fell

* Bp. Michael received this letter on September 13, 1826, and penned
the following instructions to his Consistory:

> The Church's property is that of the poor; therefore God will bless
> this project. The Consistory is to allow the priest to use excess church
> income both for the school and for poor Aleuts.

Word of this approval reached Unalaska only in June of 1828, and immediately Fr. Veniaminov began making use of its provisions. In the years
that followed not only was the school improved, but a six-bed hospital, staffed
by what we would now term a "paramedic," and a foundling home accommodat-
ing twelve orphan girls (1831) were established in Harbor Village.

upon Fr. John's shoulders, and he accepted the challenge, instructing the villagers in the rudiments of carpentry and other building trades, and seeing the work push forward well into the winter. By December the door and windows had been framed, and the altar area was covered by a roof.

As the New Year began, another "building project" of fundamental importance to the Church of Unalaska was begun in Harbor Village. Fr. John by now felt confident enough in the Aleut language (although he still never preached publicly without an interpreter) to begin translating the *Full Catechism*. By early March he had completed the first section and sent it for review and criticism to Tigalda Island, to the man whose name eventually would find its way to the title page as his co-author, John Pankov, reputed to be the finest translator in the region.

A first draft of the entire catechism was completed and checked by Pascha, and since his responsibilities in supervising construction work looked as though they would preclude any travels that summer, Fr. John continued his translating far into the spring. For a while he even entertained hopes of sending a copy home to Irkutsk with the summer mail to begin what would surely be a lengthy process of obtaining authorization to publish it, but in the end his other work forced him to abandon this plan, for fear that "by haste any errors might be admitted" to the translation. The reward of seeing work on the church step-by-step nearing completion, however, compensated for this, and on the Wednesday after Pascha, as the barrel and cupola were completed, a special prayer-service was conducted to bless it and the large cross which would be set atop it. Next Sunday a three-barred shadow fell upon the ground where, after a final "prayer-service of thanksgiving to the Lord God for all the good things we have received in this chapel," the sad but inevitable job of razing the decrepit old structure was begun. Services went on in a tent pitched nearby until Ascension Day when, the rubble having been removed, the tent was transferred to the hallowed old location, where the old altar and iconostasis were set up for Liturgy that day. Finally in June all work was completed. The sturdy spruce walls were neatly hung with sailcloth. The old icons were brought in and hung in place. The old iconostasis was also set in place—a temporary measure, since Fr. John intended personally to build a new one in the future—and the Church of the Ascension was ready to be consecrated. This took place on June 28, 1826, the second anniversary of the Veniaminov's arrival on Unalaska.

A visitation to build up the Church in the eastern region was long overdue by the time all necessary arrangements were completed in 1827. The previous year's delay now proved fortunate, however, as Fr. John, a systematic presentation of the Christian faith in the Aleut language in hand, began his summer's travels.

The distances involved in visiting the eastern region were far too great to be attempted by kayak alone. A ship would have to transport Fr. John, his interpreter and several Aleut guides over 250 miles of open ocean to Unga Island, the farthest outpost within his jurisdiction. They left Unalaska April 17 on what should normally be a sixty-hour passage, but faced the whole way with fierce headwinds they arrived only on the twenty-eighth. Once there, however, Fr. John was "greeted by each and everyone with evident joy" and set to work as he had in the past. In each village, when the people had been gathered together, his Catechism was read, and it created in everyone great joy and a desire to have a copy for themselves. Those who knew Russian acclaimed the accuracy of his work, and everyone gladly signed a petition to the bishop requesting permission to have it printed and distributed.

After several days' work on Unga, and after observing the Feast of the Ascension marooned by winds on a deserted island, Fr. John first set foot on the Alaskan Peninsula on May 14. He found that as a rule the able-bodied men throughout the region were already gone to sea on the hunt, and he had to begin ministering to those left behind—the women, the old, the young and the infirm—while these were being summoned back. Preparing large numbers of people with scarcely any knowledge of the Christian faith worthily to receive the sacraments kept Fr. John working far into the night almost daily. The very rites themselves consumed whole days, scores of confessions and many weddings being performed in every settlement. Everywhere his efforts were rewarded, however, by the sincere reception which the people gave his word and by their profuse gratitude for his having come to them bearing the Good News of the Christian faith in all its truth. Modestly Fr. John would remind them, however, "that it is *God* Whom they ought to thank for allowing me to come to them and to be in such a distant land, enlightening them with the Holy Gospel—and also that they ought to pray to God for *me*, that I might be able to visit them again."

Twice in the course of his travels in these regions it was proved indeed just how vital such prayers were. By the end of June Fr. John had reached Deer Island, the farthest point west of Unga Island he would attain that year, and he began his return trip through the villages he had just visited. In each of these he generally found a few new faces who had been absent on his first stop, and he ministered to them before passing on. Leaving Morzhovoi he was asked by the Russian-American Company to transport some cargo for them to Unga, and he readily agreed. An empty kayak would not sit right in the water anyway, and rather than using rocks for ballast he might as well be carrying something useful. Some 180 pounds of walrus tusk was thus loaded aboard his craft and off they paddled into calm winds. Once at sea, however, the wind's intensity grew and whipped up heavy waves which soon flooded his heavily-laden boat. The party hurried for shore, where fortunately the sea calmed before the surf line and the danger passed.

On the final day of his travels, however, Fr. John found himself in even graver danger. Thirty miles offshore in rolling seas his kayak again began to take on water rapidly—rapidly enough to require bailing every fifteen minutes. There were no islands in the vicinity, and a brisk tailwind precluded any thought of turning back. Fr. John describes what followed:

> By then I'd grown accustomed to being at sea, and hoped, moreover, in God who "guides a man safely in the way he should go." Thus we overcame our

fear, and other than seasickness I observed no fear
or discomfort in anyone...I was, however, continually in danger of losing my life, for (as they
say) "there's not a single board here to save you
from death—just skins."

Fr. John reached Unga safely and boarded a Company
ship to return home to Unalaska. First, however, he and his
Aleut guides (who now left him to join the hunt themselves)
gave thanks to God for protecting them "in this frail boat"
and asked for a safe completion of his travels. In alternating
headwinds and dead calms the voyage took over a week, and
even then the last night was spent helplessly becalmed in the
channel within sight of land, in constant danger of being
swept out to sea by strong currents. With much paper work
awaiting him ashore, Fr. John paddled in next morning and
hiked through the hills to end his first visitation of the eastern
regions on Sunday, June 12, its forty-ninth day. "And thanks
be to the Most-high God," he records,

> it ended safely, healthily, and joyously. Furthermore,
> if I may dare say so (since mine was just to plant
> and water; it is for God to make it grow [1 Cor.
> 3:6]) it was truly useful and successful as well;
> indeed, with sincere pleasure in soul and heart I
> can state that it was not without success or value,
> for there was not a single village in which I failed
> to serve and administer the sacraments, to teach
> the faith and law to each and everyone, and to ex-
> plain to them the sacraments which I had adminis-
> tered. And they (the Aleuts) thanked—and still
> thank—me for this.

Four days after his return home the brig *Golovnin*
arrived with evidence that Fr. John's pastoral labors were not
going unheeded at home in Russia. The year's supply of mail
included a pectoral cross awarded him by the Holy Synod.
It seems that the official reports and meticulous journals
submitted to Bp. Michael struck the hierarch with the extent

of the young missionary's labors during his first year in Unalaska, and when he received confirmation from the Russian-
American Company of the impact his mission was having on
the colonies, he reported to St. Petersburg:

> . . . for his praiseworthy and exemplary behavior, and
> moreso for his holy obedience and willingness to
> fulfill it on the Island of Unalaska, the Priest Ve-
> niaminov is, in my opinion, worthy of being awarded
> the pectoral cross, as this will awaken in the is-
> landers greater attention and respect for their Pas-
> tor, for his teachings, and for his ministry . . .

On June 21, before the beginning of Liturgy, Fr. John placed
this mark of distinction so extraordinary for a priest his age,
around his neck with devotion and humility.

Among the dispatches which Fr. John in turn had readied
for shipment to Russia that summer were his translations.
With them he enclosed an explanatory letter (or "Humble
Request") to Bp. Michael and petitions signed by the Aleuts
who had heard and read his work and attested to its accuracy.
Fr. John writes:

> During the three years I have been here, I have
> considered my most important duty to be teaching
> the Word of God to the flock entrusted to me—and
> this I have fulfilled to the best of my ability. How-
> ever, inasmuch as the Aleuts live scattered . . . over
> large distances, I have also made translation my
> duty. And so, with the help of God the Word, I
> have translated the *Full Catechism* into the Fox-
> Aleut language, and now have the honor of pre-
> senting it to you.
> I humbly ask YOUR GRACE to allow me to
> send it and the Russian text as written to a printer,
> and once printed to make use of it in the local
> school and for distribution among the Aleuts . . .
> I had no other object in translating this than
> that the Aleut who reads or listens to the *Catechism*

in his native tongue might understand and learn
from it what he ought to believe and do for his
salvation. ... I dare not assert that the translation
is free from insignificant errors—for this is the first
work to be composed ... in a language which has
as yet no [written] grammar; I do, however, dare
assert that with regard to *important* errors I have
neither tolerated through negligence or laziness—
no moreso inserted with aforethought—anything
contrary to the Orthodox Faith or Christian law ...
Nevertheless, I dare not consider my work perfect,
but humbly ask YOUR GRACE to make corrections.

Since many Aleuts can understand Russian, I
consider it wise to print it together with the Russian
text ... In my opinion this can be of profound
value, inasmuch as those who understand Russian
can read the *Catechism* in Russian, while those who
do not can read it in Aleut.

As concerns printing expenses—if only YOUR
GRACE will allow it to be printed—I have asked the
Chief Manager of the Russian-American Company ... to bear the expenses on its account and to
print 800 copies for this region. I hope that they will
accept and fulfill my request ...

Having completed his correspondence, Fr. John took
advantage of a ship leaving for the Pribilof Islands to make
his second trip of the summer, and his first pastoral visitation
there. On July 1 he offered a prayer-service for those wishing
to travel by sea and boarded ship. In the morning they left
harbor but were soon becalmed while still in sight of land.
The next day, a Sunday, the ship's whole crew kneeled with
Fr. John on deck as he repeated the petitions of the Liturgy,
and three days later they arrived off St. George Island. The
low, treeless profile of this island, so unlike the soaring
Aleutian chain, was shrouded (like them) in the usual dense
fog as they approached. Again only the squawks of seabirds
signalled their existence, but by afternoon as he was taken
ashore to perform his ministrations (the ship being unable

to remain for lack of safe anchorage) the skies cleared and remained so for the remainder of his visit.

The sole reason for the existence of a Russian colony on this cold and desolate mound of rock in the middle of the open ocean was plainly visible in the racks of drying hides and mounds of rotting carcasses too numerous to dispose of properly. These poisoned the village's air but did nothing to destroy the spirit of the inhabitants. After a day spent completing their Company chores (which could not be interrupted) they came to listen to Fr. John with all the attention he had seen in their relatively more fortunate brethren at home. For his part, Fr. John undertook his ministrations with full energy. In the morning he chrismated 32, in the afternoon he married eleven couples, and in the evening after vigil he heard 51 confessions. By next morning, July 9, when he served Liturgy in a tent and married one last couple, everyone in the village had been duly instructed and nourished with the sacraments.

Fr. John planned on leaving for near-by St. Paul Island next day after a prayer-service and an individual visit to each family's yurt and to the Company barracks, but a calm fell over the island, and it was Tuesday, the twelfth, before they completed the sixty-mile crossing. When Fr. John at long last stepped ashore on its sandy beach, the entire population was there to meet him. They took him through their less pungent and more prosperous village to the chapel which they themselves had built in 1821 and dedicated to Sts. Peter and Paul and then on to the governor's wooden house, where he spent the night in luxury rare on his travels anywhere in the islands. In the morning as his ship left to explore for islands suspected to lie to the southwest, Fr. John gathered the people into their well-appointed little chapel to teach them, as usual, through an interpreter. At their request he also celebrated a prayer-service to Sts. Peter and Paul and blessed some water. That day 41 people were chrismated. On Thursday another 32 joined them, and after vigil Fr. John spoke with all the children. This daily cycle continued over the next four days, and by Monday, when the ship returned to fetch him, Fr. John had heard another 103 confessions and performed thirteen more weddings. As he departed the people stood on the beach filled with profound gratitude towards their zealous pastor.

It was Fr. John's fervent hope to be home by August 1, for the anniversary of his first Liturgy on Unalaska had become the occasion for great festivities in Harbor Village. By the afternoon of July 31, Mount Makushin was in sight, but the winds died as they approached land. "Faith in God will not be put to shame," the priest remarked, and to be sure at dawn a brief but brisk tailwind sufficed to push the ship into harbor. The church bells rang out as the anchor plunged into the water and again that afternoon to summon the people to worship as Fr. John was being rowed ashore to begin the Hours. At their conclusion the now-traditional procession formed and moved first down to the stream to bless the waters and then circled the whole settlement. After giving thanks to God for his second safe voyage of the year, and unable by reason of the late date to undertake a third one to the nearest eastern islands, Fr. John settled back into his normal routine for another winter.

CHAPTER 5

THE SHAMAN

Early in April of 1828 a delegation of four kayaks arrived in Unalaska to conduct their priest to Unimak Island for his second planned visitation. He, however, was determined to stop first at near-by Akun Island, which he had not yet visited, and so mid-morning on April 12 five boats paddled out of Captain's Harbor on what was destined to be one of the most memorable trips of Fr. Veniaminov's entire ministry in America.

The eighty-mile voyage to Akun was remarkably calm and free of headwinds, and as they approached the rocky shoreline the whole village stood waiting. As he stepped ashore the priest sensed an atmosphere even more festive than usually attended his arrivals, and he inquired why this should be so. "Why, Fr. John," he was told, "we knew you'd set off and would arrive today, so we came out all full of joy on shore to meet you."

"Who told you I'd be coming today, and how did you know that I am Fr. John?"

"Our shaman, old John Smirennikov, told us: 'Wait. A priest will come today. He's already on his way, and he'll teach you to pray to God.' He even described your appearance to us—just like we see you now."

"Can I see your shaman?"

"Sure. He's not here right now, but when he comes, we'll tell him and he'll come to you himself."

Fr. John was amazed by this incident, but put it out of mind as he began his usual busy round of services. In the morning he gathered all the Aleuts in a tent and through

John Pankov taught them to confess their sins. On Saturday he chrismated 46 people, and after vigil he began hearing the confessions of all who had gathered from outside the village. Among them was Smirennikov, but the "shaman" behaved so properly that Fr. John paid him no special attention and, in fact, during confession neglected even to discuss with him why the Aleuts referred to him in this way. On Sunday Smirennikov along with all the rest received Holy Communion, but afterwards went immediately to his chieftan to complain about this priest who had failed to ask him about a name which he found so disagreeable—since he was most certainly *not* a shaman. Fr. John was informed in due time of the old man's displeasure and sent for him immediately to have an explanation. Smirennikov met the messengers on the way and informed them: "I know Fr. John wants to see me, "and I'm going there now."

Fr. John looked forward to this meeting, for through Pankov he had learned of several extraordinary incidents involving the old man, including these three which he later reported to his bishop:

1. In October of 1825, the wife of one Theodore Zharov, chieftain of the Artel Village, had her leg caught in a fox trap and was beyond medical help. She was at the point of death, having been wounded by all three of the trap's $3\frac{1}{2}$-inch long iron teeth. Her relatives secretly asked this old man Smirennikov to heal her, and he, having given it some thought, replied that in the morning she would be well. Indeed, to everyone's amazement, in the morning she stood up, walked about, and to this day feels no pain.

2. During the same winter (of 1825) the local inhabitants were extremely hard-pressed for food, and several of them asked Smirennikov "to give them a whale" (in their words). He promised to see about it. Very soon thereafter he informed the people that they should go to the place which he would designate and there they would find a whale. They

went and in the place he indicated they did indeed find a whole, fresh whale.

    3. Last autumn I had meant to go to Akun, but financial matters from Russia prevented this. All the people of Akun were waiting for me, and even sent someone to fetch me. He [Smirennikov], however, boldly insisted that I would be coming not that autumn but in the spring, and indeed contrary winds did prevent me from leaving until it became too late to travel at all. Thus I put off until spring my plans to go there . . .

The old man, too, was pleased at having this opportunity to talk and he answered all of Fr. John's questions candidly and freely. The breadth of Smirennikov's knowledge of the Gospel and of the Church's prayers amazed the priest. "Can you read?" he asked. No, replied Smirennikov, he could not, and as their discussion continued it became clear to Fr. John that there was no "normal" way for him to know these things. Hampered by a lack of qualified interpreters, earlier missionaries had contented themselves with baptizing all the natives (no mean feat in itself) but had done little more to Christianize them. "Though they came to believe and prayed to God before my arrival," Fr. John records, "they scarcely knew in Whom they believed or to Whom they prayed." John Pankov, the only competent translator then in the region, disliked and shunned Smirennikov, who, thus cut off from any contact with the Russians, had no way of knowing the theology that he consistently proved he knew.

How had he known Fr. John before they ever met? How could he describe him with such accuracy or confidently foretell to all the Aleuts the time of his arrival? Smirennikov replied quite simply that two companions had informed him of these things.

"And just who are these two 'companions' of yours?" Fr. John asked the old man.

"White men," he replied. "And they told me that very soon you're going to see your family off on shore and sail away to see some great man, and you'll talk to him."

"And where are these 'white men'? What kind of people are they? What do they look like?"

"They live near-by, in the mountains. And they visit me every day." The old man then provided a description which tallied very closely with the way in which the Holy Archangel Gabriel is portrayed on icons: in a white robe with a rose-colored band across the shoulders.

"When did these 'white men' first appear to you?" asked the priest, and Smirennikov proceeded to tell a story so amazing that Fr. John was inspired to report the whole of it to his bishop, "for although the grace of God has not grown weak," he writes, "nor can it ever do so—still, in these latter days such things as these have become quite rare, or are, at the very least, not widely heard of." Here follows Fr. John's report:

Soon after he was baptized by Hieromonk Macarius, first one and later two spirits appeared to him but were visible to no one else ... They told him that they were sent by God to edify, teach and guard him. For the next thirty years they appeared to him almost every day, either during daylight hours or early in the evening—but never at night. On these occasions: (1) They taught him in its totality Christian theology and the mysteries of the faith ... (2) In time of sickness and famine they brought help to him and—though more rarely—to others at his request. (When agreeing to his requests that they help others, they always responded by saying that they would first have to ask God, and if it was His will, then they would do it.) (3) Occasionally they told him of things occurring in another place or (very rarely) at some time in the future—but then only if God willed such a revelation; in such cases they would persuade him that they did so not by their own power, but by the power of Almighty God.

Their doctrine is that of the Orthodox Church. I, however, knowing that even the demons believe—

and tremble with fear [Jas. 2:19], wondered whether or not this might be the crafty and subtle snare of him who from time immemorial has been Evil. I therefore asked him, "How do they teach you to pray, to themselves or to God? And how do they teach you to live with others?" He answered that they taught him to pray not to them but to the Creator of all, and to pray in spirit, with the heart; occasionally they would even pray along with him for long periods of time.

They taught him to exercise all pure Christian virtues (which he related to me in detail), and recommended, furthermore, that he remain faithful and pure, both within and outside of marriage (this perhaps because the locals are quite given to such impurity). Furthermore, they taught him all the outward virtues . . .

Next, I asked him if they had appeared to him that day after confession and communion, and whether they had told him to listen to me. He answered that they had appeared to him after both confession and communion, and had told him not to talk with anyone else about the sins he had confessed, not to eat anything rich right after communion, and to listen to *my* doctrines but not to the traders (i.e., the Russians) living here. They even appeared to him on the road that day, told him why I had summoned him, and instructed him to tell me everything; he should not be afraid, for no evil would befall him. I then asked how he feels when they appear to him, happy or sad? He replied that if he has been doing evil when he sees them, he feels remorse; at other times he feels no fear.

Inasmuch as many consider him to be a shaman and he does not wish to be considered one, he asked the angels several times to leave him and never appear again, but they replied that they were not devils and had not been instructed to leave him. In answer to his question as to why they appear to no

one other than him, they replied that that was what
they were told to do.

Following this conversation Fr. John asked Smirennikov
if he could see these spirits of his. "I'll ask," the old man replied and walked away.

Fr. John then departed[7] for several days to preach and
minister to the people on Tigalda, Avatanok and Unimak
Islands. When he returned to Akun, his first question to
Smirennikov as soon as they met was, "Well, did you ask
these 'white men' if I could see them, if they'll receive me?"

"Yes," he answered, "and they say they'd like to see
you, only—why do you need to see them if you're teaching
us the same things they are? Anyway, come on. I'll take you
to them."[8]

Something unexplainable then happened to Fr. John, as
he reports to the bishop:

> I was filled with fear and humility, and thought to
> myself, "What if I really *were* to see them—these
> angels—and they were to confirm all that the old
> man said? How *can* I go to see them? I'm a sinful
> man, unworthy of talking to them. If I *were* to decide
> to see them it would be nothing but pride and pre-
> sumption on my part. If I were to meet real angels
> I might exalt myself for having such great faith, or
> start thinking too highly of myself ... No, I'm un-
> worthy; I'd best not go."

He adds further in his report to Bp. Michael:

> ... by all that he [Smirennikov] had said above
> and confirmed by an oath ... by the freedom, fear-
> lessness and certain satisfaction with which he spoke
> —and even moreso by his upright life—I was con-
> vinced that the spirits which appear to this old man

---

[7] Another version has Smirennikov returning that same day.

[8] They purportedly also said some things complementary to Fr. John which
he in humility declined even to report.

(if indeed they do appear) are not devils, for although the devil can indeed at times transform himself into an angel of light, he never does so for purposes of exhortation and salvation but always for the destruction of man. Inasmuch as an evil tree cannot bring forth good fruit, these must be ministering spirits sent for those who wish to inherit salvation.

Fr. John's report ends with his resolution of the situation:

Therefore, in order that his faith and hope in the One, Almighty and Omniscient God might not in some manner grow weak, I ventured, even before receiving permission from Your Grace, to give him the following exhortation: "I see that the spirits which appear to you are not devils; therefore, heed their doctrines and exhortations whenever these contradict nothing I have taught you in the general assembly. To those who question you concerning the future or who seek your help say that they should ask God, the Father of all. I do not forbid you to heal people: just be sure to tell anyone whom you decide to heal that it is the power of God which performs it and not your own. Recommend that they pray diligently to the One God and thank Him. Neither do I forbid you to teach others, but do no more than exhort those of tender age. Tell no one—*not even me*—about the future." Then I told and commanded the other Aleuts who were there that none of them was to call him a shaman or to ask about or for anything from him, but from God alone.

At dawn the next morning Fr. John returned to Unalaska, arriving in the evening, but this was not the end of the amazing story of John Smirennikov. In Irkutsk Bp. Michael shared this tale with many of his acquaintances, "outstanding in mind and heart," and all were duly impressed. Thanking

Fr. Veniaminov for his detailed report, the bishop wrote this
letter in reply:

> ... I thank you also for your wise advise and per-
> fectly proper exhortations both to Smirennikov and
> to his fellow Aleuts that they no longer falsely call
> him a "shaman," and, furthermore, that this shaman
> not seek or desire the glory of a miracle-worker. I
> tell you sincerely and frankly that by not allowing
> your curiosity to surpass your faith you are more
> blessed than those who, like the Holy Apostle
> Thomas, must touch everything in which they be-
> lieve. However, just as in our church hymns Thomas'
> doubt is called "good," I (and many others with
> me) wish that you would consent to visit and speak
> with the spirits which appear to Smirennikov (if he
> is still alive), doing so for the greater glorification
> of our pious faith. No precautions are required for
> this beyond your pure faith and prayer of the heart.
> Remember only throughout your meeting with these
> spirits to say the Lord's Prayer; you should also recite
> it together with them. Speak with them of nothing
> but the destiny of your parishioners, the newly-
> converted Aleuts. For their sakes you may ask these
> angels to ask from God whatsoever good you wish.
> *Sat sapienti.*
>
> Whatever God grants you to know through the
> Gift of His Christ, inform me when convenient,
> either by letter or in person when in the future we
> shall have a welcome meeting.
>
> Asking God's blessing upon you, I remain your
> well-wishing servant,
>
> † MICHAEL, Abp. of Irkutsk

Mail deliveries being what they were, however, it was
over three years later when this reply reached America, and
by then John Smirennikov was dead. He had forseen the day
and hour of his passing, and when the appointed time had
come he gathered his family together, lit a candle before an

icon, prayed and bade farewell to all. He then rolled over on his bed towards the wall and peacefully surrendered his soul to God.

One of those in Russia who found inspiration in this story was Andrew Muravev, a man who in later years came to know Fr. John quite well, and who left us this very fitting analysis of the entire incident:

> Once again, one scarcely knows at which to be amazed—the miraculous gifts of the old Aleut or the humility of the missionary who in patience is denied a singular opportunity to satisfy his obviously holy curiosity in such an unusual matter, simply in order not to transgress the commandment of obedience. The old man's premature death, however, vindicated his actions by showing clearly that these revelations had been necessary for himself, his family and his people only for as long as the Aleutian Islands remained spiritually neglected. Now, however, by the grace of God, people have come to work towards their salvation, and the heavenly guides concealed themselves once again.[*]

---

[*] Muravev writes further:

It is comforting to read about such miraculous Divine Providence towards savages, sons of Adam *who, though forgotten by the world, were not forgotten by Providence, but because human means were lacking, were fed through the faith of one of their elders upon the saving faith—even though this was preached to them only in part.*

(Emphasis in the original. Cf. *Epokha* 1866, pp. 105-6.)

CHAPTER 6

THE PRICE AND FRUIT OF MISSIONS

"The ministry on Unalaska Island which I began on 29 July 1824 I do not wish to continue beyond mid-1831."

Although Russian subjects signing on to go to America in any capacity were obliged to pass no more than five years in service to the Company before free passage home was guaranteed them, these words from Fr. Veniaminov doubtless provoked surprise and shock when they arrived in Irkutsk. This all the more so since they came in the same shipment with his report about Smirennikov and other dispatches which as in past years showed clearly that his ministry was bearing fruit. When one reads, however, the full text of this "Humble Request" to Abp. Michael, one can appreciate the sorrow behind it and the reasons why it was granted.

> The ministry on Unalaska Island which I began on 29 July 1824 I do not wish to continue beyond mid-1831. Neither the distances involved in traveling between far-flung islands nor any such reasons lie behind this; I am simply unable to continue my ministry here—a ministry which has been spent with joyous heart—because of my health, which is already poor and still declining in the climate here, and yet is so essential for the travels which are needed if the Aleuts are truly to be helped.
>
> Therefore I humbly ask YOUR EMINENCE that YOU select someone to succeed me in my work, and allow me (once he arrives) to return to Irkutsk

with my whole family, and that YOU issue YOUR
most merciful archpastoral resolution to my petition . . .

Fr. John wrote this painful letter long in advance of his
planned departure, knowing how slow the process of finding
a replacement was apt to be. Specifically, the ailment which
threatened to put an end to his missionary work in America
was arthritis in his legs, caused by their being held sixteen
hours and more at a stretch virtually motionless in kayaks
whose thin hulls offered virtually no protection against
frigid sea water. Even when he finally was able to climb
out of his boat, most of the time was spent in exposed, usually
cold locations. Never could he really claim to be comfortable
while on the road.

Despite such conditions, for as long as he remained
pastor of the Unalaskan Church, Fr. John was determined to
continue traveling and visiting his people. And so, after completing his correspondence, he took advantage of a Company
ship westward-bound to pay a visit to Umnak Island.

The purpose of this short trip was to consecrate the
newly-completed chapel on the island, the second in a chain
of "prayer-houses" which Fr. John envisaged stretching
throughout the islands. Work began on it soon after his first
visit, using plans which he himself had drawn. Lumber for
it was requested from the Russian-American Company, but
when the tender *Unalaska* arrived in Nikolski after ten days
of fighting rough seas it was obvious to the "architect" that
the Aleuts had made do with their usual building materials,
the remnants of ships wrecked at sea which washed up in
abundance on their shores. Still, they had done an admirable
job, producing a spacious chapel with a cupola piercing the
foggy sky. Inside was an iconostasis and an altar table. It was
the afternoon of August 15, the Dormition of the Theotokos,
when they arrived, and that evening vigil was served for the
first time in the new house of God. In the morning before
Liturgy, St. Nicholas' Chapel was dedicated according to the
rite for the blessing of new homes.

The *Unalaska* left several days later, taking the normal northern route home, but Fr. John stayed behind, hoping to spend more time ministering to his flock and in particular to visit by foot and kayak those living in isolation along the southern shores of the two islands. He saw many people there for the first time, and tried through them to establish contact with their nomadic brethren whom he had not yet met. It was the last day of August before Fr. John reached home, but even then he was to find no rest for several weeks, for envoys from the nearby islands lying to the northeast were waiting to request that he pay them a visit too, and he was disposed to go. On September 12 his yearly travels finally ended, and to mark the passing of another busy year he blessed the site of a new bell tower and began construction on it.

The next year, 1829, was again one of extensive travel, beginning soon after Pascha with Fr. John's normal biennial visitation to the eastern regions, bringing to the people there a far more detailed presentation than before of the doctrines of Christianity: Who Christ is and the obligation of each Christian to imitate Him in humility, patience and suffering in order through them to become perfect.[10] But the truly historic visitation that year was as yet to come. Fr. John was home on Unalaska for only two weeks when the year's mail arrived on the brig *Golovnin* which, he learned, was scheduled still to visit Bristol Bay and the Pribilof Islands. Fr. John had long hoped to "sow the Word of God in the North"(or at least, he adds, to "learn about the 'soil' there"), and having standing permission from his bishop to do so, he seized upon

[10] This trip produced an entry in Fr. John's diary which illustrates the very point he was preaching about, and is most striking both by its expression and by the fact that it is unique in his extant writings:

Today and the past two days were very boring and rather sad for me, for I never expected our kayaks would be able to arrive against the [prevailing] strong east wind by today or even tomorrow. This, in addition to my poor health and an almost total lack of provisions, greatly upset me. (This was, however, the first time in all my travels that such unpleasantness had overtaken me.) Nevertheless, God Who comforts everyone deigned today to give me joy. First, my health, which had been troubling me considerably as a result of a cold and the complete lack of anything to remedy it, improved noticeably after noon; secondly, beyond all hope our kayaks appeared at four o'clock.

this opportunity. The manager of the Company's Sitka office, Cyril Khlebnikov, was aboard the *Golovnin*, and gladly granted permission for the priest to join them. He even went so far as to change their scheduled visitations to include St. George Island, thereby allowing Fr. John to visit all his parishioners in that isolated region.

By June 20 all preparations were completed, and although a calm lay over the island, a prayer-service for those about to travel was offered in the chapel and everyone went aboard. By morning the winds had freshened and the expedition was on its way.

At noon on its eighth day at sea the *Golovnin* dropped anchor before the mouth of the Nushegak River to await the safety of high tide before attempting to navigate its treacherous estuary where on the sandbars more than one ship had met an untimely end. By evening they had gone as far upstream as possible by ship and anchored for the night. They sat surrounded by a world of green. The summer air was filled with fragrances of birch and alder. Clumps of spruce trees with their delicate new growth rose from muddy earth which not too many days before had been locked in winter's lingering grip. Now ferns and cotton grass and a multitude of berry bushes made this an altogether different world from Fr. John's rocky island home. At dawn he packed a kayak with the supplies he would need for his ministrations and paddled off, arriving mid-morning at Fort Alexander.

This minor wooden stockade, just ten years old, was built as protection for the fur industry. It had taken over twenty years after Fr. Juvenal's murder back in 1796 for economic interests to lure the Russians back onto the Alaskan mainland, and in 1829 Fort Alexander still remained almost exclusively a Russian enclave. A handful of natives lived and worked inside as servants of the Company, but no native villages were to be found in the vicinity—not because they were forbidden, but because the inhabitants of these forests lived as nomads, showing up outside the gates each year in May and again towards the end of August to barter their wares, but never in groups of over 100-150. When Fr. John arrived, there were only five such nomads to be found, and with little prospect

at present of doing missionary work, he turned his attention
first to ministering to those inside the fort. On his first Sunday
he chrismated eight children (including one native Aglemiut)
baptized by laymen soon after birth, and in a tent celebrated
Divine Liturgy. That day, he records, there were

> at my invitation 5 savages who had happened to
> arrive and who watched the Mystical Service with
> the greatest of attention. Afterwards I told them
> (through an interpreter) that we had been offering
> here, in a spirit of humility and thankfulness, the
> Bloodless Sacrifice to the true God, the Creator of
> heaven and earth and of all mankind. They listened
> attentively.

Seven more natives arrived that evening, but when by July 2
no more appeared to be forthcoming, Fr. John decided that
this would have to suffice for a beginning. He invited all the
natives to his quarters in the fort and sought to convince them
to listen to his message. All fourteen agreed.

> Then, calling to help Him without Whom we can
> do nothing, I told them (through an interpreter)
> that there is no other God, than the One Whom we—
> and many others—worship. I told them Who this
> God is, what He has created, what pleases Him and
> what displeases Him. Finally, I told them that man
> was created not simply for a temporal life here but
> for life eternal, and what we must do in order to
> receive this blessed eternity. I dared not—and could
> not—speak any more than this, for my interpreter was
> not overly competent.
>
> Having taught them thus I asked what *they*
> thought. They replied that now they believed. One
> of them—quite unexpectedly—asked me, "How is
> it that I think and do things that I don't want or
> desire to think or do?" I answered that everyone is
> that way, and so forth. Therefore, the more one con-
> quers himself, the greater the reward that he will

receive there in eternity. This is the Christian's most
essential duty, and for this one needs God's help,
which is received through prayer, etc. Finally, I asked
each of them individually if he wished to be included
with those who believe in the true God, and all of
them (except one) voluntarily consented. One of
these then said, "I would be included eagerly, but I
am a shaman." I told him that if he were to abandon
his shamanism he could be included among the
believers. He agreed. Afterwards I told them about
what they must do and ended by telling them that
they would receive no gifts. They replied, "We require none." Then, although nothing prevented our
proceeding with the Sacrament [of Baptism] I
ordered them to think about it more thoroughly and
to give me their answer next day. (The one who did
not express a desire to be baptized I dismissed in
peace.)

In the morning, inasmuch as the natives were unchanged
in their intention to be baptized, Fr. John set up his tent by
the river bank and proceeded with the rite. One by one they
were required to renounce the devil, "and the Nushegak became for them the Jordan River."

After baptizing them, Fr. John gave each new Christian
back his former clothing rather than the traditional new white
shirt that their godparents wished to provide them. The cheap
copper cross which he placed around each one's neck would
have to suffice as a symbol of the new life they had entered.
"I did this," he explains,

intending that the shirts... not become for other
savages a false incentive to accept baptism, or a
contrivance as had once happened among the
Chugach. These at their baptism were as usual given
some little gifts which *for them* were *very* valuable indeed; then they, having been baptized by
one priest and receiving the gifts offered them, would
next year go to another priest—or even return to

the same one a while later! For the local savages
shirts are a very valuable and important thing.

Fr. John continued his ministrations to everyone in the
fort, and by Friday, July 9, he was finished. Several native
women, as yet undecided about accepting this initiation for
themselves, sought baptism for their children, and Fr. John
obliged them. Before leaving Fort Alexander he empowered
its pious commandant to baptize anyone who came requesting
it, but on strict condition that he likewise never offer gifts
to any of them. At dawn on Saturday the *Golovnin* began the
trip downstream, and once they were safely out at sea again,
under sail for the Pribilofs, Fr. John offered a prayer-service
on deck to thank God for their safe passage thus far and for
having allowed them to fulfill their good intentions on the
Alaskan mainland. "Thus," he records in his diary, "were
the first fruits of the Word of God sown by my unworthy hand
in this wild but fertile soil."

The voyage to the islands did nothing to spoil the missionary's exuberance. The sky was clear, the sea was calm
the whole way, and they averaged over 130 miles a day, driven
by steady breezes. On Sunday, July 14, after serving the Hours
on deck, they sighted St. Paul Island shrouded in its customary
fog. Fr. John spent thirteen busy days in the Pribilofs and
returned home to Unalaska on the last day of July.

CHAPTER 7

HOME LIFE AND LABORS

Fr. John's homecoming from the north was made even more joyous than it would normally have been in the wake of a successful mission, by the news that in his absence a second daughter had been born to his wife, Catherine, on June 27. Both daughter and mother were in fine health, and it was decided to postpone the child's baptism until the radiant Feast of the Transfiguration, five days hence.

Olga was the Veniaminov's fifth child. Innocent was now six years old and one of twenty-five students enrolled in the village school. Catherine was five, sons Gabriel and Alexander were three and one respectively. They together with the other children in Harbor Village occupied much of their father's free time.

Catechism, the sacred history of the Old Testament, Russian grammar, simple arithmetic, reading and writing were the subjects taught in school—whenever cold did not prevent its opening. But just as his own education had early assumed a broader scope, so Fr. John sought to open new horizons to his children as well. He told them stories and played ball with them whenever time was short; whenever possible he made a point of taking them on walks in the hills surrounding the village, where he taught them the secrets of nature. (Eventually these walks proved their practical value as well, for when Fr. John judged there were enough he talked the children into using all the rocks they had been gathering to lay a path from the house to the door of the church.)

Fr. John still enjoyed broadening his own mind by reading, and he spent his evenings avidly consuming everything sent him from Sitka or Irkutsk. In his carpenter's shop he continued to work with his hands, and especially in the early years there were plenty of building projects around the church and house. Once most of these had been completed he enjoyed making organs and clocks. In any project he tried always to involve the children. He could no more stand to see them idle than he could himself endure having nothing to do. Regularly they made the candles used in church, and whenever there was something to be built each child found himself with a task to accomplish. For the youngest there were such vital tasks as holding the hammer or handing over the tacks. For the older ones there were more responsible things to do, such as planing or gluing together the parts. No one, however, was allowed to become frustrated at his work, for a good explanation of what was to be done preceded every project, and simple rewards awaited everyone who performed his duty well.

The depth of the shallow stream near the house was monitored by a device of Fr. John's invention, and if the children were found to have nothing to do at either of the appointed times each day, they would be summoned together and asked, "Well, kids, who can tell me the water level first?" and they would bound off, barefoot, to the opposite bank, take the reading and scamper back again. The "winner" received his reward—usually the wild berries native to the island which the children liked so much. By including them in his projects, Fr. John found that the most important of these could be continued even in his absence.

This was fortunate, since the Veniaminovs' house had become by 1828 a small meteorological observatory. Mounted on the shady side were a barometer, a thermometer and a home-made anemometer. Both at home and on his voyages, Fr. John kept a daily notebook of temperatures, humidity, cloud formations, precipitation, tides and currents, wind velocities and like natural phenomena. To these he added careful notes about the flora and fauna he found throughout the islands.

This work received an added impetus in the summer of 1828 with the unexpected arrival in Captain's Harbor of two

naval sloops, the *Seniavin* and the *Möller*, en route from
St. Petersburg to the Bering Sea on a mission to chart these
still largely unfamiliar waters. It was almost accidental that
the expedition even stopped at Unalaska at all. It had no real
business there, but had been convinced by the Chief Manager
in Sitka to drop off a shipment of grain for the inhabitants of
Harbor Village and at the same time to hire there a kayak
and its crew to aid in collecting data close to shore on the
islands that they would be visiting. The winds, however, which
truly rule the region, held the expedition in harbor for nine
straight days against its will, thus giving Fr. John ample time
to become well acquainted with the skipper of the *Seniavin*,
Theodore Lütke.[11]

Naturally inquisitive, intelligent, and largely self-trained,
Lütke shared much in common with the missionary priest,
and the two developed bonds of mutual respect and friend-
ship. Fr. John describes as "enlightened and dedicated" this
pious young navigator and geographer who, his reputation
already well-established even before this expedition began,
was as a result of it destined to be elected to the Academy of
Sciences and to become co-founder of the Russian Geographic
Society. To him the priest entrusted his notebooks.

Lütke for his part was instantly aware of how fortunate
this meeting would prove for science and readily accepted
the responsibility. In his memoirs of the voyage he records:

> Father John studied in the Irkutsk Seminary and,
> still in his prime, came here where with the full zeal
> of youth he abandoned himself to his duties—and
> not just to those connected with being a pastor, but

[11] Theodore Lütke (or Litke, 1797-1882) was by 1828 a decorated naval
veteran and an acclaimed scientist. His first book, a description of four previous
voyages to the Bering Sea in 1821-1824, was being published in St. Petersburg
and was beginning to draw even greater attention to its author in the scholarly
world. His description of the present voyage would win him a prize from
the Academy of Sciences and election to it as a corresponding member. By
1843 he was promoted to the rank of Vice-Admiral; in 1845 he founded the
Russian Geographic Society; in 1846 he became president of the Marine Scientific Committee, and in 1864, president of the Academy of Sciences itself. In
1866 he was ennobled. Lütke was the first of many persons of influence and
means whom Fr. Veniaminov was destined to meet.

to those also which serve to advance the natural sciences.

In a short time he learned the Aleut language sufficiently well to be able to translate the *Catechism* and thus (in addition to the humble and intelligent way in which he dealt with them) earned the trust of the islanders to such a degree that every year as he visits the outlying locales of the Unalaskan District he always finds some people ready to convert to the faith. (At the same time, his earlier spiritual children are beginning to become Christians in more than name alone.)

His time free from pastoral duties he devotes to observing nature, making most of the needed instruments himself. From his industry we can in time expect substantial data on the Aleutian Islands and their inhabitants.

The significance that this meeting would have for Fr. Veniaminov, however, he could not foresee. Lütke was destined to become, as it were, an "agent" in St. Petersburg for the priest's scholarly work, the first important contact he would make in the capital. Fr. John began sending him materials regularly and enthusiastically, declaring in a letter, "For as long as I shall live here [on Unalaska] I shall never cease making additional observations. Please allow me to say just how pleasant it is for me to conduct such observations!"

In September of 1828, Fr. John set out on his second voyage of the year, to nearby Akun Island. It was in all respects a "routine" trip; they were bestormed at sea, twice forced ashore on deserted islands, once almost capsized by a pod of whales—but once there, together with John Pankov, "having invoked the help of God the Word," he began work on the monumental task of translating the Gospel into Aleut.

In their enthusiasm they completed two chapters during their first night of work. In two weeks, through "unremitting labors" and "with the help of God and the prayers of the Holy Apostle and Evangelist Matthew," they had finished the entire book with the exception of two troublesome verses—

Mt. 7:17 (for which not a single word in the original had an equivalent in Fox-Aleut) and Mt. 9:17, whose content they found unclear. The Passion narrative they augmented from the other Evangelists.

Back on Unalaska work continued into the fall and winter of 1830. In December a finished draft was ready to begin soliciting outside criticism. One interpreter, Daniel Kuziakin, gathered everyone whom he could night after night and read the text to them until the whole Gospel had been read through five times. Only in one place did he find an expression too weak, and the correction which he proposed Fr. John found most appropriate and incorporated it. A second interpreter, Stephen Kriukov, the zealous creole in charge of the office on Unimak Island, also reviewed it and found no errors at all.

With the arrival of spring Fr. John prepared to end his ministry on Unalaska. All of the potential obstacles to his leaving as planned had vanished. Abp. Michael had succeeded in obtaining for the Veniaminovs a firm promise from the Russian-American Company to pay their traveling expenses home to Russia.[12] Furthermore, as a result of the Company's decision to close its Sitka office and transfer the personnel to Kodiak, it would no longer be necessary to await a replacement from Russia. Fr. Sokolov could simply move out to Unalaska and cover Kodiak as well for the time being.

There remained on Unalaska, however, certain unfinished projects for Fr. John to attend to in the meantime. He had been carving a new iconostasis for the Church of the Ascension which he hoped still to see finished. A school for orphan girls had opened in March and he would have for several months to continue overseeing its initial development. Finally, there lay before him one more trip to the outlying areas of his parish after one last Pascha, which was destined to be memorable, for in preparation for it he had specially translated the appropriate lection from the prologue to St. John's Gospel: "In the beginning was the Word." That year, 1831, history was

---

[12] He was not, however, able to obtain for the missionary a pension from the Company. Although it agreed that he was surely deserving of one, its charter contained no such provisions.

made, as for the first time ". . . the Gospel was read in Church
Slavonic, in Russian, and in Fox-Aleut (by the priest, the
cantor and a creole—Zach. Chichinev—respectively)."

The last visitation was itself memorable, as we read in
Fr. John's report to Abp. Michael:

> . . . on Unimak, where almost all of the inhabitants
> of the western portion of my parish were gathered
> together, I read to all those gathered the last three
> chapters [of Matthew] while the creole Stephen
> Kriukov listened to them and translated [what they
> said] into Russian. All listened and understood and
> afterwards expressed their desire to have such books
> for themselves.
>
> Despite all this (and the fact that I am convinced
> that inasmuch as this is possible—given the present
> state of the language—this translation is both faith-
> ful to the original and comprehensible) I am not
> sending it to you as yet, planning still to check it
> more carefully, to give it to others to read and to
> read it whenever possible to those who know
> [Aleut]. Next year I shall have the honor of bringing
> it to YOUR EMINENCE together with the *Cate-
> chism* which I am now beginning to translate with
> zeal and attention.[13]

Fr. John arrived home on Unalaska on June 11, 1841,
to find his parishioners busily at work putting in place his
as-yet-unfinished iconostasis as a surprise for him, and as he
waited for a Company ship to arrive from Sitka, he put the
final touches on it in order to bless it before leaving.

---

[13] The reason for Fr. John's beginning a new translation of the *Catechism*
is found in an ukase of the Holy Synod dated November 14, 1828. While
agreeing in principle to the publication of such materials for use by the natives,
the hierarchs found that the original Russian text underlying his translation
did not correspond with that prepared by Metropolitan Philaret in 1823 and
subsequently sanctioned for exclusive use. It was decided, however, that once
the Aleut translation was made to correspond with this official text, Abp.
Michael would be authorized locally to sanction its publication by the Russian-
American Company without further recourse to St. Petersburg.

This event took place with great solemnity on the seventh anniversary of the Veniaminovs' arrival on Unalaska, but by then it was no longer a pressing matter, for the mail ship which arrived on July 18 brought from the Consistory in Irkutsk official word that on June 5, 1830, Abp. Michael had fallen asleep in the Lord. Clearly the Veniaminovs' plans for returning home to Russia would have to be postponed until a successor for the See of Irkutsk could be chosen,[14] and for several days Fr. John and his flock mourned and prayed for the soul of the man whom he had hoped soon to see again in person—the hierarch who had helped train him in seminary and who ordained him to the holy priesthood, that "most caring father" who over the years had labored ceaselessly from afar to ease his difficult work in this distant land, and who had, in fact, inspired that work, as we read in one of Fr. John's last letters to him:

> ... emboldened by YOUR EMINENCE's example, YOUR mercy and benevolence, I shall try to conduct my ministry after YOUR own heart, and will to the end of my days pray to the Source of joy for YOUR health, which is so precious to us all.

For Stephen Veniaminov, however, this news did not require a change of plans. Ready to resume the seminary studies which he had abandoned in his youth, he prepared with his young Aleut wife Melany and their year-old son Theodosius to return to Irkutsk. With him would also go his nephews Innocent and Gabriel, themselves now old enough to enter seminary, and their grandmother who at age 66 was now ready to go home and spend her final years in peace.

---

[14] A quick succession of hierarchs—Irenaeus, Meletius, Innocent and Nilus—in the Diocese of Irkutsk in fact made it years before the transfer was completed.

CHAPTER 8

END OF AN ERA

By the time summer's second ship sailed into Captain's Harbor on July 4, 1831, Fr. John was prepared to discuss travel arrangements for the coming year with its distinguished passenger, Baron Ferdinand von Wrangell, the new Chief Manager of the colonies. Fr. John's growing enthusiasm at the prospects of a second visit of the north—Nushegak—now eclipsed all the sorrow and disappointment of recent days, and while Wrangell was more than happy to oblige him by arranging the transportation that he would need, he was more disposed to talk in broader terms about how to keep this now-famous missionary in America.

He informed Fr. John first that the proposed transfer of the main office to Kodiak—upon which his own trip home had hinged—had been called off. Then he began impressing upon him the need to have a really good priest in the largest city in Russian America (where, incidentally, both the weather and the amount of travel required would be, by comparison with Unalaska, considerably less strenuous on his health). We have no details of their conversation, but its outcome is clear from a letter which Fr. Veniaminov soon afterwards wrote home to Irkutsk. He reviewed for the as-yet-unknown hierarch the promises made to him by his late predecessor and then continued:

> ... however, despite the fact that (as everyone well knows) the main factory will remain (and probably permanently) in its present location, I humbly ask YOUR GRACE to allow me to leave my present duties and that YOU select for me a replacement ...

Futhermore, I have the honor of reporting to
YOUR GRACE that should there be a vacancy, and
should YOUR GRACE consent to appoint me there,
I should be pleased to serve in Sitka for as long as my
health permits, but in any case for no longer than
five years.

Fr. John was destined to spend another two years on
Unalaska before his transfer came through. He saw to it,
however, that the time was well-spent in visits to his parishioners and in completing and systematizing all the materials that
he had been gathering in this isolated land.

In 1832, after an absence of three years, Fr. John returned to visit his northernmost parishioners. Accompanying
Baron von Wrangell aboard the galliot *Mariner*, he and a
translator arrived on July 8 at Fort Alexander on the Nushegak
River. There he found that through the commander's zeal
the Church had increased by seventy members from among
various local tribes. These were Fr. John's first pastoral concern, and on his first Sunday he gathered them to teach them
about the God Whom they now served and hoped in. Next
morning they were chrismated and on Wednesday, together
with the Russians and creoles living in the fort, they received
Communion for the first time. In the afternoon he went on ex-
horting everyone to be good Christians, zealous for their God
and kind in their relations with all men. The Chief Manager
was so moved by all he saw that he ordered a log chapel be
constructed in the fort to accommodate the growing number
of the faithful. It would replace one they themselves had
begun to build of driftwood. Fr. John provides the following
evaluation of his visit:

Several of the first-born of the local Church (i.e.,
those whom I baptised in 1829) had no sooner heard
of my arrival than they came and gave me joy by
recounting their initial successes in the path to Christianity. Some brought their families along for me to
baptize, and I fulfilled their wish . . .
Thus, the Church of Nushegak (or better, the

North American Church), whose formation began in 1829, now consists of some 220 people (excluding Russians and creoles). Our hope for the local Church—for the dissemination of Christianity in the region—is very great indeed, and (one might say) very sure: for one needs only to begin and the local Church will multiply to several thousand in a very few years.

On July 15 the *Mariner* departed for the Pribilof Islands. There Fr. John found that his long absence had left much work to be done. Many newborns had to be chrismated, many elderly and sick required special attention, and the whole population needed exhortation and instruction. Their zeal for the faith was as strong as ever, for whenever he began to preach they would drop everything and come, and would listen attentively for as long as he was able to go on. Such zeal did not deserve the little attention which he could pay them, and so, as he reports to his bishop, being concerned for their welfare—for who could tell how long it would be before he or any other priest would be able to see them again—he decided at their own request to "leave several particles of the Reserved Holy Gifts for the sick, giving appropriate instructions to the local manager about preserving and using them in time of extreme need."

In the spring of 1833 Fr. John visited the extensive eastern region of his parish, and in 1834 the western villages, and so completed his ministrations in the Aleutian Islands. Both of these trips, however, were particularly fruitful, for he carried with him and read at every opportunity a lengthy treatise on the Christian life which he had spent the winter of 1833 composing. The title of this first original work in the Aleut language was: *An Indication of the Pathway into the Kingdom of Heaven.*[15]

By the summer of 1834, Fr. John Veniaminov had indeed, in the words of the conclusion to this treatise, ". . . inasmuch as I was able . . ." shown his parishioners "the Pathway into

[15]A full translation is included in volume 2 of the present work.

the Kingdom of Heaven," and was able openly to declare
that

> ... no difficulty, no danger on the way—however
> great—was able to stop me from visiting the inhabit-
> ants of this area. They are good sheep of Christ's
> flock—even exemplary, I must say frankly, in terms
> of their zeal, and rare in today's world for their zeal-
> ous and constant hearing of my teachings. Further-
> more, their simple, sincere gratitude for this is a
> tremendous satisfaction for me—and one of the
> greatest rewards on this earth.

The time had now come, though, to begin putting all things
in order and to hand them over to his successor.

On June 3, 1834, word came from Sitka that a replacement was on the way. He was Fr. Gregory Golovin, newly
ordained and sent from Siberia. He arrived in person thirteen days later, and over the next two months as Fr. John continued his preparations for departure, the two priests became
well acquainted. Finally, on the tenth anniversary of his arrival on Unalaska Fr. John recorded in his diary:

> I celebrated Liturgy and a service of thanksgiving
> to the Lord God Who has enabled me in good health,
> safety and (if only I am able to see and to judge by
> what I see) some measure of success to complete my
> active ministry on Unalaska. Today I also handed
> over to my successor all the Church archives and
> papers.

The days flew by, recorded tersely yet poigniantly in
Fr. John's diary:

> [Aug. 1] At my successor's invitation we con-
>   celebrated Liturgy and the blessing of
>   waters at the stream. . . .
> [Aug. 12] I celebrated my last Liturgy on Un-
>   alaska.

[Aug. 14] At the Hours, served by the Priest Golovin, I delivered to all the local inhabitants who had gathered a speech
which I had written for the occasion. It
was on the text, "In a little while you
will not see me anymore, and then a
little while later you will see me"
[Jn. 16:16]—*about how we will all
without fail see one another there, in
blessed eternity.* Immediately afterwards I boarded ship, being seen off by
each and everyone with sincere gratitude
and regret—as witnessed by the tears in
the eyes of every Aleut. That same day
at one o'clock we raised anchor and
sailed for Sitka. Thus ended my sojourn
on Unalaska, lasting 10 years and 17 days
(i.e., from 29 July 1824 to 15 August
1834).

CHAPTER 9

THE TLINGITS

The Veniaminovs reached their destination in safety on August 22. By now there were only seven of them: Fr. John and Catherine together with five of their children: Catherine, Alexander, Olga, Paraskeva and Thekla, for Fr. John's mother and his two oldest sons, Innocent and Gabriel, had returned to Russia in 1832 with brother Stephen and his family.

Their new home, Sitka, was essentially the same thriving seaport and commercial city that they had visited in 1824. Some 1300 people, mostly Russians and creoles, lived within its walls—thick walls which, with the bristling gun emplacement further up the hill, served as a constant reminder of how one quiet Sunday afternoon in 1801 twenty-four men, women and children in the fort of "old" Archangel had perished in a treacherous attack by their "neighbors," the Tlingit Indians.[16]

Filthy and repulsive, utterly savage and bloodthirsty, vengeful and irrational—such were the things Fr. John heard from the Russians about these people. And yet, as far as he himself could see, the few Tlingit women who with their Russian husbands were allowed to live inside the compound seemed, all things considered, decent and intelligent, good housekeepers and devoted mothers, pious Christians. Furthermore, outside the walls, all indications were that the Tlingits were not as wild as they had been in 1824, and everything he saw of their material culture—the bold lines and color of their

---

[16] From the natives' own name for themselves. The Russians referred to them as "Koloshes," a term Fr. Veniaminov felt was derived from the Aleut word *kaluga*, for the lip-plugs worn by the women.

art, the perfection of their intricate carvings and woven goods—all pointed to a keen intellect which gave him hope that, using on them the methods employed so successfully among his beloved Aleuts, a mission here might bear fruit after all. His earliest complaint thus was that:

> I haven't yet been able to gather much information about them that is *trustworthy*, for although I'd like to become acquainted with them—as I did with the Fox-Aleuts among whom *I lived* and who opened their hearts to me—these [Tlingits] can only be watched, and so my observations must remain merely superficial.

With impatience Fr. John observed the many impediments to converting the Tlingits to Christ: their own fierce pride and independence compounded by the lamentable witness they received to the Christian faith. The Russians in Sitka remained for the most part an utterly impious lot, while the baptized Aleuts were treated so poorly as servants by the Company that rightly or wrongly it appeared to the Tlingits that in accepting the white man's religion, they had forfeited the freedom they had once held so dear. It is doubtful if these conditions would have changed significantly in many years, had not an act of Providence occurred which in Fr. John's words marked "the border or boundary-line at which the reign of rank ignorance ended and their enlightenment began—or will begin."

In January of 1836, a smallpox epidemic then raging up and down the Pacific coastline finally struck Sitka. A creole child was the first to fall ill, and soon the whole city was infected. Innoculations stemmed the tide among those living inside the compound, but once it touched the Tlingit villages outside the walls victims began falling a dozen every day. In three and a half months about 400 adults—almost half the native population of the region—were dead, and hardest hit among them, naturally, were the older people—the very ones most firmly entrenched in their superstitions and in blind hatred of the Russians and the cultural innovations which they had brought with them. One of these innovations was the vaccine which kept the entire Russian population healthy despite all the dire spells cast upon them by the Tlingit shamans in recompense for bringing this horrible disaster upon them. The vaccine was even strong enough to deliver them from food purposefully infected with the disease and then sold them. The shamans—no less than the common folk—perished as they danced and chanted and practiced their surest cures with great confidence and fervor. This sharp contrast between the Russians' continued health and the shamans' utter failure to stem the tide of death caused the faith of the younger Tlingits to be shaken and the old ways seriously questioned.

The least hostile among them began to understand why this contrast existed and started turning to their old enemies for help. The Russians readily agreed, and Dr. Blaschke, the colonial physician, zealously and energetically administered the vaccine to any and all who would allow him to do so. And when none of those who received it fell ill, those who were still wavering became convinced. The shamans' influence was permanently damaged, and the Tlingits began coming in droves, many from great distances, voluntarily to receive the protection which only months or weeks before could not have been forced upon them.

It is against this backdrop that we must read Fr. John's account of how his missionary work in New Archangel began. It demonstrates once more one of his favorite premises, that "all of man's good enterprises are brought to fruition solely by the will of Providence, and then only at the appointed times; and that Providence often uses not only ordinary incidents, but even our own weaknesses, for good."

> Among the goals I set myself when settling in New Archangel was that of trying to speak to the Tlingits about the True Faith. I arrived in New Archangel towards the end of 1834 but had no opportunity that winter even so much as to meet them, other matters (with the Aleuts) keeping me occupied. During the summer the Tlingits customarily disperse for

fishing and the like, while in the autumn of 1835—
again for rather important reasons—*I* was unable to
begin. I planned then to begin—without fail—next
winter and mentioned this to the colonial Manager
[John] Kupreanov, who readily offered me whatever
means and finances I might need—I had only to begin.
Circumstances and events—none of them unimpor-
tant—once again prevented me, but now at times,
I must openly confess, there was also in me a certain
reluctance and unwillingness to start. I was forced
to postpone my plans from day to day until finally
I began to grow ashamed of myself. Meanwhile, the
Feast of Christ's Nativity was approaching, and I
made a promise to myself that without fail I would
begin my work by the end of this holy season (i.e.,
by January 7 or 8). Now, who will fail to be amazed
by the winds of Providence? The smallpox broke out
among the Tlingits on January 3 or 4—just the time
we had decided to begin our visitations. Had I succeeded in beginning my discussions with them before
the epidemic began, the Tlingits would probably
have blamed all of their grief and destruction on
me—the Russian shaman or sorcerer who had brought
this evil upon them. Before me no Russian priest
had ever set foot inside a Tlingit door (either to
bring them the blessing of peace or simply to satisfy
his own curiosity). The consequences of such an
ill-timed visit on my part would have been stag-
gering: their wholly natural enmity towards the
Russians—which by then had all but vanished—could
easily have been revived. They might have killed me
as the prime cause of their misfortune—but even this
would have been nothing in comparison with what
might have followed: had I visited the Tlingits before
the epidemic, the road would probably have been
blocked for perhaps fifty years to those who would
wish to preach the Gospel, for these would henceforth be looked upon as heralds of destruction and
death.

Thank God, everything worked together for good! The Tlingits are not today what they were a year ago, and even if they will not soon become Christians, they are at least at the point of listening— or at the *very* least of *beginning* to listen—to the Word of Salvation.

With this "real opportunity here for great and worthwhile work" (1 Cor. 16:9) opened to him by God, Fr. John began studying the Tlingits' culture, language and traditions in depth.

Although ethnically distinct from all the other peoples in the region, the Tlingits shared with them all a shamanistic faith, that is a belief in a Creator of the universe who is not, however, in control of its activities. For the Tlingits this being was El,[17] who loves man yet sends upon them in his anger disease and misfortune. Furthermore, El has a son whose origin is unknown but who is far more loving than his father and often intercedes for those with whom El is angry. The whole key to the Tlingits' religion was the legendary life of El, and Fr. John learned as much as he could about it in order to know how (and how not) to preach Christ to them.

The study of their language went very slowly, and although he devoted at least two hours a day to it, as late as 1836 he was still lamenting that "it seems as though it will be ages before I'll be able to speak Tlingit."

The first real breakthrough towards converting these people came only in 1837, when Fr. John visited Fort Dionysius east of Sitka on the American coast. There, outside the compound walls, in a latticed enclosure he celebrated Divine Liturgy for the first time. He informed the local Tlingits of the service well in advance, and some 1500 of them assembled for the occasion. The respect and decorum with which they watched this new and incomprehensible spectacle amazed Fr. John and earned them his respect. He recalls:

[17] Fr. John saw in this name—the same as one Hebrew word for God—a sign that while "their traditions are but a mixture of lies and fabrications, even so . . . in their mythology can be seen traces of true history, as for example, in their tradition of the Flood."

... not only the adults, but even the children made
no noise whatsoever, nor did they do anything un-
seemly during the service, which lasted more than an
hour. I had thought in particular that there might
be some sort of commotion when they saw their
neighbors whom I had baptized that same day approach Holy Communion together with the Russians
(for although I had baptized them only with the
consent of their chieftains and relatives, this might
not have been known to all). Even then, however,
nothing resembling a commotion or grumbling occurred—they simply paid even greater attention.

On another occasion Fr. John served Liturgy on the same
site and afterwards performed a funeral at the cemetery. Again
the Tlingits came to observe, and again they were as well-
mannered, decorous and respectful as on the first occasion.
In fact, during the funeral, when two Tlingits—unaware that a
service was in progress—happened by singing their own songs,
the chieftain immediately sent out to have them stop, and they
obeyed, although they had never been hushed in this manner
before. After services the people would flock to visit Fr. John,
and he for his part never let pass an opportunity to relate to
them some bit of truth from the Gospel. All who had an
opportunity to do so listened to him with rapt attention and
great curiosity, and often they asked amazingly astute questions.
For instance, as Fr. John was leaving Stakhin a chieftain asked
him, "What will there be after death for the people who did
good here?" This question filled the priest with great joy,
and as always he tried to provide as full an answer as possible.
The first ship to reach Sitka from Stakhin brought greetings
from these people and a request that Fr. John return to them
again as soon as possible.

In time Fr. John's patient approach began to bear fruit
as it had on Unalaska. Whenever possible he sat with the
people and talked in simple, vivid terms. He was in great
demand among them and was received everywhere with what
he discovered to be great and sincere hospitality. Those whom
he baptized were held in high esteem among their fellows,

and the Church grew many-fold among these intelligent and gifted people who not long before had been mortal enemies of the Russian invaders.

CHAPTER 10

FORT ROSS

Even as Baron von Wrangell had promised, Fr. John's assignment in Sitka did not require the extensive travel which had characterised his earlier ministry and had so endangered his health on Unalaska. Besides nearby Stakhin there were but a few outlying posts falling within his jurisdiction. One of these, however, lay about 1500 miles to the south, nestled on the California coastline near San Francisco. In 1836 Fr. John learned that a Russian-American Company ship was due to pay an extended visit to New Albion, and he immediately seized upon the opportunity to minister to his parishioners at Fort Ross.

On Tuesday, June 30, the usual prayers for seafarers being said, he and a cantor joined the crew on board. Early next morning the ship cast off, only to lose a day at roadstead before strong northerly winds filled the sails and drove them steadily towards their destination. Steady breezes and clear skies then prevailed for over a week before, at their desired latitude, they became becalmed. On Thursday, July 16, they dropped anchor in a sheltered bay and Fr. John stepped ashore on California soil.

He did so, however, not at Fort Ross, but at Bodega Bay to its south. It seems that when the Russians were first reconnoitering the area, fear that their planned encroachment might be met by a show of Spanish force had dictated that strategy take precedence over convenience. Therefore when a site was found some twenty-four miles away which promised rich soil and ample pasturage, good stands of timber and abundant water supplies—plus security from attack by virtue of its steep shoreline—it was decided to build the fort there. Visitors, however, found compensation for their inconvenience in the the luxuries of housing and the bath which Bodega offered, as well as in the scenic ride northward up the rugged coast road which led them to their ultimate destination.

As his horse trotted along at a moderate pace, Fr. Veniaminov had time to gather a first impression of the region. "One must confess," he writes, "that California's good, clear air and pure blue skies, its location and the vegetation native to the latitude can at first startle and disarm those born above 52° latitude and who have never been below that—especially an inhabitant of Unalaska and Sitka!"

After about five hours on horseback, a last tall hill was crossed and the redwood stockade of Fort Ross came into view. Built by the Company in 1812 to house those sent to hunt fur seals on the offshore islands, it had grown into a center for farming, ranching and above all, trading, but by 1836 it was nearing the end of its days under the Russian flag. Still, 260 men and women—Russians, Kodiak Aleuts, creoles and local Indians—lived within its aging walls, and they had not seen a priest in years. In the east corner of the stockade was tucked a small wooden chapel topped with cupola and belfry. Even by Alaskan standards its interior was extremely plain,[18] and it gave every indication of extremely rare use— a condition which Fr. John set out to rectify immediately.

First he declared a solemn fast for all those wishing to receive the sacraments. All children in the compound were chrismated and all married couples sacramentally united. A daily cycle of Vespers, Matins and the Hours—with religious instructions interspersed—was established. Almost immediately, however, his work was halted by a cold. The Russians assured him that this was the common fate of them all— the California sun which he found so pleasant brought rapid changes in

[18] Plainer even than the chapel of SS. Peter and Paul in the Pribilof Islands, where just thirty Aleut families lived in dire poverty. It seems that the political tensions with Spain (and later Mexico) which prevented Russia from annexing outright this strip of California coast also made them wary of building and consecrating a church there, even though visiting seamen had donated considerable funds towards just such a project.

temperature which caused this physical plight. When he was able to resume his teaching he found that he had to work with various groups individually: with the Russians, as adults and as children; with the Aleuts through one interpreter, and with the local Indians through another. As people came to realise their sinfulness and seek repentance, he heard their confessions: 46 in a single day. As some inhabitants returned to the fort from duties away, he had to begin the whole cycle several times to accommodate them. On August 1, Fr. John chrismated two adult Indians and celebrated Liturgy. Afterwards the traditional blessing of waters took place at the nearby stream, and the whole population of the fort walked in solemn procession around the stockade walls.

When his work was scarcely half-way over, Fr. John's ship left for a visit of Monterrey and San Francisco, planning to return for him before proceeding home to Sitka. Eleven days later, however, he learned that revised plans precluded this stop and that he would have to meet the ship in San Francisco.

And so, Fr. John's visit to Fort Ross came to an abrupt end. He set out on horseback in the company of a sea captain named Becker, another of the Russians' current guests. Their first night out was spent in the open and although much of his life had been spent under such conditions, it was to be a memorable occasion, for never before had Fr. John slept outside the boundaries of the Russian Empire.

Around four o'clock on Monday afternoon, August 24, the travelers reached the Franciscan mission of San Rafael, to be graciously received by its jovial and outgoing rector, Padre José Lorenzo de la Concepción Quijas. The need to rejoin his ship prevented Fr. John from accepting more than a single night's hospitality there, so in the morning he set off across the bay to San Francisco. Arriving at the Presidio on Wednesday morning, Fr. John was disappointed to learn that his haste had been pointless. His ship had not yet returned from Monterrey, and had it not been for the fact that his traveling companion's own craft was moored in the harbor, he should have been hard pressed for a place to stay.

Fr. John had enjoyed his visit to California and had

learned enough about the area to wish to see more. He had heard that around the southern half of the bay there stretched rich lands belonging to the Franciscan brothers sent at the end of the previous century from Mexico to convert the native populations to Christianity. Their fertile fields, well-tilled and bountiful, and graced with clean white churches and other stone buildings were the envy of every Russian who saw and spoke of them. But these same visitors told other stories, too, of despotic cruelty towards the Indians—a cruelty so out of keeping with the manner of the one priest Fr. John had met in San Rafael that he was filled with curiosity and hence not entirely disappointed when word came that their departure for Alaska would have to be delayed until mid-September at the earliest. Accompanied by the captain of his ship, Fr. John set out on September 2 on a tour of the southern bay area.

They spent the night crossing the bay in a bark, reaching shore just before dawn to find at their disposal horses belonging to their destination, the nearest mission: San José. There they were well received by the rector, Padre José Maria de Jésus González Rubio, a young, well-educated cleric with whom Fr. John soon became friends. The two discussed theology— in Latin—and as Fr. John recalls, "I had to explain myself in it as best I could," but at least he—unlike most of his companions in seminary—could at long last claim to have reaped some benefits from something to which he had devoted so much time and energy in his youth. Fr. Gonzáles Rubio was a most gracious host during the three days the Russians spent at San José. He offered his guests tours of the extensive lands with their (indeed) rich fields and fine orchards, the workshops, the school for the Indians and the well-supplied vestry. Four times the Russians attended mass, and Fr. John had his first opportunity to witness the Roman rites of baptism and burial. Contrary to the rumors he had heard, Fr. John found the Indians well-treated and content with their clerical masters. On September 7 it was time to be moving on.

Fr. González Rubio accompanied his guests down the road to the neighboring mission of Santa Clara. Here too the rector, Padre Rafael de Jésus Moreno, and another priest received them cordially and provided a tour of their own

extensive property. Once again Fr. John had an opportunity
to observe the Roman eucharistic rite—this time celebrated
by three priests simultaneously on three separate altars, "each,
of course," he notes, mystified, "in a whisper."

On August 9 the tour of the missions came to an end as
Fr. John and his companion began the two-day journey back
to port in San Francisco, where Fr. John attended one more
mass.

Elsewhere in his writings, Fr. John tells a charming story
about his contacts with the California missionaries. In Sitka,
as on Unalaska, Fr. John continued a favorite hobby of his
youth, the building of barrel organs. The quality of his work
soon earned him a reputation, and through the traders who
came down from Sitka twice a year the Spaniards learned of
his abilities and placed an order for one of his instruments.
Fr. John gladly obliged, and a new organ was delivered to
them with a roll of sacred music in place. Hearing this the
padres seemed genuinely pleased, but their pleasure turned
to unabashed joy when the second roll was inserted. Fr. John
with amusement recalls that "those Jesuits [sic] are probably
still praying to God to the strains of our merry [Russian]
dance music!"

CHAPTER 11

"IN A LITTLE WHILE YOU WILL NOT SEE ME"

In Sitka Fr. John resumed his writing. The careful documentation of every aspect of his life in Alaska had consumed a large part of his energies since late 1833, as his days on Unalaska were drawing to a close. He had collected a large amount of data over the years which he now systematized and organized into several long manuscripts to send to Russia to Theodore Lütke for presentation to the Academy of Sciences.

The first of these was an extensive description of the geological, geographic, climactic and other physical aspects of the region, together with a detailed ethnographic study of the peoples. Completed in February of 1834, it was entitled *Notes on the Islands of the Unalaska Region*.[19] The next two works were devoted entirely to the Fox-Aleut language. One was a 1200-word Aleut-Russian dictionary, the other a *Trial Grammar of the Fox-Aleut Language*.[20] With characteristic humility he wrote of this latter work:

> I considered it almost useless to compile a grammar
> of a language such as Fox-Aleut. The Aleuts have
> no need for one—they are able to communicate their
> thoughts one to another without grammar, and will
> in all likelihood soon abandon their language any-
> way. Nor do foreigners have a need for it. Seeing,
> however, the avidity, the indefatigability, with which

[19] For excerpts, see volume 2.

[20] Intended to be included in volume 4 of his collected works by Barsukov, but never issued.

many a scholar seeks to gather information of any
sort, and the interest with which even the most in-
consequential discovery of this sort is received by
them, I decided, if not to compile a full grammar of
Aleut, then at least to give an account of certain rules
of its grammar, on the supposition that this will
prove useful for some understanding of its origins
and for historical conjectures.

For himself the effort at systematizing the language had
proven a useful exercise which, as he writes,

opened for me a new light on the Aleut language,
and I see that at times I had been pronouncing and
writing words incorrectly in my translations, not
understanding their roots—although I had obtained
the correct sense.

These new insights he continued to apply even after his transfer to Sitka, to the *Indication*, the *Catechism* and the Gospel
according to St. Matthew.

By the spring of 1836, he was able to declare concerning
all his compositions that, "... given the present state of this
language the translations are accurate and as clear and pure
as possible." The next step was to have them published.

This, however, presented a problem. In 1833 the Holy
Synod had received Fr. John's petition to have his Gospel of
St. Matthew printed but decided that inasmuch as the Bishop
of Irkutsk had no means of verifying the accuracy of the work,
and doubting that the Aleut language possessed adequate
terminology to express "accurately and with full force ...
the lofty truths contained in the text of the Gospel," it had
postponed final decision on the matter, while allowing him
to make additional copies of his manuscript to give to the
Aleuts to read and criticize, "in order that making use of
such notes he will gradually bring it to the greatest impact
and perfection ..."

Therefore, on April 24, 1836, Fr. John had sent the following "Humble Request" to Abp. Meletius of Irkutsk:

I do not wish to continue my ministry in the Russian-American colonies, begun in November 1823, beyond May of 1839. I am forced to leave this ministry and to expedite my departure from the colonies by the following circumstances:

The *Catechism* which I translated into Aleut was printed with an unavoidably large number of errors, and I am absolutely determined to reprint it completely. In order that this second edition meet its goal as perfectly as possible, I consider it necessary that the work be done under my personal supervision.

However, inasmuch as for it to be printed I will have to be in one of the capitals, I plan to go from here to St. Petersburg on a trans-world Government ship which is scheduled to arrive here at the end of 1838. This means will be good for me (for many reasons) and useful for the ship's crew as I will be able to serve as ship's chaplain for almost a year.

Therefore, I humbly ask YOUR EMINENCE to relieve me of my present duties, to give YOUR ARCHPASTORAL blessing to a second edition of my *Catechism*, and to furnish me, along with permission to leave for St. Petersburg, a passport both for the trip to and for my stay in St. Petersburg . . .

As we shall see, permission came, and on the very day of his departure from America Fr. John brought to an end his literary works by writing a preface to the Gospel according to St. Matthew, which forms a fitting farewell to those whom he had loved and served so long and faithfully:

My Christ-loving readers and brethren!
By the Word of God was all created; by the power of the Word of God is all that was created sustained. The Word of God is food for man; it nourishes his soul. The Word of God is water to quench his thirsty soul. The Word of God is a lamp

to lighten the darkness of man's heart until daylight
finally dawns. The Word of God is also Light itself;
that is, the Word of God shows in man's heart
clearly and vividly all of God's works—and even
God Himself. Without the Word of God man is
spiritually hungry, thirsty, blind and dead.

Therefore, from the very beginning of the
world, God Who loves each person spoke many times
and in many ways to our ancestors through the
prophets and finally through His only Son, Jesus
Christ. And, in order for people to possess His Word
openly, God commanded those whom He had enlightened to write it down in Holy Books which are
called "the Bible." Now, these holy books are available to virtually all the peoples of the world in
their own languages, but not as yet to you Unalaskans. And so, in order for you also to have the
Word of God in your own language, I have written
down for you one book of the Bible, written by the
Apostle Matthew. I first translated it in 1828, together with John Pankov. In 1832, working with
Simon Pankov, I made corrections to it, and finally,
with Peter Burenin I reviewed and corrected it
thoroughly. I then sent it to the priest James Ne-
tsvetov, who examined it and, by adding a few
words, made it understandable to the Atkhans as
well. Nevertheless, I tell you that there are in this
book a few words which do not fully express the
Russian words, for your language lacks full equiva-
lents (these non-equivalent words are printed in a
different typeface). Therefore, do not think that
this translation will never require corrections; neither
become attached just to its words, but try to grasp
the full meaning and spirit of the Divine Word.
And if there are some words that you cannot understand, ask someone who can. Or better yet, ask Jesus
Christ zealously, and He will illumine you and make
you understand. For, indeed, the Gospel is lofty in
its Wisdom, and even the most learned cannot with-

out illumination from God comprehend the full spirit of the Scriptures.

My brethren: Read. Hearken. Believe and put into practice the things you read. Become wise and be saved! We ask you to pray for us who worked on this as we now depart from you.[21]

---

[21] In this preface one finds first expressed the prudence which was to characterize all of Fr. Veniaminov's linguistic endeavors. He looks to the future, to the need to correct and improve any translation, and warns of the dangers which lurk in a refusal to do so—a refusal such as occurred in Russia when the service books were corrected in the days of Maximus the Greek and Patriarch Nikon.

PART THREE

HALFWAY AROUND
THE WORLD
AND BACK AGAIN

HALF AROUND THE WORLD
AND BACK AGAIN

On April 14, 1838, the 400-ton Finnish-made ship *Nicholas I* sailed into Sitka harbor, having completed an eight-month round-the-world voyage from St. Petersburg. For the people in the colonies, it meant a rich cargo of badly-needed supplies and materials. For Fr. John Veniaminov, it meant a long-awaited passage home.

Permission to join the *Nicholas* on its return voyage had been granted readily by the new bishop of Irkutsk. Nilus, himself formerly a missionary to various Siberian tribes, could well appreciate the problems faced by his American priests and the need to have these problems presented forcefully before the Holy Synod. By the time permission arrived in Sitka (in October of 1837) just such a presentation was readied, a document which Fr. John entitled *A Review of the Orthodox Church in the Russian Settlements in America, Together With My Opinions as to How Their Condition Might Be Improved.*

All hands were due aboard the *Nicholas* on November 8, 1838. That morning Fr. John served a last prayer-service in St. Michael's Church, and in fulfilment of John Smirennikov's prophecy, "saw his family off on shore." Of the five children still in Sitka four would accompany their mother home to Irkutsk, while the youngest, Thekla, would sail with her father to St. Petersburg and enroll in a girls' school to prepare herself for a career in education at home in Irkutsk.

The voyage began quite uneventfully by North Pacific standards. Heavy seas and shifting winds gradually gave way as they approached the tropics, and after 43 days at sea the *Nicholas* reached the port of Honolulu, Hawaii. There the complement of ten officers and thirty-one crewmen under the command of Captain-Lieutenant Eugene Berens took twelve days to rest and take on additional provisions before setting sail for Cape Horn. Continued fair tropical winds made this leg proceed so smoothly that Berens decided it possible without losing too much time to stop over for a few days in Tahiti.

One can well imagine the amazement and delight of the Russian priest and naturalist, born and raised in the frigid depths of Siberia, who had spent all but six weeks of the last fifteen years of his life in what he termed the "eternal autumn" of the Alaskan coast, at stepping now into the lush, exotic "eternal springtime" of Tahiti: this "earthly paradise" of palms and leafy bread trees, yellow bananas, golden pomegranates; fields of jams, sugar cane and pineapples; flowers whose heady fragrances saturate the air, and birds whose brilliant colors and enchanting songs please both eye and ear. In later years he would fondly recall his four days spent in Tahiti to refute the Russian proverb: "You know as much about that as a pig knows about oranges." With characteristic humor he notes:

> Insofar as I was able to observe, given a variety of fruits from which to choose, the pigs on Tahiti —and there were quite a few there—seemed invariably to prefer oranges. Hence the proverb is incorrect: pigs know pefectly well how oranges taste!

On February 2 the *Nicholas* weighed anchor, and encountering brisk winds sailed steadily towards the Cape. By March 29 they were safely in Rio de Janeiro, after a 54-day passage which remarkably saw neither illness to the crew nor damage to the ship even during several day-long storms which hit while they were doubling the treacherous waters off the tip of South America. On April 10 the final passage to Europe began, with stops in Falmouth, England, and Copenhagen, Denmark, before entering the Russian port of Kronstadt on June 22, the entire voyage having taken seven months, fourteen days, of which thirty-two were spent in various ports. Three days later, on June 25, 1839, Fr. John Veniaminov, priest of the Church of St. Michael the Archangel in Sitka,

Alaska, set foot for the first time in the northern capital of the Russian Empire.

The agenda Fr. John prepared for his first day in St. Petersburg was characteristically busy. He had first to stop by the Consistory to clear up complications with his passport. He would then be free to pay visits to the city's ruling hierarch and to the Ober-Procurator of the Holy Synod. At his very first stop, however, he met face-to-face for the first time in his life the stark realities of Russian bureaucratic life:

> I arrived in Petersburg from my round-the-world voyage and went first to the Consistory, not—I must confess—without some sinful pride on my part, thinking that they would treat me with special curiosity—newly-arrived from America, wearing a pectoral cross and a medal [1] to boot— decorations not seen on many a priest my age even in the Capital! I approached the department chief whom I was told to see. He gave me a "haughty look and with arrogant heart" [2] and asked, "What d'you need?" "I'm from America. Please validate my passport," I replied. He took my passport, put it on his desk, and went on with other matters. I took a seat and began watching him impatiently. And what happened? Well, to my amazement I saw him look over other documents and pile these one-by-one on top of my passport, until finally there was a whole stack there. I could stand it no longer. I got up, went over to him and said, "Sir, do me a favor. Don't hold me up. I still have to see the Metropolitan and the Ober-Procurator."
>
> "Just take it easy. I've got a whole lot to do besides your passport," he mumbled, and taking out a quill pen (steel ones weren't yet in use by clerks) he inked it and wrote in large figures on a clean sheet of paper "25 rubles." At first I failed to under-

[1] The Order of St. Anne, Third Class, awarded Fr. Veniaminov by Imperial ukase dated January 12, 1835, "in recognition of his zealous service and continual efforts in spreading the Christian faith among the Aleuts and other savage nations . . ."

[2] Ps. 101:5.

stand, since the "bribery system" was in use neither
in Irkutsk nor in America. He looked at me, crossed
out the "25" and wrote "15." With this I understood
—but pretended still not to get the message. Finally
this *sub-ego-cuius* (i.e., the clerk—a [Latin] play-on-
words we used in the old days: *sub*—"under," *ego*—
"I", and *cuius*—"who") crossed out the "15" and
wrote, "AT LEAST 10." at that I lost my temper
and said: "Sir, I've already told you. I'm from America— a *savage*. I come with no appointment and tell
you what I need—and what do I get? 'You'll get
yours'—and the money pours into the coffers . . ."
The department chief saw that the battle was lost
and validated my passport. Later, when the Ober-
Procurator and I had become close friends, I told
him this story. He laughed merrily and said, "Where
else can they get it? You know, with their low salaries, they're paupers."

Despite this incident, Fr. John managed to keep his remaining appointments that day and was introduced still deeper
into the new and unfamiliar ways of cosmopolitan church
life. His first stop was at the local bishop's residence. Metr.
Seraphim, the 76-year-old president of the Holy Synod, had
been a key figure in the successful fight against foreign mystical
movements which, although unheard of in Fr. John's part
of the Empire, had for years shaken the intellectual elite of
the northern capital. Having received his blessing, Fr. John
presented to him letters from Bp. Nilus and outlined the
reasons for his trip. He then went to do likewise to the Ober-
Procurator.

In Nicholas Protasov, a forty-year-old Jesuit-trained
former military man, Fr. John met the real center of power in
the Russian Church. His nineteen-year career as Ober-Procurator had just begun in 1836, but already he showed the strong
direction his administration would take. On behalf of the
Holy Synod he accepted for review the young missionary's
Review of the Orthodox Church, a report in which by means
of careful statistics and documentation, Fr. John called upon

the ecclesiastical authorities to "increase the number of churches in the colonies, form a permanent mission in North America, and appoint clergy and missionaries to it under a dean as accountable as possible to the diocesan bishop." Protasov was most impressed with the young priest and with the engaging stories he told about the Aleuts. His invitation to come again whenever he wished opened to Fr. Veniaminov one of the most important doors in St. Petersburg.

The Holy Synod was not scheduled to meet again for several months, and so Fr. John secured permission to visit Moscow, hoping to attend there to several projects beneficial to overseas missions. His first stop in the ancient capital was at the local bishop's residence, where he met by far the most famous and respected figure in the Russian Church of the day.

A bishop since the age of 34, ruling bishop and member of the Holy Synod since 1819, in charge of the Diocese of Moscow since 1821, a fine linguist, distinguished theologian and pedagogue, a trusted confidant of both the reigning tsar, Nicholas I, and his late brother—Metr. Philaret, then 57 years of age was, in despite his failing eyesight and growing feebleness, at the pinnacle of his prestige and power. No decisions of Church or State were made without consulting him. A man outwardly of great power, intellect and eloquence, and inwardly of sincere devotion to the solitary life of the monastic, he nonetheless had a reputation for both haughtiness and coldness. Fr. John soon found him otherwise, and the metropolitan, for his part, found to his delight in the already famous young priest a humble worker, a man of genuine simplicity, truthfulness and clarity of mind—all the characteristics he sought to inculcate in the priests he trained. To the young cleric, Philaret opened not only his own apartments at the Trinity Cathedral, but his heart as well, and the two developed mutual bonds of affection and respect which would only strengthen as the years went by. Whenever opportunity arose he said of Fr. Veniaminov, "there is something apostolic about that man."

No less enthusiastic was the response of Moscow at large. The exotic tales of far-off lands and savage peoples which the Muscovites now heard would themselves have sufficed to captivate their minds and inspire their generosity even if the fame of their American visitor had not gone before him. But by 1829 Russian society had already learned much about him and his work through reports by Lütke, von Wrangell, and seamen who had met him in the colonies, and through the steady stream of manuscripts which he, as a corresponding member since 1835, had been sending to the Academy of Sciences.

For several months Fr. John enjoyed the city's warm hospitality. He lived in the metropolitan's residence, was driven about in the metropolitan's carriage, served with the metropolitan at the latter's request at the altar of the great Annunciation Cathedral in the Kremlin. Almost every evening he spoke with the metropolitan and his flock of the needs and opportunities of missionary work among the peoples of Russian America. Everywhere doors opened to him and his work. Relationships were formed with some of the noblest families in Russia—the Sheremetevs, Sverbeevs and Chaadaevs—which resulted not only in immediate donations of badly-needed funds, church wares, vestments and icons for Alaska (which, indeed, the less affluent hastened to provide as well), but more importantly in a continuing support for the cause of mission which was destined to outlive both Fr. John and those who heard him speak.

In October of 1839 Metr. Philaret left for St. Petersburg for the beginning of the regular winter session of the Holy Synod. Fr. John remained in Moscow, endeavoring to secure publication of his scholarly works which did not fall within the Synod's provenance. The first article which met with success was published in the journal *Syn Otechestva*[3] in November. It was entitled, "The Mythological Traditions of the Tlingits Inhabiting the Northwestern Shore of America." A second treatise, entitled "Characteristic Traits of the Aleuts Inhabiting the Fox Islands," was published next in a collection edited by Karl Ernst von Baer and Grigorii Helmerson entitled *Beiträge zur Kentniss des russischen Reiches und der angränzenden Länder Asiens*. It attracted special critical at-

---

[3] No. 11, pp. 40-82; also published in part in the Journal of the Ministry of Public Education (*Zhurnal Ministerstva narodnago prosvieshcheniia*).

tention in Russia, including this appraisal in the Journal of the Ministry of Public Education:

> It breathes a patriarchal nobility, the paternal love of an honorable pastor, Fr. Veniaminov, for his half-savage flock. He is, as it were, proud of the noble traits in the Aleuts' character while at the same time recognizing their deficiencies. In his every opinion we recognize the sacred bonds of the Christian faith linking these pious people with their zealous spiritual mentor.

In November of 1839 an invitation came for Fr. Veniaminov to appear before the Holy Synod, and he returned to St. Petersburg where he continued to enjoy Metr. Philaret's hospitality. On the day appointed, Fr. John presented his report, touching in particular upon the hardships which priests in Alaska were required to endure and which hampered the success of their work. He described for the bishops the geography of the Aleutian Islands, the nature of the people and the difficulties encountered in converting them to Christianity. He described his travels in kayaks and his voyage around the world. His stories, so sincere, so entertaining and so highly captivating, awakened in the Synod an interest in and sympathy for the needs of the American flock.

Several days after his appearance Fr. Veniaminov was elevated to the rank of archpriest by the Holy Synod in recognition for all his labors. At Christmas Day Liturgy, during the Little Entrance, Fr. John was led before Metr. Philaret who prayed for him, made over his head the sign of the cross and exclaimed, "Blessed is God! Behold, the servant of God, John, is a Protopresbyter of God's most holy Church—of the Holy Archangel Michael on the Island of Sitka—in the name of the Father, the Son, and the Holy Spirit. Amen."

On January 24, 1840, the Holy Synod received for its consideration Fr. John's *Review of the Orthodox Church* and nineteen days later two more petitions concerning publication of his other theological works in Aleut. The Synod acknowledged the value of these works and the need to have them published. In particular praise was reserved for the *Indication of the Pathway into the Kingdom of Heaven*, which they recommended be issued in Slavonic and Russian as well as in its original Aleut.

Amid all this success and acclaim there came from Irkutsk the shattering news of the death several months before (November 25) of Fr. John's wife, Catherine. His first thoughts were for his orphaned family, and he immediately sought permission to go to join them. Metr. Philaret did his best to console him in his grief and, following standard procedures in the case of clerical widowers, offered the suggestion that Fr. John become a monk. No immediate answer, however, was possible. Such a monumental decision would require a long and painful spiritual search, and as a first step he obtained the metropolitan's blessing to make a pilgrimage to the Lavra of the Holy Trinity and St. Sergius north of Moscow. There in the monastery Fr. John offered a memorial service for his wife and spent several days in prayer and meditation. He returned to St. Petersburg, his turmoil unresolved. Fortunately there was more work there to occupy his mind.

In his absence the Holy Synod had taken the following decision concerning Fr. John's report:

> With pleasure the Holy Synod perceives in this *Review* that the seed of the Word of God planted among the savage and pagan tribes of that region has not been fruitless. Providence is blessing the activities of the Russian-American Company which spares neither labor nor capital for this holy work. The Church of Christ founded at the end of the last century in the Aleutian Islands has now grown to number some ten thousand souls among its members (in addition to Russian settlers).

Furthermore, it accepted in full his assessment of the mission's needs and adopted the following concrete resolutions:

First, to designate the Church of St. Michael in Sitka a cathedral, thus allowing the assignment there of an increased staff of two priests, one deacon, three minor ecclesiastics and one prosphora-baker; a catechetical school would, in addition, be attached there. The existing churches in Kodiak, Unalaska, and Atka would each continue being served by one priest, two minor ecclesiastics and a single prosphora-baker.

Second, to appoint a Dean of Clergy to manage all present and future churches and clergy in America. This would be the senior priest of the Sitka Cathedral. The junior priest there would serve as Assistant Dean, but under the Dean's complete control. (The Russian-American Company formally recommended that Fr. John be given this responsibility.)

Third, to delegate to Fr. Veniaminov responsibility for compiling and submitting to the Holy Synod a set of special instructions based on his own experience to guide all clergy working in America. This was done in view of the vast distances which separated the American Church from its diocesan center in Irkutsk, which in turn rendered difficult, if not impossible, any effective episcopal direction of Church life—a cause for real concern considering the importance of the work being done there.

Finally, to inform the Chief Manager of the Russian-American Company of these resolutions and to arrange with him a financial plan which would allow its implementation. If the plans should exceed the Company's means, the tsar might then be approached directly for assistance. In response, the Company reiterated its firm commitment "to help the State in transforming the American Orthodox Church and spreading Her saving doctrine to nations still darkened by paganism." It did not dispute the need for higher salaries for the missionaries in order to attract a higher over-all quality of clergy (of Fr. Veniaminov's calibre, they stated), in order that the natives not be alienated from the Gospel by seeing a disparity between the priestly calling and the actual priests who came to serve among them.[*] The Company pledged its continued willingness to sacrifice its capital towards this project, but noted that it would have to begin limiting that sacrifice somewhat, whereas the Synod's plan would require at

---

[*] The Company did, however, protest the contention that salaries were insufficient to live upon, citing the fact that employees often returned home to Russia after five years with considerable savings.

least a doubling of expenditures for salaries alone. In the end
it asked only that it not be burdened beyond its means.

By next fall Fr. John had prepared the required report,
and on November 6 the Synod met to hear and discuss it in
light of the Company's response to the entire project. The
result was a total endorsement of Fr. John's instructions, which
thereby obtained canonical force for all missionaries within
the Russian Empire. The spirit of their author is clearly seen
in the opening exhortation of these *Instructions to Priests
Assigned to Convert Non-Orthodox and to Lead Those Converted into the Christian Faith:*

> To leave one's homeland and go to far-off, savage
> lands void of many of the comforts of life in order
> to turn to the path of Truth people still wandering
> in the darkness of ignorance, and to illumine with
> the light of the Gospel those who have not yet seen
> this saving light is truly a holy work, like that of the
> Apostles. Blessed is he whom the Lord chooses and
> confirms in such a ministry! More particularly, bless-
> ed is he who with zeal, sincerity and love works to
> convert and enlighten such people, enduring the
> labors and sorrows he encounters in his field of
> ministry! Great will be his reward in heaven. But
> how horrible for him who is chosen and confirmed to
> preach the Good News but who fails to do so! More
> horrible yet for him who traverses land and sea in
> order to convert others, and then makes his converts
> children of hell moreso than himself!
>
> Thus, O Priest, as you undertake this work for
> which you will either enter into the joy of your Lord
> as His good and faithful worker, or receive condem-
> nation as a hypocritical, evil and lazy servant—may
> the Lord God preserve you from the latter and grant
> you the desire and the strength to achieve the
> former . . .

With this, all of the tasks assigned to Fr. John by the
Holy Synod were completed. He had done everything in his

power to assure the further development of missionary work in America, and had seen to his own publishing interests. Now he was free to go home.

In the year that passed since news came of Catherine Veniaminov's death, Metr. Philaret's attempts at persuading Fr. John to accept monastic tonsure had not abated, and yet for three reasons the young priest found it impossible to take this step. First and foremost, there was his large family in Irkutsk; second, there was the fact that the active life which a missionary must lead would preclude full observance of the equally demanding monastic rule; and finally, there was his conviction that he could continue being of service to the Church and to his nation as a priest without becoming a monk. Still in inward spiritual turmoil, Fr. John decided to visit the very birthplace of Russian monasticism, Kiev. There he prayed and, as he had the relics of St. Sergius, venerated the great wonderworkers asleep in the Caves. The people of Kiev were just as pleased with their famous visitor and amazed at the tales he told, but they were no better able than the Muscovites to offer peace to his troubled soul. Fr. John returned again to St. Petersburg to face Metr. Philaret.

Now, however, there was a difference, for in Fr. John's absence the wise old prelate had used his influence with the Imperial family to remove at least one of his objections. He informed Tsar Nicholas of the plight of the Veniaminov children and obtained from him permission to enroll them in schools in St. Petersburg. Innocent, Gabriel and Alexander[5] would be transfered from the Irkutsk Seminary to the one in the capital. Olga (aged ten) and Paraskeva (aged eight) would join their sister Thekla in the National Institute for Girls, and all would enjoy imperial patronage and high-placed guardians.

Then and only then did Fr. John feel free to make the momentous decision. Discerning in these events the hand of God and remaining faithful to his calling, he decided to become a monk. On November 24, 1840, his wife's namesday

---

[5] This is the last reference to the youngest Veniaminov son. The only conclusion possible is that he died some time between this and the arrival of the other two boys in the northern capital.

and the first anniversary of her death, Fr. John Veniaminov submitted the following petition to the Holy Synod:

> I desire to enter the monastic calling—without, however, abandoning the ministry given to me among those who have been and are being illumined in the Christian faith in our Russian-American dominions. Therefore, most humbly I ask the Holy Ruling Synod to sanction and to bless my entry into the monastic calling.

The Synod acted quickly to approve his tonsuring and elevation to the rank of Archimandrite, and so instructed Metr. Philaret in an ukase dated November 27. Two days later, during vigil in the Chapel of St. Sergius in the Trinity apartments, Fr. John Veniaminov was tonsured by the metropolitan and given—at his own request—the name of Innocent, in honor of the first Bishop of Irkutsk.[6] His sponsor was Bp. Nikodim of Krasnoiarsk. During the next morning's Divine Liturgy the new Hieromonk Innocent was elevated to the rank of Archimandrite.

On the third day of his participation in the "angelic life," the second half of the Aleut John Smirennikov's prophecy was fulfilled. "You will see your family off on shore," the old man had said, "and go to see a great man and talk with him." And indeed, precisely at noon on December 1, the nervous new archimandrite was conducted directly from church into the imperial offices for a meeting with Tsar Nicholas I.

Innocent presented the pious monarch with an icon of the Savior, and a routine conversation began with polite questions about his background, his education, his work in Alaska,

---

[6] In the course of a renovation the remains of Bp. Innocent (Kulchitskii) were uncovered and found to be intact and incorrupt. State officials conducted a thorough investigation and testified both to their physical condition and to numerous testimonies about miracles performed by the late missionary hierarch. In 1800 the Holy Synod had these data carefully reviewed by a clerical commission, and on the basis of its findings ordered in 1804 that throughout Russia St. Innocent's memory be celebrated on November 26. For Siberian Russians in particular he became the object of intense devotion, and his silver-encased relics in the Ascension Monastery were the center of pilgrimage for the entire region.

about the natives and so forth. It was not long, however, before it turned to the more substantial matters for which he had been summoned to this meeting.

"I have approved the Kamchatka Diocesan project," said Nicholas, in words which could only puzzle his companion. "But who should be appointed bishop?"

"The Holy Spirit will inspire in Your Majesty's heart the holy idea of whom to elect."

Nicholas thought for a moment and said, "I wish to make *you* Bishop of Kamchatka."

A stunned Fr. Innocent replied, "I am wholly at Your Majesty's command. Whatsoever pleases You is holy in my sight."

"Very well. Communicate my words to the metropolitan."

The Tsar bowed, and the Archimandrite left his presence but remained until the end of his stay in St. Petersburg a frequent visitor to the court, entertaining the future Tsar Alexander II and the royal children with his tales of natives and kayaks and other exotic things.

The project to which the Tsar alluded was first considered by the Holy Synod on the very day of Fr. Veniaminov's tonsure into monasticism, and its decisions were as follows: (1) to establish in Russian America an episcopal see to which would be subordinated the parishes along the Pacific seaboard in Kamchatka and Okhotia, thus removing these territories from the Diocese of Irkutsk; (2) to fix the bishop's residence in Sitka, headquarters of the Russian-American Company in Alaska; (3) to designate the new district the "Diocese of North America and Kamchatka"; (4) to permit the bishop and his clergy (inasmuch as the establishment of the usual complement of diocesan structures—consistory etc.—was clearly impossible) to modify the usual liturgical and administrative procedures in accordance with local circumstances and necessities, "observing only essential church order and lawful means of operation, but following the example of ancient simplicity"; and (5) to maintain at then-existing levels the financial support given to the diocese as a whole. These decisions were submitted to Tsar Nicholas by the Ober-Procurator on November 30 and were duly approved.

Next day Nicholas received for final selection the required list of three candidates deigned by the Holy Synod "most capable and worthy of this ministry." They were: (1) "the Archpriest John Veniaminov, former missionary to the region who by his own petition has been allowed by the Holy Synod to receive monastic tonsure and elevation to archimandrite"; (2) Archimandrite Gennadius, Abbot of the Monastery of St. Paphnutius in Kaluga; and (3) Archimandrite Nicodemus, Abbot and Rector of the Dormition/St. Trophimus Monastery and Seminary in Viatka. Of the three, clear preference was expressed for the first since by reason of

> his long service to the Russian-American Church he has already demonstrated his outstanding ability and true worth, and has by his stated voluntary consent to return to this ministry in his former calling demonstrated his true zeal for the ministry of the faith and, therefore, gives us full hope of a new blessing by God upon his ministry should he be elevated to the episcopate.

As we have seen, Tsar Nicholas selected Archimandrite Innocent, a man of whose apostolic efforts in the mission field he already enjoyed personal knowledge. His only modification was to change the name of the diocese to "Kamchatka, the Kuril and Aleutian Islands." When the Ober-Procurator objected that "there is not a single church in the Kuril Islands," Nicholas replied, "he will build some."

The imperial ukase was signed and returned to the Synod. The consecration was set for December 15, and Metr. Seraphim of St. Petersburg was to be chief celebrant. On December 13, in the presence of many dignitaries, Archimandrite Innocent was officially elected to the episcopate in the chambers of the Holy Synod. The Bishop-elect then delivered the following speech:

> O Leaders of the Orthodox Church, chosen by God!

What can I say at this moment of such importance for me? Should I express my gratitude to you for electing my humility, and to our Christ-loving Sovereign for consenting to this election—whereby I am given in this higher ministry both the possibility of being of greater value to my Church and nation and a taste of spiritual comfort as well? But my gratitude ought to be expressed not in words but in deeds—of service to my Church and nation. Therefore, what *can I* now say? I find nothing more proper than to confess before you the wonderful will and mercy of the Lord which He has shown to me, to the glory of His Holy Name. "Bless the Lord, O my soul, and forget not all his benefits!"

When it pleased this holy body to have my bishop choose a presbyter for the newly-illumined Christians on Unalaska Island, I was among those called to the ministry, but being terrified by its difficulties, I grew faint-hearted and evaded it. Our merciful Lord, however, did not allow my carnal, earthly will to contradict His heavenly destinies. The bishop himself called the ministry he set before me "apostolic," but I paid no attention to its importance. Then, in the presence of my bishop, the simple tales of our countryman about the Aleuts' zeal for the Christian faith changed all my thoughts in a single moment and kindled in me a flaming desire to go to America. Even more amazingly, I had heard these tales before, but it was only then, in the presence of the one who had the power to invoke the Grace of God, that it acted upon me, and my desire was irresistibly drawn to the precise place that I previously had fearfully and stubbornly evaded. The Lord was and is so merciful to me that despite my unworthiness He did not and has not taken away from me my desire to serve in America. He gave me first the desire, then the strength to endure all the difficulties of my journey and my ministry. To Him alone and to His All-Holy Name be glory, for never

once during my trip to America nor during my stay
there—in bitter circumstances which pained my heart
—was my weak heart troubled by any word of grumbling or remorse over my chosen lot. Blessed be the
Lord Who perfects His power in weakness and Who
chooses the humble and unworthy!

Now, too, in this election—so very unexpected!—
by Your Holinesses, I perceive the same all-directing
will of my Lord: the circumstances which forced me
to travel completely around the world from those
far-off lands to this capital; Your Holinesses' kind
attention to my meager labors; the arrangement of
my domestic affairs in such a way as to make possible
the ministry before me—the more these things are
unexpected the more clearly I perceive in them the
finger of God. May the Lord accomplish His will
with me always and in all things! I firmly hope and
believe that the Lord Who has guided my steps so
wonderfully, Who now grants to me this new lot of
ministry through the blessing of Your Holinesses,
by whom will be invoked upon me the blessing of
Him Who made fishermen into Apostles and Who
through grace heals that which is infirm and provides
that which is wanting—this same Lord will grant me
new and greater strength to fulfill my ministry.

Lord, all my hope is before You and from You:
do Your will in me and through me. Bless me to
serve You with the blessing which cannot be taken
away. Grant me new desire and new strength to be
of use to my Church and my nation. O Lord Jesus
Christ, may the new light of the grace of the episcopate which You now find worthy to pour out upon
those distant lands be a sign, the dawn of illumination through our Orthodox Faith for all the pagans
living there.

O Holy Virgin Theotokos and you Holy Apostles, you bishops and righteous ones, and all the
company of heaven—I fervently ask you: pray to
the Lord for me! I pray you, God-chosen Fathers and

Leaders of the Church on earth: accept me in your prayers and pray to the Lord that His grace and mercy may be with me forever.

On December 15, 1840, Archimandrite Innocent was consecrated to the episcopacy in the Cathedral of the Kazan Icon of the Theotokos by Metr. Jonah, Abps. Cyril of Podolsk and Joseph of Litovsk, and Bp. Benedict of Revelsk.

A month later Bp. Innocent prepared to return home to America. On January 10, 1841, he bade farewell to Metr. Philaret, who in keeping with all he had done for him in the past now provided his new fellow hierarch with a letter to the Abbot of the Holy Trinity-St. Sergius Lavra requesting that he present him with an icon from the monastery's treasures, and empowering Innocent to select any of the monks to take with him to serve in Siberia or Alaska.

In Moscow Bp. Innocent settled in the Monastery of the Miracle,[7] where he began the considerable task of packing for the long trip ahead all of the contributions which the Muscovites in their generosity had given to his mission. Several times he traveled to the Lavra in hopes of finding suitable candidates for missionary work, but these were very few. On his final visit there he celebrated the Divine Liturgy in the Trinity Cathedral, and later, under a bright winter moon, he set out a last time for Moscow while the monastery bells rang. On January 30 he was bound for Siberia, taking not only two sleds full of material gifts, but the blessings and well wishes of the inhabitants of the two capitals who over the months had come so to love him and his flock.

On the 2600-mile trek to Irkutsk, Bp. Innocent planned his route in such a way as to spend at least one night in each diocesan see, resting from the rigors of travel to be sure, but more importantly talking to the local bishops in order better to prepare himself for his new ministry by taking advantage of their collective experience.

One can well imagine Bp. Innocent's feelings as he first

---

[7] The so-called Chudov Monastery inside the Kremlin walls, named for the legendary miracle by the Holy Archangel Michael, was built in 1365 by the saintly Metr. Alexis of Moscow.

caught sight, far off through the haze to the south, of the
snow-capped mountains which marked the Chinese frontier.
To those familiar with the region these proclaimed that
Irkutsk was near. The bells of the Ascension Monastery were
the first to welcome home this far-ranging traveler. The monks
joyfully assembled to receive his blessing and accompany him
to the church where he would celebrate a prayer-service and
venerate the relics of his new patron saint. He then hurried
on to the city itself.

The bells of every church in Irkutsk rang out to welcome
home its first son to become a bishop. Bp. Nilus stood at the
head of the crowds who thronged the streets to see their former
deacon and priest home again. On the first Sunday after his
arrival Bp. Innocent celebrated Liturgy in the church where,
twenty-four years before, his ministry had begun.

The choir sang majestically as he entered the church,
and one-by-one the clergy—his former schoolmates, their faces
filled with amazement—came up to kiss the cross and receive
his blessing. As he stood in the center of the church he paused
a moment to gaze around the familiar interior before venerating the icons and being vested for Liturgy. At the conclusion
of the service Bp. Innocent gave his blessing to every one of
the people who came to see him—a crowd so dense and excited
that the police on the street were a loss to keep order.

Later that day in Bp. Nilus' residence, one of Bp. Innocent's former teachers, the Archpriest Parniakov, came to
pay his respects. Although by now quite elderly he fell to
the ground touchingly at the bishop's feet. Innocent, however,
hurried to raise the old man up. "You ought not to kneel
before me, but I before you, for through you I went out into
the world," he said, and then he himself knelt before his
former mentor.

Bp. Innocent remained in Irkutsk for over a month, enjoying Bp. Nilus' kind hospitality and increasing his retinue
and supplies. "Time has flown for me here," he wrote to a
friend in Moscow. "I hardly managed to look around and
it's time to be off for Yakutsk. My God! The changes I find
in Irkutsk, and almost all for the worse..." His cause for
complaint was certainly not in the bishop or in the kindness

of his former neighbors and friends. Nilus gave him from his own vestry four sets of episcopal vestments and various other articles, and organized a citywide drive which resulted in the donation to the American missions of over 150 vestments and other badly-needed items. Finally Bp. Innocent and his enlarged retinue of eleven—three deacons, a student from the Academy, two seminarians and five churchmen, all but three of whom had been recruited in Irkutsk—left for Yakutsk, down the path which he and his family had taken some eighteen years before. Their first stop was the village of Anga, the house where the bishop was born, and the graveyard in which lay the remains of his wife and parents. Innocent arranged for a distant relative, Fr. George Dobroserdov,* one of the best, most conscientious and pious priests in Irkutsk and a recent widower who wished to become a monk and continue his studies in the Academy, to accompany his children to St. Petersburg and gave them letters addressed to their new benefactress, Barbara Sheremeteva. Bidding them farewell, Innocent's retinue set off for Yakutsk arriving on May 28. Fourteen days later they set off for Okhotsk, and to their surprise and great delight found that "the Okhotsk Road which so frightens everyone—and which indeed *is* difficult and dangerous during the rainy season—was most favorable to us. We could complain more about dust and lack of water than of mud and rain." By July 1 Bp. Innocent found himself for the first time within the boundaries of his own diocese, but the local clergy were still unaware of the changes which had placed them under his spiritual care.

The band reached the Okhotsk seaboard on July 15 and there enjoyed over a month of much-needed rest before the

---

* Later Gerasimus, Bp. of Astrakhan (1809-1880). Like St. Innocent a graduate of the Irkutsk Seminary (where he too received a new surname: Dobroserdov—"Good-Hearted"—for not having turned in a comrade who had beaten him), he married and while serving as a priest continued to teach. On January 3, 1841, his wife and three of their four children were killed, and the grief-stricken widower petitioned to be sent to the Academy. In St. Petersburg, where he delivered the Veniaminov children, he completed his studies, was tonsured a monk in 1845, taught in various seminaries for eight years, and from 1850 until his death occupied a number of vicarial and diocesan sees in Russia. Throughout his long career he enjoyed a reputation for piety, strict asceticism and mysticism.

brig *Okhotsk* was ready to put out to sea on the last leg of
their odyssey. The clergy made good use of this time to
minister to the people of the region, who for a variety of
reasons had not seen a priest since 1837.

By local standards the morning of August 20 dawned
incredibly fine as the *Okhotsk* sailed out of the estuary and
into the Sea of Okhotsk. Indeed, throughout the voyage around
the tip of Kamchatka and on to Sitka, they enjoyed good
traveling weather and stopped only once en route (to minister to hunters on the isolated island of Simushir in the Kuril
chain). "In a word," Bp. Innocent wrote, "everything is fine
and well. I take all of this as a new sign of God's good graces
towards the work I am about to do."

Meanwhile in Petropavlovsk, the chief port of Kamchatka, the Archpriest Procopius Gromov was stirred from
bed early one morning by the cry of a trader returning from
Okhotsk: "Congratulations on your new bishop!"

"I'm sick of change!" he mumbled, half asleep. Such
news could hardly impress the priest, for in the seven years
he had spent in Kamchatka since leaving Irkutsk, he had seen
three bishops. One more change was unlikely to make much
difference.

"No, no!" said the messenger. "Congratulations on *your*
bishop—for Kamchatka! And guess who!"

"I'm no prophet."

"John Veniaminov—only now he's Bp. *Innocent*!"

An hour or so later a naval officer delivered to Fr. Gromov
a letter addressed to him in a very familiar hand. He opened
it and read, "Can you believe your eyes, my friend? *I'm* your
Bp. Innocent!" The letter went on to advise him that a visit
of Kamchatka was planned for next year, and in preparation
the new hierarch wanted simple catechetical instructions for
the children to be introduced in all the churches.

Word soon filled the city, and a prayer-service was offered in the cathedral to celebrate the joyous news. No one
had heard of or from Fr. Veniaminov in over three years. No
one knew of his leaving America, or of his trip to St. Petersburg, or of his wife's death—much less of his consecration to
the episcopate.

PART FOUR

"APOSTLE TO AMERICA"

CHAPTER 1

"DANGERS ON THE HIGH SEAS"

September 25 dawned with clear skies and fresh tail-winds, the twentieth straight day of fair weather. Bp. Innocent was thus able to assemble all hands not in a stuffy cabin but on deck beneath billowing sails to celebrate the Hours of the Feast of St. Sergius. That same day Cape Edgecumbe first came into view. By dusk it loomed large above them and already clear were the rocky harbor islands and thickly-forested coastal mountains surrounding Sitka, their crests already white with snow. The spectacular northern lights provided a fitting backdrop for Vigil that evening as the ship's crew besought St. John the Evangelist to "dispel the darkness of the nations." When these words were repeated next morning at the Hours, the *Okhotsk* already lay safely at anchor opposite the fortress of New Archangel, and when Bp. Innocent finally stepped ashore to be welcomed by the civil authorities and the entire population of the city, this theme was still very much in his heart. On September 28 the first Pontifical Divine Liturgy was celebrated in Alaska, and afterwards Bp. Innocent recorded his impressions on arriving home:

> Finally, thank God, I am in America and in good health. Thus God, Who in 1799 did not see fit for Bp. Joasaph to reach Kodiak, now desires for me to be in Alaska. He has looked down upon His creation, people so long lost in spiritual and intellectual darkness, and has sent—and brought—us to show them the Light of Truth. Now, so to speak, it is in *our* hands. But will anything come of us? Will we—with

147

our meager strength—do anything? And moreso,
with our laziness? Oh, that laziness! Without it we
could be clothed in the strength of the Apostles
themselves, for everything is possible for those who
pray. But laziness does not allow us all to pray. . . .

Hieromonk Mishael's zealous preaching of the
Word is beginning to penetrate the hearts of our
neighbors, the Tlingits. Already some eighty persons
are ready to be baptised, but I am in no hurry . . .
All of us, from the sacristan—indeed from the bell-
ringer—on up, *all* of us are nothing more than instruments of God. If it pleases the Lord, the bell-
ringer's simple tolling can suffice to touch the heart
of one upon whom He looks down. Apparently Grace
has acted upon many through my word . . . Oh, if only
the Lord would bless me to realize my ideas! Then
with flaming words would I write to you of my joy!
But all is in the hand of God. Amen.

In the next few months Bp. Innocent proved that he had
indeed put himself and his mission in the hand of God, and
that he himself would do everything in his strength to realize
his truly apostolic work. A new mission was planned for
Nushegak, headed by the bishop's new son-in-law, Fr. Elijah
Petelin.[1] The newly-authorized pastoral school opened with
twenty-three native students under the supervision of one of
the hieromonks recruited by the bishop in Russia. A second
such recruit was sent to Kodiak to begin studying the local
languages, and a third began fruitful discussions with the
Tlingits. As spring arrived Bp. Innocent himself prepared to
set off on a first episcopal visitation of the entire diocese.

"In order to act as thoroughly as possible," he writes in
a report to the Holy Synod,

in ruling the diocese entrusted to me, I must certainly
have data as reliable as possible concerning the con-

[1] Fr. Elijah, son of the manager on Unalaska when the Veniaminovs first
arrived there, was one of the first native children to enroll in and finish the
school. He married the oldest of the Veniaminov girls, Catherine.

dition of all churches and clerical staffs, their needs and so forth. I have, therefore, established for myself as a definite duty to survey the entire diocese at the earliest possible opportunity.

But the entire diocese (i.e., the churches in America, Kamchatka and Okhotia) cannot be surveyed in under a year, and one cannot return to Sitka within sixteen months. However, this great length of time is required not so much by the expanse of space as by difficulty and inability in communicating.

Necessary arrangements were made with the Russian-American Company and free passage secured for Innocent aboard the schooner *Kwikpak*, which was already scheduled to make a trip to Kodiak on official business. Although the tiny ship was well-laden with cargo and thirty-nine passengers even before Bp. Innocent and his retinue of five (a deacon, a cell-attendant and three cantors) were booked aboard, the bishop could not resist trying to squeeze in seven more travelers bound for duty in Nushegak. For one thing, this would give him a little more time with his daughter and first grand daughter before duty separated them. Company officials offered no real opposition to this request, for the resultant crowding would surely prove but a minor inconvenience on a trip which normally required just three days and nights and rarely lasted over twelve, even in March, the region's stormiest month.

And so, on February 12 they left, but scarcely had they gone ten miles from land before fierce headwinds drove them back to harbor. Four days later they put out again but with no greater success. Finally, on the nineteenth, with clear skies and favorable winds they left harbor a third time and that same day finally lost sight of shore. "I had begun to think," wrote Innocent, "that perhaps Kodiak was such a forsaken place that it had been decided that no bishop should see it. I must admit, I was troubled not so much for myself as for those with me in the ship. If I were to die, I reasoned, then obviously that was *the* best time for it to occur, considering the condition of my soul. And then, I reasoned, I'm useless any way ..."

For over four hundred miles the voyage was ideal, until

the evening of February 23. Suddenly the *Kwikpak* began to
roll and pitch violently. The captain and the bishop both ran
up on deck to investigate. The ocean did not appear to be
particularly rough, nor had the wind shifted noticeably. The
boatswain and pilot were asked what they thought. "A big
change is coming," they replied solemnly. An earthquake,
they surmised, perhaps lasting a minute or two, must have
caused the sudden rocking, and if this were so the full consequences would soon be felt. And indeed, the winds very
quickly changed. With frightening power they washed in over
the bow, lashing the men on deck and forcing the helpless
ship off course. Heavy rains pelted them, and the old timbers
shook as wave after wave crashed over the decks. The captain
reckoned them to be at least 265 miles from the nearest land.
Only the watch was allowed to remain on deck. Fifty-two
people were forced into the hold to find for themselves room
to sit wherever cargo storage would allow. As the days went
on without change, passengers and crew sat in darkness, silence
and often intense cold, with no opportunity to go up on deck
for fresh air—indeed even to move about down below to warm
up and loosen cramped muscles. Despondency grew. Food,
which should have been abundant—considering that the cargo
included flour and salted beef—soon became unavailable as
water supplies dwindled so low as to preclude its use in
cooking. Careful rationing was begun, each sailor being
allotted two bottles per day, and each passenger one and a
half for all purposes. Day by day the danger of death by
starvation and thirst increased, and despair set in. In order
to ward off this dangerous condition Bp. Innocent whenever
possible read the Hours with added petitions for a favorable
outcome to their voyage.

Finally, on their twenty-ninth day out of Sitka, at 5 A.M.
on March 15, they sighted land about 65 miles off. The winds
calmed and the skies cleared. Relief spread among the passengers. The captain recognized that they were off Spruce
Island, just northeast of Kodiak Island, but shied away from
heading ashore, fearing that another shift in the winds would
drive them uncontrollably into the shallows. He favored instead putting out to sea again and heading for the safer

anchorage of Three Saints Harbor at Kodiak. The crew, however, was too hungry and thirsty to obey and threatened mutiny. Only through Bp. Innocent's intervention was peace restored. The captain was persuaded to head straight for shore, Bp. Innocent remaining on deck the whole time in virtual command of the ship.

A short way from shore they dropped anchor and fired the ship's cannon as a signal of their desperate need for provisions. The tearful passengers and crew joined Innocent in kneeling on deck to thank the Lord for sparing their lives, and as he stepped ashore the bishop's first words expressed the relief everyone felt: "My legs hurt!"

Despite all the privations no one had taken ill. Even the child born at sea five days before the ordeal ended emerged healthy (despite the fact that the mother's ration of water had not been increased, so desperate had the situation become). "I consider all of this," Innocent wrote, "as an obvious sign of the Lord's mercy to us."

The danger had indeed been very great, as Bp. Innocent himself describes:

> Had we left Sitka on the 12th (i.e., when we first set out) one can assume that we would still not have reached Kodiak any earlier than March 18, for as the inhabitants of Kodiak confirmed, strong easterly and southeasterly winds (i.e., straight headwinds) blew constantly into harbor from the beginning of February on. In such a case our voyage would not have been without calamity—all the more so as after our first return to Sitka we took on ten additional days' provisions. But the Lord did not allow calamity to befall us. Glory to Him Who makes all things work out well!

The *Kwikpak* remained moored at Spruce Island for a week before crossing the channel to Kodiak, there depositing the bishop and his retinue and then continuing on its own course. Before departing, however, all of the passengers came to Bp. Innocent to receive his blessing for the remaining part of their voyage and to thank him tearfully for having taken command and rescued them.

Word of this occurrence soon spread throughout the diocese and into Russia, and years later, in 1866, Bp. Innocent received from a certain Abbot Damascus the following version of the event which had reached the monastery in Valaam:

> One of the pilgrims who happened upon our monastery from America told me of the Creole Gerasimus' story of the life of a missionary monk named Herman who was tonsured in Valaam. There is much information in this story which witnesses to the grace of God which enlightened and enlightens the Elder. Included in this information is something especially touching Your Grace, allegedly coming directly from you. This is it: you were carried on the waves for thirty-six days by a powerful storm while in sight of Spruce Island. All were in despair. You offered a prayer-service during which mentally you asked Fr. Herman to save you from drowning. Immediately a favorable wind appeared, turning you once more toward harbor. Quickly you celebrated a memorial service on the Elder's grave. You were holding a book in your hands when Fr. Herman appeared to you by the Cross, wearing his mantle and cowel. The book fell from your hands, and the vision disappeared . . .

Fr. Damascus went on to ask the bishop to verify the truthfulness of this account. Whether he did or not is unknown. There exists, however, the text of the abbot's letter written over in Bp. Innocent's hand with corrections which read:

> We maneuvered in a powerful storm for twenty-eight days in sight of Spruce Island. All were in danger—from lack of water. I said to myself, "Fr. Herman, if you have found favor with God, let the

winds change." And this is precisely what happened. A quarter of an hour had not passed before favorable winds appeared. I quickly served a memorial service on the Elder's grave. I saw nothing.

During his stay on Kodiak Island Bp. Innocent celebrated Liturgy every Sunday and on the Feast of the Annunciation. On the first Sunday he preached a sermon, on the second he gave instructions to the pastor and his flock, and on the Annunciation he held discussions with the people through an interpreter.

He also examined the church's archives, gathering data about the inhabitants of the region and in particular about the bay area where he proposed establishing a new mission. To this end he studied with and exhorted the sacristan who was learning the local Kodiak dialect. While organizing the files in the church, Bp. Innocent came upon a letter which read in part: ". . . Johnny has begun walking and frequently recalls his uncle . . ." This letter, written in a familiar hand, was addressed to one of the monks who in 1799 had set off from Irkutsk in the retinue of the newly-consecrated Bp. Joasaph and a few weeks later perished with him at sea. The "Johnny" in the letter was Innocent himself, now Bishop of Alaska.

Having accomplished his tasks on Kodiak Island, Bp. Innocent boarded the brig *Providence* [*] to return to Sitka. Five days later they sighted Mt. Edgecumbe, and at five o'clock on the evening of April 8 ther lay safely at anchor in the harbor.

The conditions of the church on Kodiak comforted Bp. Innocent greatly. As late as 1840 it had been without a permanent priest, and this made quite credible and a cause for real apprehension the tales which had reached him of continuing shamanism there among people still in the process of emerging "from darkness into the light." In fact, he had heard that so powerful were the old beliefs that not only was a general reversion taking place among the natives, but that the more superstitious Russians were in fact being "converted"

[*] *Promysl.*

to them. Happily, however, the bishop found that the new priest, with his zeal and piety, and the new governor, who provided not only any and all material support the mission might need but also in his own person an all-important example of a truly Christian life, had together succeeded in working wonders with the local population. Whereas in the past few people had bothered to attend church and virtually no one fasted or repented of their sins, now at every feast the church was overflowing, and more than 400 persons took an active part in the Great Lenten Fast. These findings lifted the hierarch's spirits as he prepared for the major travels just ahead of him.

CHAPTER 2

THE RETURN

As it had throughout the ten years he spent as a priest on Unalaska, Pascha signaled the beginning of more extensive travels for Bp. Innocent, a round trip journey of some 12,500 miles throughout the entire diocese projected to last over a year. He would visit Unalaska and Atka during the summer, cross the Pacific to Petropavlovsk by summer's end, tour Kamchatka during the winter, and end in Okhotsk early in 1843. His return to Sitka would have to wait until the autumn of 1843, as ships are held icebound in Okhotsk until at least mid-July.

Arrangements with the Chief Manager were made, and the bishop left his clergy detailed instructions governing the long period he would be away. With a retinue of six (a deacon, four singers, and his cell-attendant, who served also as subdeacon and scribe) he boarded the brig *Okhotsk* on May 4, 1842. Next morning, aided by a steamship, they put out to sea. For twelve straight days winds were good, and on the evening of May 16 they first sighted the Shumagin Islands, which belonged to Bp. Innocent's first parish in America, the Church of Unalaska. Next morning, and for the next three days, strong headwinds blew, preventing their approach to Unga Island until the morning of the twentieth.

Bp. Innocent thus describes his reunion with his former parishioners, none of whom knew that there existed such thing as a bishop, much less that their former pastor was now one:

Several pages could be devoted to a description of

how the Aleuts met me there and everywhere, and how I met them . . . But I will be brief. They met me as a father whom they obviously remembered quite well. (I will say no more.) And I met them as children, as brothers, and as true friends whom I love (now I am bragging) with pure Christian love.

The first thing which brought me special joy and comfort was seeing with my own eyes that my translations into Aleut had not been stowed away somewhere but were being read—and even by the women, one of whom (a Creole) amazes everyone with her clear, intelligent and sensible reading.

Next morning, May 21, Bp. Innocent conducted a prayer-service in a tent and afterwards preached to the people. That evening there arrived quite unexpectedly from Unalaska the parish priest, Fr. Gregory Golovin. As he paddled his kayak up to shore, as he did every second spring, he was amazed to find, standing there in the crowd to greet him, his predecessor in the parish now wearing the monastic veil and insignia of a bishop. He no more than his parishioners had any idea that a new diocese had been formed or that Innocent was in charge of it. Next morning, on the personal antimension (which he had surrendered to Fr. Golovin when he left Unalaska) Bp. Innocent celebrated Liturgy and once again gave Holy Communion to his beloved Aleuts.

On May 23 the *Okhotsk* set sail for Unalaska, taking Fr. Gregory along, thereby sparing him 400 miles of rowing home. At 7 A.M. on May 28, the Feast of the Ascension, the *Okhotsk* dropped anchor in Captain's Harbor, in sight of the wooden church which the bishop had built with his own hands sixteen years before. At 10 A.M. Innocent went ashore as the bell summoned the villagers to services. His sermon that day was on the same text of the Gospel as on the day he left Unalaska in 1834: "In a little while you will not see me any more, and then a little while later you will see me" (Jn. 16:16). "And the Lord was pleased," he writes, "to turn my words into prophecy, as it were."

But it was far more than even the joy of reunion which filled Bp. Innocent's heart that day. As he writes:

My arrival on Unalaska on their patronal feast—and at the very hour for Liturgy at that—I consider worthy of further detail. Leaving Sitka I wished and hoped very much to be in Unalaska by Ascension, and until May 26 I did not lose hope. But on the twenty-sixth, as we entered Unimak Pass, we were met by strong head winds in the face of which we were able no more than to maintain our position in the pass. Next day the winds quieted, giving us opportunity to progress somewhat, but soon thereafter they died entirely, stranding us some fifty miles off Unalaska—and I lost all hopes of reaching there by next day. However, no more than an hour later a favorable wind began to blow—so softly, though, that we scarcely moved. After midnight it increased and moved us to the mouth of Unalaska Bay. It then turned against us, and although we were able to tack, we were so far from harbor that even with the best possible tacking we would not be able to enter before evening. Therefore I had no hope of being in church on time. Then suddenly the wind shifted. It turned favorable and brisk, and within two hours we stood at anchor in Unalaska Bay. As soon as we dropped anchor the wind increased still more, and snow began to fall, and while this did nothing to prevent our transferring ashore, had it occurred even half an hour earlier, we would not have been able to anchor and would not have been able to come ashore.

Glory—glory and thanks—to the Lord God Who has fulfilled all of my desires for good, miraculously, as it were, for even with every possible human means, it can be called a miracle to arrive on time—not early, not late—aboard a sailing ship over 2,000 miles (on steamships it is possible), especially since the strong currents at the entrance to Unalaska are always capable of effecting ships caught without wind.

Nor was Bp. Innocent's joy to be ended quickly. "I had thought to spend no more than two weeks on Unalaska," he writes,

> since the ship on which I was scheduled to travel from Unalaska to Atka (the brig *Baykal*) had planned to leave Sitka soon after us. As it turned out, however, beyond all expectation I was able to spend 38 days there, giving me the opportunity of seeing virtually every Aleut there, to the comfort of us all . . .
>
> This church, thank God, is in the same condition as I had the honor of reporting to the Holy Synod. That is, the parishioners (the natives) are zealous for the Church, pious, diligent in fulfilling the Christian duty of cleansing their consciences, possessed of an ardent desire to hear the Word of God, and now that they have received books in their own language, all who can do so read quite avidly, while of those who are unable many are learning how (including many women) and the rest listen with pleasure as others read.
>
> In this region, as before, there is not even word of crime, nor even of transgressions. The priest, the district chief and the leaders in all localities praise the Aleuts highly. For the Aleuts, seeing me was a real feast, and the Lord commanded almost all of them to see me, for though we were fully prepared to leave, we were unable for twelve full days to get out of the harbor for lack of wind, during which time almost everyone returned from hunting . . .

Finally, on July 2 the *Baykal* succeeded in putting out to sea, and Bp. Innocent was again parted from his first home and flock in America. At the time of his departure the Aleuts presented him with an eagle rug, exceedingly well-woven from native roots and grasses, just like the one they saw him stand upon during services in their church.[3] After standing two more days at roadstead, they weighed anchor and set sail for the Pribilof Islands.

Towards evening on July 5, the *Baykal* approached St. George Island and the bishop went ashore. Want of good harbor demanded that his visit be a short one. He had time only to celebrate a prayer-service and preach briefly to the people, yet he left comforted at having seen that this isolated little flock was fully as good as that on Unalaska. Two days later St. Paul Island was sighted and the *Baykal* anchored a good distance offshore. Contrary winds prevented its coming closer, and in the morning Bp. Innocent rowed ashore in a kayak and went straight to the chapel of Sts. Peter and Paul. Again his visit had to be short, for not only was the island harborless, but with no Company business to hold it there, practicality demanded that the *Baykal* move on. (From the start the bishop had known and accepted that until he reached Kamchatka his schedule would be subordinate to that of the Company ships.) Before leaving, however, Innocent heard the parishioners' request that he send them a priest of their own, whose salary they declared themselves willing and able to pay. He advised them to give the matter further thought and to repeat their request in writing.

On July 9 the ship set sail for Atka. Wind and tides cooperated beautifully and in four days land was sighted. On July 14 at 8 A.M. the *Baykal* stood at anchor and two hours later Bp. Innocent stepped ashore to be met with the usual ceremony. In church he greeted the people and conducted a prayer-service.

On Sunday he celebrated Liturgy, during which he rewarded the priest for his zeal and faithful service, and blessed both of the parish cantors to wear the sticharion. He preached in Russian and instructed the priest to translate his words for those who did not understand and to distribute a copy of the text to each village in the parish. The rest of his time on the island he devoted to looking into parish affairs and giving instructions and admonitions wherever necessary.

[3] He in turn sent this rug as a gift to Metr. Philaret of Moscow.

On July 24 the bishop's party hoisted anchor and set sail for Kamchatka aboard their third ship since leaving Sitka, the galley *Seafarer*.[4] With them went the priest from Atka who, after seeing his bishop safely ashore in Petropavlovsk, would continue on to pay a pastoral visit to Bering Island. Listless winds caused the voyage to drag on for over two weeks, however, so that when on August 8, still 165 miles from her destination on the peninsula, the *Seafarer* encountered strong south winds, she changed course to run with these to Bering Island, which lay approximately the same distance away. Two days later she lay at anchor offshore of the island where the remains of the discoverer of the Aleutian Islands, Vitus Bering, lay at rest.

Bp. Innocent spent two days ashore, then, leaving the priest behind, he reboarded the *Seafarer* after Liturgy to continue on his way. With good breezes the passage to Kamchatka was now accomplished in just three days.

[4] *Morekhod.*

CHAPTER 3

PETROPAVLOVSK

Five distinct mountains lying far to inland of the peninsula—their summits wrapped in perpetual clouds and their rugged upper slopes of granite presenting an unlikely vista of both glacial ice and volcanic smoke and ashes—combine to give the majestic central coastline of Kamchatka a primeval and altogether unhospitable air not at all unlike that of the Aleutian chain upon first approach. The fact that seamen quite routinely have to spend a few extra days at sea at the end of their long voyage searching for the elusive entrance to harbor did little to change their estimation of this port. The *Seafarer* was kept three days in just such pursuits, and had made her way only partially up the narrow channel before darkness overtook her, forcing her to anchor there for the night. At nine o'clock, however, the mood aboard was changed with the arrival of a welcoming party sent from shore, led by the Dean of the Cathedral of Sts. Peter and Paul, the Very Reverend Procopius Gromov.

As morning dawned, nothing spoiled this new mood, for the *Seafarer* quickly made her way into the sunken volcanic cone which forms and gently shelters Avacha Bay. Beneath brilliant skies they pulled up to the docks and moored. A plank was swung over to the deck, and at its foot stood in welcome the district governor and most of the population of the foremost city of the region. The clergy stood in their most resplendent vestments, the military in full dress uniforms; civil servants wore their frock coats; their ladies were in silk; and the hot sun which bore down upon this show of gold transformed their company and helped conceal from their esteemed visitor — and in the excitement, even from themselves — the poverty and isolation in which these people really lived.

At 10:30 Bp. Innocent stepped down the plank to shore. Governor Nicholas Strannoliubskii and Fr. Gromov gave their official welcoming orations, and the whole population formed an escort to the cathedral, where all gave thanks to God for the safe arrival of their archpastor.

It was after this, in the next few days, that Innocent began to realize the real plight of this village called a city. The quarters he was given were in one of the few wooden houses in Petropavlovsk, and it was these alone which gave any indication that this settlement of tattered huts scattered across the otherwise streetless and gardenless hillside plain had not in fact been abandoned by its Russian masters. This was curious, for an abundance of natural vegetation made it clear that the land could easily support agriculture, and yet it was a known fact that the port was regularly plagued in winter by hunger and scurvy. Apathy was clearly at fault here, and this too was peculiar, for it stood at odds with the spirited reception the people afforded him both upon his arrival and again on August 22, when all turned out in anticipation of an event few of them had ever witnessed in their lives.

At nine o'clock the cathedral bells announced that the clergy had begun escorting Bp. Innocent from his apartment to church for Liturgy. Fr. Gromov recalls:

> One can imagine how touched these children of the desert were, seeing for the first time the majestic hierarchical liturgy, hearing for the first time a word of exhortation from their Chief Pastor. The second hierarchical activity never seen before in Kamchatka was an ordination to the deaconate and another to the priesthood.

The sight and sound of this immense man adorned in the splendor of the Byzantine court inspired the choir, and together they (again in Fr. Gromov's lively characterization) helped these poor and isolated Siberians to relive the experience of their ancestors sent by St. Vladimir to Constantinople to find the true faith. For the remainder of that day all thought of wordly affairs was abandoned to the spirit of celebration.

From the start Bp. Innocent's stay in Petropavlovsk was destined to depend entirely upon the weather. He arrived at summer's end—at a time when the picturesque and luxuriant inland valleys become vitually impassible to travelers. And even if the extra effort were made—and considerable it would be—to visit the settlements in these parts immediately, this would do nothing to speed the bishop's return home to Sitka, for as we have seen the port of Okhotsk is ice-bound until midsummer. Zeal on the part of the bishop would serve only to burden unnecessarily the local peoples at the time they were busiest laying in provisions for the long and rugged winter ahead. Therefore it was decided to put off any travels until winter's cold had created a smooth, efficient route for him to follow.

This ensured the bishop ample time to examine in detail the particulars of church life in the chief port and to become re-acquainted with his old friend from seminary days. Fr. Gromov was very much a part of the active schedule which Innocent established for himself and adhered to strictly throughout his stay. We include here its particulars on the assumption that it is not at all atypical of his life in general during these years.

Every morning the bishop arose in time to attend six-o'clock Liturgy in the cathedral. This was followed by a cup of tea, and then work began. Until noon he would read over the deanery journals covering the past two years. (In two months he was to write over 150 pages of resolutions dealing with what he found there.) Precisely at twelve o'clock he ate a light lunch and then spent the afternoon either discussing ecclesiastical matters with Fr. Gromov or taking an active part in repairing the damage done to the cathedral by an earthquake just before his arrival. (It had left the south wall pitifully propped up by beams.) On feast days this part of the schedule differed, for after personally celebrating Liturgy in the morning, Innocent would spend the rest of the day visiting with various officials and business leaders in the port. Evenings were spent quietly with Fr. Gromov, either in continuation of their official discussions or in pleasant reminiscences of their earlier days. Precisely at eight o'clock each evening the two friends were brought a light supper consisting of a glass of gin and bitters, a small portion of bread and salted fish, and a glass of Madeira to conclude the meal. Precisely at ten o'clock the bishop would retire for the night.

In the course of his inspection Bp. Innocent found everything in order. Following the instructions sent him the year before, Fr. Gromov had established classes for the children every Saturday evening after Vespers. "Such classes," wrote the bishop, "will bring profit—whether great or small, but profit nonetheless; and indeed, one can state that they have already brought some, for insofar as I have seen, every child without fail prays as he passes by the church. (This was all the more significant since before his coming the children had roamed the streets in unsupervised and undisciplined mobs.) Furthermore, Fr. Gromov had established the practice whereby every Sunday and at each feast a sermon was given or read, while on normal days during the communion of the clergy, one of the clergy not celebrating was assigned to read to the people a portion of the New Testament in Russian. Petty quarrels, so common in many places among the clergy, were unheard of in Petropavlovsk. "The local clergy," the bishop declares, "are very good. The Archpriest is an educated, strict, energetic and loyal man. His activity and persistence must be credited with making the clergy what they are, and even explains the bureaucrats' zeal for the Church. When they arrived here, they were not what they are today." The archives were an example of precision and good order; contributions were significant. The only problem lay in the near-by village of Avacha, where convict laborers and a few cossacks were causing considerable disruption. In fact the only murder to be committed the year before anywhere in the entire diocese had occurred there.

With good reason, therefore, was Bp. Innocent pleased with the work of his old friend, and in gratitude he invited Fr. Gromov to his apartment on September 2 to celebrate his "pre-monastic" namesday, the Feast of St. John the Faster. There he presented him with an autographed copy of his Aleut *Gospel According to St. Matthew* together with a gold-plated pocket watch. On the Feast of the Elevation of the Holy Cross (September 14) Bp. Innocent blessed his friend's son to wear the sticharion and ordained one of the cathedral staff to the deaconate in preparation for his approaching travels. On September 17 Bp. Innocent consecrated a new chapel attached to the cathedral which during his stay his own hands had helped build.

One day Bp. Innocent asked Fr. Gromov, "Very Reverend Father,[5] when are you going to show me your parish school?"

"Whenever Your Grace would like to see it. It's on my way home, so I'll come with you. I'd like myself to see what sort of a school we have."

"What?! You mean, you're not in charge of it?"

"No. Neither I nor my predecessor was found worthy of heading it, although both of us are seminary graduates."

"Then why did Bp. Nilus tell me in Irkutsk that you're the supervisor?"

"Bp. Nilus wrote me, too (but unofficially) asking me to put some order into the dismal school. But I didn't know if I should interfere in someone else's business on the basis of an unofficial letter, and so requested written instructions—which I never received."

"Then who *is* in charge?"

"Fr. George Loginov holds the title of 'dean.' "

"Oh? Is that so?" said the bishop, and he set off to see the school.

A few hours later he returned and asked Fr. Gromov to come over to his apartment. "What a mess!" he lamented. Fr. George has no money, no firewood, no flour, no reserve supply of fish, no candles—he has *nothing!* The tin plating has come off his dishes, so when he cooks fish in them it sours and make him sick. What a mess! Very Reverend Father, I ask you humbly—*please* accept the job of supervising the school."

"Your Grace! You can demote me to bell-ringer and I'll gladly go, but to work in the school . . . I put in over eleven years in the Irkutsk Seminary teaching two courses, so I've

[5] The standard form of address for an archpriest. It is not at all as formal sounding and aloof in Russian as in English.

repaid the debt for my education. I don't owe the system anything any more. I just *can't* accept the supervisor's job in the Kamchatka school under present conditions."

Innocent then approached Fr. Gromov and said, "It's not your *bishop* asking you to do this, but your old friend John Veniaminov. And he's asking you *with tears!*"

"But Your Grace! The supervisor hardly gets any salary at all, and you know I have a family and debts."

"I'll try to get 1200 rubles a year salary for you, and if they won't give it, I'll pay it myself."

After this, what more could the priest say? He accepted the difficult task on faith in this promise. The church life of Petropavlovsk was now in order. (Later Fr. Gromov found out that his faith had been fully justified. "Well, do you believe what you read?" Bp. Innocent asked him one day after Liturgy. "Come on," he added, and led the way to his apartment. There he produced an ukase from the Holy Synod reorganizing the school and making clear that in the future the Governor of Kamchatka was to take seriously his responsibilities as trustee of this institution.)

CHAPTER 4

KAMCHATKA

"Autumn is wonderful in the port of Petropavlovsk," writes Fr. Gromov,

> bright, warm, quiet. As it draws to a close with October's passing and as November—gloomy, severe, blustry November—begins, it brings with it the long-awaited passage into the peninsula's interior. During the summer this region, covered as it is with tundra and intersected by rivers and streams, is impenetrable. The return of snow provides the only possible road.
>
> The time the bishop spent in Petropavlovsk brought new life to the port: hierarchical services at the feasts, the pleasure simply of seeing a bishop in Kamchatka, strolling down the isthmus or through the hills surrounding the port, or visiting its residents in all simplicity, regardless of their station in life. His cheerful disposition, his edifying discussions alternating between ethical matters and splendid practical lessons—all of this bound the residents of Petropavlovsk to Innocent so tightly that when he left, we felt our desert had become a desert once again . . .

On November 26, Petropavlovsk celebrated the memory of St. Innocent of Irkutsk, a very special feast throughout Siberia and Kamchatka, made even more special by the presence among them of their bishop celebrating his namesday. This

167

past, however, the time was at hand for Innocent to resume
his travels through the diocese.

"What will I need on the road?" he asked Fr. Gromov,
by then a veteran of some eight trips up and down the
peninsula. The priest listed the most essential pieces of equipment and then suggested keeping with him on his sledge "a
supply of gin, bread and dried fish, for at times passage can
be blocked for long periods of time by blizzards and one can
become cut off from food supplies ahead. Oh yes . . . and you'll
also want to have along a bottle of water under your *kun-
lianka* (otherwise it'll freeze) in order to quench your thirst."

"Ha! Ha! Ha!" laughed Bp. Innocent. "We'll be traveling
on *rivers* the whole time and I have to keep a supply of water
anyway!"

"As you wish," smiled Fr. Gromov.

On November 29 the city turned out to see its bishop
off, and many of the officials, headed by the governor himself,
traveled with Innocent the first ten miles or so up the eastern
coastline to the village of Avchina before, with his blessing,
turning back to the port.

Though a seasoned traveler on horseback and aboard
ship, Bp. Innocent was a novice to the modes of transportation
used in Kamchatka. "More than 3300 miles," he writes, "I
traveled from Petropavlovsk to Okhotsk by dog team and
partly on reindeer, but I never even saw a horse." Instead,
locomotion through the dense, wolf-infested woods was provided by teams of dogs, six pairs per sled, rapidly and rather
reliably—unless in a moment of inattention the driver should
relax the reins just as the lead dogs caught an alluring scent
across their path. Then the traveler could be overturned and
dragged for miles helplessly crying "Ko! Ko! Ko!" to convince
the beasts to stop. Indeed, the imaginative novice could see
in the very vehicle which the canines pulled a sign of the
dangers he faced. Bp. Innocent provides the following vivid
description:

The vehicle in which I travelled could very well be

termed a coffin, except that it was lined with bear
fur instead of canvas or calico. It was no wider than
36 inches at the head and eighteen at the foot; no
taller than 21 inches at the head, and sixteen at the
foot. It differed, too, from a coffin first in that there
was at the head, behind on top, a plate or collapsible
seat attached, and secondly, it was on runners. Quite
often we had to travel along narrow roads cut deep
into the snow which seemed like long graves. The
coffin and the grave were ready— one had only to
close one's eyes, arrange one's hands, and be interred.[6]
But blessed be the Lord Who preserves me! Despite
all the harsh changes in weather, water, food, etc.,
I and all with me were perfectly healthy, and not
one of us encountered any unpleasantness—except
for frost and blizzards!

And, one might add, the very thing of which Fr. Gromov had
warned at the outset.

Several days out, gliding over smooth ice after a good
salty fish dinner, Innocent was lulled to sleep. Fr. Gromov,
too, napped in the sledge ahead. He awoke first with a terrible
thirst, and quickly drank most of his supply of water. Then,
seeing they were less than a half hour out of the next village,
he poured out the remainder of his supply. Just then came a
voice from behind. "Very Reverend Father! I am in great pain
in this fire![7] Give me some water!"

"I just poured it out," Fr. Gromov called back.

"Why, you no good. . . !" joked the bishop, and his first
words upon reaching the village ahead were, "Make me up a
reserve bottle of water!"

The travel plan adopted by Bp. Innocent was comprehensive: north from Petropavlovsk up the eastern side of the

---

[6] This was precisely the greatest danger in traveling in Kamchatka. Blizzards
could develop rapidly and trap those unfamiliar with the warning signs beneath
deep snow drifts in narrow valleys.

[7] Lk. 16:24.

peninsula through the villages of Malkinsk, Milkovo, Kliuchi and Nizhne-Kamchatsk, then back through these same villages to Malkinsk, across the peninsula to Bolsheretsk and on up the western coast to Dranka. From Dranka they would trace around Oliutor Bay, back across the peninsula to the tip of Penzhino Bay, and along the coast of the Sea of Okhotsk through Gizhiga, Yamsk and Tauisk to Okhotsk.

The first stop was at Malkinsk, some 91 miles out of Petropavlovsk. They arrived on November 30. There the bishop found an old hospital chapel established "in order to heal the souls of those whose bodies are being healed here." However, as both it and the hospital were badly situated, far from the therapeutic mineral springs and therefore virtually unused, Innocent decided to close it down and transfer the clergy elsewhere.

By December 2 they were in Milkovo, some 206 miles out of Petropavlovsk. There Bp. Innocent found the dedicated parishioners building themselves a church. He praised their zeal but quickly redrew their plans. The building on which they were working was badly suited to the climate (being too tall), their financial means (which were meager) and the particular plot of ground selected (which was already settling). With the priest and chief carpenter he went over the new plans and estimated that the project should be finished within a few years—about as long as their old building could be expected to last. On December 6 he celebrated the St. Nicholas' Day Liturgy and, as everywhere, preached to the people about the Christian's most basic duties. Next morning he and his party departed.

By midnight of the ninth they arrived in Kliuchi, a Russian and creole village in the midst of many Kamchadal settlements. In the morning at their pastor's request the bishop admonished the people briefly to be zealous and diligent in their faith, but then, since the weather appeared excellent for travel and since he was planning to return within a few days, he set off again for Nizhne-Kamchatsk, some 55 miles away.

Early in the morning of December 11 Bp. Innocent reached the first milestone in his land travels through Kamchatka, 175 miles out of Petropavlovsk. The Dormition Church there was the oldest in the entire peninsula, and its founder, the Monk Ignatius, was the grandson of the man sent by Peter the Great to bring the region into subjugation to the Russian crown. With the founding of Petropavlovsk, however, the village's strategic value had been lost, and by 1841 it was the smallest parish in the entire diocese, numbering a mere 250 people. With a general shortage of clergy it would be extravagant to maintain such a church in operation. Its few people could be added to the Church in Kliuchi nearby (by Kamchatkan standards) without too great a burden on anyone. This being his conclusion, in a report to the Holy Synod Bp. Innocent nevertheless makes the following interesting observations and recommendations:

> Since (1) the Church in Nizhne-Kamchatsk was the first to be established in the Diocese of Kamchatka, (2) missionary archimandrites were the first to come here, and (3) there was once a hermitage here, directed (so to speak) by an abbot—therefore, as a monument to the beginnings of Christianity in the Diocese of Kamchatka (and, therefore, to the mercy and grace of God), this church can be left standing, despite the small number of parishioners.
>
> Furthermore, there is in the entire territory of the Diocese of Kamchatka no place where a person zealous to save his soul, who has felt the urge to live in solitude, can go to be free from the noise and cares of the world; no place where a minister of the Church who has lost his family or is no longer able to continue serving the Church can find calm haven; no place where those who have sinned can find good correction, etc.—to put it plainly, there is in the entire Diocese of Kamchatka no monastery. The closest one is in Yakutsk, some 660 miles from Okhotsk along the most difficult of roads. And while such a distance is not, of course, by local standards great, how many people will be found willing to leave forever their native land, their relatives and close friends, and go to a foreign place where he has no

relatives, no acquaintances to help him should he find himself in need thereof? And could a person, born near the sea (and all the churches in the Diocese of Kamchatka save one are located by the sea), a person who has eaten foods for the most part taken from the sea, a person accustomed to breathing salt air—could such a person live far from the sea, without his normal diet, breathing dry air, and not experience a change in his health (especially in old age)?

For these reasons, we must have a monastery in the Diocese of Kamchatka. And since such a large number of clergy live on [the peninsula of] Kamchatka (in this respect, Okhotia can be included in Kamchatka), the monastery ought to be located in Kamchatka. And, taking into account communications and means for building and supporting a monastery, there is no better place in all of Kamchatka than Nizhne-Kamchatsk. Ships visit here several times a year from Petropavlovsk; thus all supplies needed by the monastery can be provided. The Kamchatka River area abounds in the finest, strongest timber, very good for building; thus it would be very convenient to build a monastery here. The Kamchatka and adjoining rivers and lakes abound also in fish, including the best in all Kamchatka (the king salmon); thus we are prepared to feed the monks. There are very many places nearby for growing hay; thus livestock could be introduced to bring not only foodstuffs but considerable income to the monastery from the sale of meat. Only one thing is lacking—hands to build the monastery and perform the usual chores within it. But for both of these the best hands are those of the Yakuts. The Yakuts are excellent carpenters and the best cattle-breeders around. And to be assured always of having even the best Yakuts, one could arrange hiring through the Governor of Yakutia, for among the Yakuts there are many who have indicated a desire to come to Kamchatka for temporary work.

Once the monastery has been built, the actual parish in Nizhne-Kamchatsk can be abolished. The church can become the property of the monastery, and serve initially as its cathedral. The parishioners can be added to the Church of Kliuchi, and the clergy either remain for the time being at the monastery or be transferred elsewhere wherever needed, at their present salaries.

On the evening of December 13 the bishop's retinue left Nizhne-Kamchatsk to return to Kliuchi, where several days were spent reviewing parish affairs and conditions in the old-age home and orphanage attached to the parish (the largest in the entire diocese). On the fifteenth Innocent celebrated Liturgy and preached to the people concerning the most essential duties of a Christian. On the seventeenth they set off once more, southward bound along the Kamchatka River through the fourteen Kamchadal villages which separated Kliuchi from the Cossack fortress of Bolsheretsk 440 miles away on the western shore of the peninsula. Towards evening on December 23 they arrived, having come back to within 175 miles of where their land travels began.

In Apacha, the last of these villages, Innocent found a small population of Kamchadals who had been forcibly resettled there from farther north by the civil authorities after conflicts arose with their village priest. Checking into this with the authorities and learning from them that the people maintained it was the priest who was the real cause of the disturbances, the bishop determined to learn the truth.

He turned first to Fr. Gromov, who as Dean of Clergy had been aware since 1839 that a problem existed in Icha and had done everything in his limited power to remedy the situation—but without success. From the refugees themselves the bishop learned of false accusations against them by their former priest, of beatings at his hands, of refusals to hear confessions or administer communion, of demands for sable furs in payment for performing weddings and of long refusals to grant this sacrament to those unable or unwilling to pay. Fr. Alex-

ander Snovidov was in general described as a stern man with
very little tenderness.

Learning these details had proved no mean task for the
bishop. The Kamchadals were, as Fr. Gromov well knew, a
peaceable and simple-hearted people, honest but intensely
suspicious of any attempts at eliciting information about
others. Therefore it was with considerable amusement that the
priest sat back to watch the people file happily one-by-one into
his old friend's hut to receive his blessing, but emerge completely downcast. "Boy, is *he* mad!" one soul muttered. But
Fr. Gromov, who knew both Innocent and the people, found
when he went in that the hierarch was in his usual good humor;
the truth simply had to be ascertained. And when they left
Apacha for Bolsheretsk the preliminary verdict was terse:
"Yes, we'll have to teach the priest in Icha a good lesson."

The great Feast of Christ's Nativity was celebrated in
Bolsheretsk, the bishop serving and delivering simple sermons
and instructions to the people, testing the children in the parish
school and visiting with the parishioners. On the morning of
December 28 they set off again towards the north, taking
along the priest from Bolsheretsk in anticipation of the unpleasantness ahead in Icha. Next day they were in Kolovsk,
a village of some 45 inhabitants located only half as far from
Bolsheretsk as from Icha, but included within the latter's
jurisdiction. Yet another indication of trouble came as these
people asked to be transferred into the jurisdiction of the closer
parish. In each of the last four villages along the road to Icha
the people were asked to confirm the stories which the bishop
had already heard. They told how in the last year seventeen
villagers had gone to Icha to confess their sins and receive
Holy Communion, but only four (all children) had received
the sacrament. The rest had been turned away, the priest
claiming to be ill. On the last day of 1842 Bp. Innocent and
his entourage entered Icha and immediately went to the church
for a prayer-service.

Afterwards, standing solemnly at his place in the middle
of the people, and vested in his episcopal mantle, Innocent
asked the large crowd which had assembled, "Are you satis-
fied with your priest?"

"Yes!" surprisingly, was their unanimous reply—including the young Kamchadals who now asked forgiveness for all they had foolishly spoken against him in the past. The bishop then turned to the priest. "Fr. Alexander, what do you say?"

"I forgive them with all my heart."

And so for the time being the matter rested. Next morning Bp. Innocent came to inspect the church, and finding everything in order, was about to question one of the tribal leaders when he found him being taken aside by the priest.

"What did he just whisper to you?" the bishop demanded.

"He says, 'Don't tell all you know.'"

This confirmed the rumors which had reached him indirectly concerning Fr. Alexander's insubordination, and Innocent turned to the priest: "So, you're teaching your parishioners to deceive me, huh?" He forbade Fr. Alexander to exercise his priesthood until a complete inquiry could be made. The clergymen accompanying Bp. Innocent were ordered to begin this inquiry, and during it the parishioners all testified that the priest and his wife lived comfortably within his salary, and far from making personal gain from parish funds, they were always giving freely of their own money to others in need. Examination of the church ledgers brought to light no great discrepancies, but seemed rather to confirm all that the parishioners had said. The only crimes of which the cleric stood guilty were coarseness with his people and insubordination to the bishop. The results of the local inquiry were sent to the diocesan chancery for a further opinion, and pending its outcome Fr. Alexander's suspension was left in force: he had failed in his pastoral duties and had lied to his bishop.[8] His place was assigned temporarily to the priest from Bolsheretsk until permanent arrangements could be made.

Leaving Icha after Epiphany, the company continued up the coast to Tigil, a village located 528 miles northwest of Petropavlovsk. There the people met their bishop with exceptional cordiality, nearly sweeping him off his feet to conduct him into church. Once inside and re-composed, he greeted them and celebrated a prayer-service.

---

[8] He subsequently died under suspension before the results of the investigation were received.

Tigil is located deep in Koryak territory, a people who among earlier missionaries gained a reputation for evil and treachery. Despite the fact that they had for years enjoyed ample opportunity to become acquainted with the Russians' way of life and religion, they, unlike their neighbors the Chugach, had fiercely resisted baptism. No more than five individuals had ever received the sacrament. The original cause of their resistance was by then long forgotten, and Bp. Innocent was determined to learn what currently prevented their coming to the Church. The answer he received brought little comfort. "Why should we be baptized? We see how the Russians live. The Russians deceive—Koryaks never do. If we get baptized, we'll just get worse."

On January 12 before leaving, Bp. Innocent celebrated Liturgy, during which he ordained a new priest for the parish. At its conclusion his sermon made a point of asking each of those present to consider whether he or she might not in some way be helping to keep the savages around them in the darkness of ignorance. At nightfall he was on his way.

Five villages separated them from the next church in Lesnov, the half-way point in the bishop's land travels, located some 845 miles from Petropavlovsk. They arrived only around midnight on January 15, and because of the hour the usual prayer-service was postponed until morning. When the people gathered then in church Innocent greeted them as was his custom and asked if they were pleased with their priest. The enthusiasm they then showed for him, the high praise they offered for his zeal for the Church, and the even more eloquent testimony to this provided by their own good Christian lives would have been comforting enough after the affair in Icha had it been just any priest stationed here, but as the people subsequently learned, the man they were praising was the bishop's own brother, Stephen.

When last we saw him in 1832, Stephen Veniaminov had after ten years been relieved of his duties as cantor and teacher on Unalaska in order to return home and resume the studies which in 1814 he had discontinued after only four years' work. It was soon apparent that immaturity more than incapacity had occasioned his earlier failure, for now he completed the course successfully, was ordained to the priesthood, and assigned to the church at Kachuga Landing. The rigorous winters of deep Siberia, however, had taken their toll on his Aleut wife Melany, so when volunteers were called for to serve in Kamchatka, Fr. Stephen stepped forward, hoping that the sea air would restore her to health. In Kachuga they were joined by an old family friend, Fr. Gromov, who was himself heading for the peninsula as Dean of Clergy. The expedition began happily enough, but this did not last long. Melany was not destined to see even Yakutsk. She died en route and was laid to rest on the banks of the Lena River, and Fr. Stephen and his four-year-old son Theodosius continued their sorrowful way. In Petropavlovsk they were assigned to the far north, to Lesnov, to find a good location for a church and to build one.

Lesnov was a large village by local standards (831 people), located on a hill (which was good for building) and near a stream (which seemed promising for provisions). By playing with the village children, Theodosius quickly learned the Kamchadal language and thus, until time came for him to go to the main port to begin his elementary education, he was not only a comfort but real help to his father in his work. As he had helped his brother do on Unalaska, Fr. Stephen taught the local men the basics of carpentry and stone masonry, and with their help he built a neat row of comfortable houses and a church. These successes came, however, only in the face of much adversity. From the very beginning the assignment had seemed virtually unworkable. The land provided scarcely any grain, the river was almost free of fish. Had Fr. Gromov not persuaded him to remain, the young priest would probably have left immediately. By the time his brother visited seven years later, Fr. Stephen was still unable to support himself adequately, and with the prospect of his son returning soon to live with him after completing school in Petropavlovsk, he asked to be transferred elsewhere.

The bishop tried to calm him. The problem wasn't as pressing as it appeared. Theodosius could study Koryak before rejoining his father in order for them together to compile a dictionary of that language. In the meantime the village needed a new church, and in view of Fr. Stephen's talents in carpentry, Innocent could not allow him to leave until this had been completed. Thus motivated, the priest was ready to set to work immediately, while his brother's retinue was content to accept his hospitality and enjoy a few days of badly needed rest.

A splendid log house, a large brick oven and the rare luxury of a Russian bath certainly lent themselves to an atmosphere of leisure, and although the time spent in Lesnov was not all lightheartedness (considerable paperwork had piled up since they left Petropavlovsk), the comfort of a warm hearth and the intimacy of family after many years produced many happy moments. One day at table after lunch a certain Deacon Nicholas in the entourage was seated opposite the bishop, facing a western window. The conversation turned to the question of life after death, and Fr. Nicholas queried, "Your Grace, if God is infinitely merciful, how can He deprive anyone of His heavenly kingdom?"

"And why do you keep twisting your head about from side to side?" Innocent countered. "Why don't you sit still,"

"Because the sun keeps hitting me right in the eye and just won't leave me in peace," the deacon replied.

"There. You've just answered your own question," the bishop laughed. "God doesn't deprive of His heavenly kingdom sinners who don't repent. They themselves simply can't bear its light—any more than you can bear the light of the sun."

Well-rested after nine days in Lesnov, Bp. Innocent, his brother, Fr. Gromov, and the rest of the party set off further northward. Before them lay the most rugged terrain that the peninsula had to offer. Fr. Gromov would be their guide for the first leg before turning back for home. Fr. Veniaminov would then see them the rest of their way.

Around dusk on their second day out, the company reached the rim of a seemingly bottomless ravine. Several crude huts stood there as shelter for anyone unfortunate enough to be caught in a blizzard, but this was all there was between them and the village of Drainka. Veteran travelers in the region tied ropes around the neophyte bishop and lowered him carefully down the cliff as he groped for footholds chopped before him into the packed snow. Fr. Gromov, for whom this was by now routine, took an animal hide and slid down the slope like a child. At the bottom the two then enjoyed several hours of rest by a fire while the sleds and dog teams were being lowered.

After sledding sixty miles up the ravine to its northernmost corner, the party found a second sheer ice cliff but this time, working against gravity, no traveler could be given preferential treatment. Each one had to climb on his own this time, hand-over-hand, aided in this arduous task by the sure knowledge that any inattention, any slip, any loss of balance however slight, could send him plunging to certain death in the darkness below. As they emerged from the depths they were greeted by the village of Drainka (or Iumgura), the last outpost in northern Kamchatka, located some 725 miles from Petropavlovsk. There, in the morning, in a chapel dedicated to St. Innocent of Irkutsk, the bishop conducted a prayer-service to his patron saint and gave his archpastoral blessings to one of the most isolated locations on the face of the earth. The second morning he celebrated Liturgy and preached according to his custom.

That evening Bp. Innocent parted with his old friend Fr. Gromov, who had to begin the long trek home in order to reach Petropavlovsk in time for Pascha. With him went two of the bishop's cantors with orders to find ship in the main post and rejoin him in Okhotsk. The prime reason for not taking them any further was that the countryside through which they were about to travel was so barren and desolate that every mouth was a burden to the inhabitants upon whom it fell to provide for strangers.

The decision was made: only those most crucial to the mission would go. This meant the bishop and his brother, whose knowledge of the land and its people would have to suffice to guide them through. The complement of Cossack soldiers normally dispatched with travelers both as guides and as guards—for among the Russians the Koryaks had a terrible reputation for restlessness, insolence and violence—

was declined for the same reason, and the reduced party set off into the wilderness.

Wilderness it was, indeed, for in the entire region there were just two established villages. For the most part the Koryaks were nomads, stopping with their reindeer herds only when necessary, and seeking shelter in vacant huts along the way only in the case of particularly violent storms. The two brothers of necessity copied this way of life, making their way slowly by day, and spending most nights under cold winter skies. From time to time they met wandering natives, who invariably came forward to greet them warmly, insisted upon feeding them and their many dogs, and even upon providing them supplies for the road—and this despite a desperate late-winter shortage of food. Such cordiality was completely out of character with the Russians' descriptions of them and this could only increase the bishop's curiosity and desire to become better acquainted with these people.

An opportunity to do so was afforded him when a violent blizzard forced the travelers to seek refuge in one of the permanent Koryak villages, Kamenets, in the district of Gizhiga.

A windowless, doorless, chimneyless structure partially dug underground, the hut in which the Veniaminovs spent over a week was typical of the region. All three of these functions were performed by a single hole cut in the roof, which was reached by a grimy, narrow board cut with a few holes to serve as rungs. Below perpetually burned a cooking fire whose smoke blinded those who sought entry or exit.[9]

These conditions were more than compensated for by the splendid treatment they received at the Koryaks' hands. Never were they insulted or offended in the least. Their supplies lay outside in the open the whole time, unguarded — and untouched. Finally, Bp. Innocent could endure the paradox no more and told the village elder quite frankly that he could not understand why his people had gained such a bad reputation among the Russians. In broken Russian the latter replied, "We good if somebody good and honest us."

[9] Innocent quickly learned that the Koryaks are violently superstitious about side doors and so surpressed any temptation to suggest this improvement to them.

Here he found the key to why there were almost no Christians among the Koryaks that he had visited, despite their frequent contact with Russians from Gizhiga. With pain he heard stories of how the Cossacks took delight in shocking and provoking the natives with behavior which even these "savages" considered criminal. Clearly there could be no thought here to converting people through Christian witness, but Innocent sought nonetheless to impress upon the chiefs and elders in every village the necessity of being baptized. In response he often heard the excuse that God had not given them any desire to be baptized, and they preferred to die in the faith of their ancestors. To the bishop's dire warnings that without this sacrament only hell awaited them after death, they replied: "What can we do? That's where our ancestors are, you know." Nevertheless, most agreed that should any of their people wish to be baptized, they would not interfere or forbid it.

A second, related objection raised in one village Bp. Innocent found quite interesting. One elder held that should they be baptized like some of their "relatives," they would anger their own god and would, like them, no longer be granted any whales or fish. In vain the bishop argued that the real reason why their "relatives" no longer hunted whales was that, having declined in numbers through migration to a point that hunting was no longer profitable, they had simply ceased to try. "It seems they feel that being baptized means receiving the right to live in poverty," he observed.

He then tried a bold argument: that the whales they *now* receive come as a gift from the God of the *Russians* and not their own. The rest of the discussion we give in Innocent's own words:

Hoping upon the Lord Who wishes that all be saved, I dared—or rather, suddenly had the idea—to say . . . "Should you ever fail to capture a whale, do this: without offering any dogs (or anything else) as a sacrifice—without performing *any* of your own rites —look straight up to heaven and say, 'Russian God, give us whale!'—and you'll see that God will give

you one." They promised to give it a try and to inform
me of the outcome. The first [elder] added that
should nothing happen (i.e., should they not receive
what they asked for) they would remain forever what
they then were ... Thus, the conversion of the Koryaks, both sedentary and nomadic, depends directly
upon the Lord Himself, for we are not now able to
do any more than speak to them as opportune in
favor of the Christian faith.

On the evening of February 22 the Veniaminovs arrived
at Gizhiga Fortress ("better 'Settlement,' " the bishop notes,
"for there is nothing even resembling fortifications here").
They had traveled 1584 miles from Petropavlovsk, and though
there remained some 990 miles to go before journey's end in
Okhotsk, the knowledge that the most arduous part was past
gave plenty for which to thank God in the church there.
Innocent then parted with his brother, who like Fr. Gromov
earlier had to hurry home to arrive in time for Pascha, while
Innocent, wishing to be somewhere with a church for Annunciation, after celebrating Liturgy several times and preaching
to the inhabitants of Gizhiga, set off again on the last leg
of his journey.

The end being in sight, it would seem, Bp. Innocent
stopped keeping the detailed diary which had occupied him
throughout his travels, but he did record one event which he
felt worth describing "for no other purpose than to give glory
to God."

In Gizhiga the natives warned him that en route to the
village of Tauisk he would hit one stretch which because of
extreme hazard was best by-passed—although this would mean
losing some time. Wishing to reach Tauisk by March 25 ("in
order if not to celebrate Liturgy, at least to *hear* it"), Innocent
decided to press on along the most direct path. In time he saw
what this hazard was—a mile's worth of shoreline rising as
sheer cliff from the sea, where the surf striking the frozen
rock at the high-tide mark had slowly formed a path (or
"braze") six to eighteen feet in width which now at ebb-tide
loomed twelve feet above the water. Clearly a rise in tempera-

ture above the freezing point of salt water could cause a fatal break in this unique road. But, the bishop reasoned, if (as they clearly did) the local inhabitants regularly used it, then it must be reasonably safe, and he decided to continue on. "But having gone out onto it," he writes,

> I almost repented for having decided upon such a clear danger—all the moreso since our last sleigh had to pass gropingly at midnight. But thank God! We all passed by safely and without the slightest "adventure." In the last village before Tauisk, at midnight, we read the Vigil service, having with us as yet no books or vestments (these remained behind). On the twenty-fifth I celebrated Liturgy in the Tauisk Church . . .

Okhotsk was finally reached on Lazarus Saturday (April 3). The bishop had been on the road since leaving Petropavlovsk for 126 days, 68 of which were spent in actual travel. He had covered over 3325 miles as estimated along straight routes, but frequent detours, both intentional and those necessitated by impassible roads, doubtless increased his total mileage by land to over 4000. By sea (including the trip to Kodiak and back), he covered another 8580 miles in 153 days, "and thank God," he writes,

> on such a varied and lengthy trip nowhere did anything unpleasant happen to any one of us, except the effects of the elements, and even then—with tremendous cold, extended stays outdoors and onboard ship, with frequent and drastic changes in air, water, food and lodgings—every single one of us remained perfectly healthy. Again, thanks to Him!

Bp. Innocent celebrated Holy Week and Pascha in Okhotsk, and then, while awaiting passage home to Sitka, he enjoyed the spring and summer months free to prepare a detailed report to the Holy Synod. In a letter to Metr. Philaret dated August 1, shortly before his departure, Innocent expresses his joy at all he saw in his travels:

> Although my flock is not very large numerically (18,500), in good examples it is far from being small. The Aleuts are not, as I had previously thought, the only ones who can (or could) share their last fish with those who are hungry. They are not the only ones who are patient, meek, obedient, peaceful, pious and so forth. Almost all of the peoples ... living in the Diocese of Kamchatka share these qualities. Only in their piety and loyalty to the Faith and the hearing of the Word of God are the Aleuts preeminent. Even the unbaptized Koryaks and Chukchi have many good traits and customs ...
>
> The more I become acquainted with these savages the more I love them and am convinced that we, for all our "enlightenment" have, without even noticing it, departed far, far from the paths of perfection. Many a so-called "savage" is morally far superior to us so-called "enlightened" people. For example, in the entire Diocese of Kamchatka one can state that there are no robberies and no murders (at least one can scarcely find a case of a Tungus, a Kamchadal or an Aleut being charged with such crimes). Furthermore, there are examples of positive virtues among these savages. For example, the first Tungus whom I happened to see and speak with (in Gizhiga) amazed and comforted me by his faith and loyalty to God. He told me about his life of near-poverty and I told him, "for this it will be well with you if you but believe in God and pray to Him." His expression changed noticeably, and with great feeling he said, "Tungus always pray. Tungus know God give all. If I just kill one partridge, I know it's God Who give all things. If I don't make kill, I know it's because God not give me anything. This mean I bad and so I pray to God." I cannot recall these words without being moved—nor after this can I

help but say in a spirit of thankfulness: "Blessed is the Lord Who reveals the knowledge of faith and truth to children but hides it from those who think themselves wise!"

CHAPTER 5

THE COMING OF CHANGE

After a month at sea, on September 6, 1843, Bp. Innocent returned home to America. His months of travel had impressed upon him the tremendous potential for spiritual growth lying in his far-flung flock and caused him to declare in one letter: "... I am happy and ready—indeed *wish* with all my soul for as long as I am able—to serve and even die here, for 'the earth is the Lord's.' "

His travels served also to remind him of a fact which from the very outset of his ministry on Unalaska had been crucial to his success: that the fortunes of the Diocese of Kamchatka were clearly and inextricably bound up with those of the Russian-American Company. The Company paid the salaries; the Company provided the food, the clothing, the fuel-oil, even the servants—in a word, all the basic needs—of himself and all his clergy. Indeed, in his absence from Sitka they had built for him, in a fine, dry location at the forest's edge, a spacious house with attached chapel, both of which on the second anniversary of his episcopal consecration he solemnly blessed and moved in. Ultimately, he realized, all of these things—and, in particular, free passage on Company ships, the very foundation of all work in the sprawling diocese—were his and the Church's only through the good graces of the Company and, in particular, of its Chief Manager in Sitka. He had no right to demand these things and was, moreover, determined not to be too great a burden on his benefactors. "God is my witness," he writes at this time, "that while I am here I can get along without such benefits, but won't my successor complain of this, while finding it harder for himself to solicit these things than it would have been for me?" He then adds, "as long as I am healthy I hope to manage all matters with the present methods," yet he could see how in the future some things (like an office staff), which would now be just a pleasant convenience, would someday become sheer necessity. Therefore, looking to the future and to the projects which he wished to see implemented, Bp. Innocent's thoughts turned naturally to what the Company could and could not do—thoughts rendered all the more appropriate as its royal charter was scheduled to expire in 1844, and its activities were under tight scrutiny as another renewal was being considered.

As always, first among the bishop's plans was education. Of the day on which he blessed his new residence, Innocent writes that it "was for me a real festival, although as yet I have not been able to dote upon my joy at having within my house a House of God." This was remedied, however, within the month, as twice a week the chapel was filled with the sounds of children—150 boys and girls, more than the total number attending the various secular schools in Sitka—listening to the catechetical lessons which had always been a hallmark of their bishop's ministry.

This school, however important as it was, marked only the beginning in the overall plan. A seminary to train indigenous clergy for the diocese also had to be formed, and having been given 10,000 rubles in 1842 to finance a building to house it, in 1843 Bp. Innocent included in his report to the Holy Synod a request for permission to establish just such a local seminary.

Innocent's hope was that, by training for the priesthood men with native insights into the people's character and peculiarities, the Church would grow and prosper in America; and his hope was bolstered by the reports he was receiving of increasing numbers of baptisms among the natives. To his joy, some forty-one long-retiscent Tlingits were, in his absence, added to the Church.[10] All missionary work in the diocese was

[10] The Tlingits were still far from pacified. At Pascha in 1842 a man named Naushketl asked to be baptized but demanded as a condition to have the Chief Manager himself as his godfather. Innocent rejected this and his

being carried out in strict accordance with the spirit and methods of his own work among the natives, the fruits of which are seen clearly in a report filed by Fr. Peter Litvintsov:

> In mid-May of 1843 I prepared to make my rounds, preaching the Word of God on Kodiak Island, which Bp. Innocent had placed in my pastoral charge. On the 15th of the month, at 4 P.M., I approached the first Aleut village, Orlovsk, situated on the shore of a small river. With me were a cantor and a boatsman. One chieftan who had seen our bishop in Kodiak said to me, "Never will I forget what our Bp. Innocent said in church. He ordered us to listen to what you say, and we won't go away until you've taught us everything good."

The same, however, could not be said concerning the bishop's own countrymen both in Sitka and throughout the diocese. They presented his single largest pastoral problem, as he reports to the Holy Synod:

> The major portion of the parishioners of the Sitka Church are Russians, simple folk from various provinces, people having for the most part neither homes nor property nor morality (or having simply squandered these). Judging by this we must say that they are the worst members both of Church and of society.

Yet, even with them he was now beginning to be able to add a positive note: when considering "the former condition of their souls, one must be amazed and give thanks to God that they are—especially now—incomparably better than they were and could have been." Some of the reasons why he felt such optimism were:

---

candidacy, seeing in the demand proof that he was as yet unprepared to receive the sacrament, for this was not conversion but self-interest. As a result Naushketl became drunk and began a fight which quickly escalated into a small native war which left two dead and four wounded.

(1) whereas before they were unaccustomed to listening to sermons (they thought this not even their duty), now almost all of them listen attentively to preaching; many of them understand it, and a few are even trying to put it into practice; (2) having been accustomed to thinking that true confession consists only in answering the priest's questions, many of them are now trying to do things to show that they have turned from their sins (or are abandoning certain sins, or are refraining from frequent lapses); one might also say that by now almost all of them know that simply relating one's sins or answering the questions asked by the priest about one's sins is not true repentance.

To guide the further growth of the diocese, Bp. Innocent issued the following set of major goals for himself and all the clergy:

(1) to confirm the piety of the flock, made up largely of newly-converted peoples not yet firm in the faith; (2) to bring back those gone astray or now straying from the path of faith (i.e., those who have returned to their former shamanism and those who have forgotten the fear of God to walk according to the will of their hearts); and (3) to spread the light of the Good News among those lost in the darkness of paganism.

In order to achieve these goals he issued pastoral instructions covering several broad areas. First, in order to facilitate the baptism of all new-born infants in outlying areas, he ordered that in each village "pious and informed" laymen be instructed in how to administer the Sacrament and then be allowed to do so using water previously sanctified by the priest and reserved for such occasions. Later, during their regular pastoral visitations the priests would complete the baptismal prayers and chrismate these children.

Secondly, where necessary, regular dispensations in the

matrimonial rules were to be granted. These concerned only
the natives living in isolated villages, however. For Russians
all ecclesiastical laws were to remain fully in force. Otherwise,
the greatest condescension was to be observed in *when* marriages could be performed (only Holy Week and the first
few days after Pascha being forbidden, rather than all the
fasting seasons of the year), in *who* could marry (the affinity
rules in Leviticus replacing the more stringent Byzantine
legislation), and in the *ages* at which marriage could be
performed. In all things harmony and good order were to be
preserved, and village elders were always to be informed of
marriage plans; no other declarations were necessary.

A third area of concern, as we read in the bishop's own
words, was the behavior of the clergy:

> Inasmuch as the Diocese of Kamchatka consists
> almost exclusively of peoples either not yet enlight-
> ened with the Light of true faith or else still babies
> in the Faith, who look therefore only upon outward
> appearances and are unable to discern the essence of
> the Faith from its rites and so forth . . . the Deans
> have been directed to pass on to parish staffs the
> detailed rules which I compiled on how they are to
> behave in church, especially during Liturgy and while
> handling sacred objects etc.

The sign that these projects would be brought to fruition
came when on October 11, 1844, the Company received from
the tsar its third charter renewal. At about the same time the
Holy Synod acted to authorize reorganization of the pastoral
school in Petropavlovsk as a seminary in Sitka. Therefore, in
the spring of 1845, Bp. Innocent set sail on a "quick" trip to
Kamchatka. His ship arrived on June 2, the eve of Pentecost,
and celebrating this feast was his only task beyond liquidating
the local school and transferring its scant material possessions
and student body to Sitka.

Work also began on quarters for the seminary. The
bishop's 10,000 rubles were already in a Russian-American
Company account bearing 5% interest for the diocese when

he approached the Company about actual construction. His well-considered proposal was as follows: The Company would receive 4000 rubles down payment once the foundations of the building were laid; the balance would be payable upon completion of the entire project. In the event that in the future the seminary should be transferred elsewhere, the Company would be obliged to purchase the building back from the diocese at the original price less 5% for each year elapsed since the time of first repair work. After a year of negotiations the Company agreed to these terms and construction began. Work ultimately required three years. Classes began on December 1, 1845, in the unfinished structure. According to the bishop's calculations the building would pay for itself within twelve years, which as it turned out is just about as long as its services were to be required. We shall see how Innocent's financial prowess ultimately served the diocese well.

These matters settled, Bp. Innocent was free in 1846 to begin his second extensive Asiatic visitation. His plans at the outset called for him to bypass the Aleutian Islands in order to use the summer months to visit the churches lying along the course of the Kamchatka River. (His first tour of the peninsula's interior seems to have convinced him that these would be reasonably accessible this time of year by boat.) The extra time this plan would gain him during the winter months would not provide the luxury of a less hectic pace of travel. Rather, it would allow him to travel the additional 600 miles past Okhotsk which was now necessary, since that port had been closed in favor of Ayan, and Ayan's territory had subsequently been added to his diocese by the Holy Synod in 1843.

Desirable and necessary as this plan might have been, it failed to materialize when the clerics from Russia whom the bishop had been expecting for over a year again failed to appear in Sitka by the time of his departure for Petropavlovsk. Therefore, if he was to give them necessary instructions concerning their duties for the year that he would be away, he would have to intercept them en route in Ayan.

All hope, therefore, for an "easy" journey was abandoned, and on May 9 Bp. Innocent, accompanied by his usual retinue and a priest en route home to Irkutsk, his tour of duty in

America at an end, boarded one of the Company's finest ships
for the voyage to Ayan. Contrary winds and a late break-up
of ice on the Sea of Okhotsk delayed the arrival of the *Heir
Alexander* [11] until June 24, yet there was still no word in Ayan
concerning the long-overdue clerics. This was very bad news
indeed for the bishop. The cathedral and seminary in Sitka
could not be left for over a year in the care of just one priest
assisted by a cantor and one of the older seminarians. Either
Innocent's travelling companion would have to postpone his
trip home to Irkutsk and return to help out, or else his own
visitations in Kamchatka would have to be cancelled. Happily,
in the end neither alternative proved necessary. On July 13
first a deacon and then a priest, both monks, arrived in port.
Their duties in Sitka were explained to them and the bishop
saw them off to America.

The Asian trip, though delayed, had been saved, and
now it began on a joyous note, for Ayan, though scarcely a
year old, already boasted—in addition to several huts, ten
wooden houses and a store—a church dedicated to the Kazan
Icon of the Theotokos, which was ready to be consecrated.
It was, as an amazed Bp. Innocent writes, "built even before
homes for the inhabitants—and such examples are surely
very few."

On July 20 at 5:30 P.M., in preparation for the solemn
consecration, the first vigil was set to begin in the new church,
and as the bishop recalls,

> the first peal of a 360-pound bell in a place like Ayan
> —where just three years before there had been no
> sign of human habitation—moved my soul (and
> many others' as well) far more than the sound of
> 36,000-pound bells in our ancient cities.

The time for a successful trip through Kamchatka by
boat was now growing rather late, so Bp. Innocent hurried
to Petropavlovsk, arriving in port on the eve of the Dormition, just in time for vigil.[12] It would be the end of the month,

[11] *Naslednik Aleksandr.*

[12] On the morning of the feast Bp. Innocent was conducted to church,

however, before the government boat *Kamchadal* could be readied to take him up the coast to Nizhne-Kamchatsk to begin his journey, but the the delay had at least one happy consequence: he was in Petropavlovsk to celebrate his fiftieth birthday and to see off to Irkutsk his old friend, Fr. Gromov.

On August 26 Bp. Innocent marked the beginning of his second half-century with a celebration to which he invited Fr. Gromov; his successor as Dean of the Cathedral, the Archpriest Eusebius Protopopov (a native Yakut who as a missionary in Okhotia had been making trial translations of sacred texts into Yakut); and the newly-arrived governor of Kamchatka. Next day they all met again on the docks. Fr. Gromov preserves the following description of the poignant scene:

> On the morning of the twenty-seventh my family received a final blessing from our bishop, who was about to be taken from our sight. Our own goodbyes would be said aboard ship. At 3 P.M. the Governor of Kamchatka, my successor and myself assembled on the [bishop's] ship. I glanced at the great three-masted transport, the *Irtysh*—upon which I was soon to sail—standing near-by at anchor, and my mind was filled with all the accidents which might befall us. Assuming that the bishop, a seasoned ocean voyager himself, would not suffer from seasickness, I asked his advice on how it could be avoided. His answer amazed me. "I can't avoid it myself. As soon as the anchor is raised I pay the usual tribute: I take to my bunk and bucket for three days, and after that I'm fine." [12]

---

greeted with the usual ceremony and led to the center of the cathedral by clergy wearing splendid new vestments. To the bishop's surprise, the vestments which he himself was then arrayed in matched them, a gift of the parishioners of SS. Peter and Paul and the population of the port at large, including many non-Orthodox. Evidently the hierarch's first visit had moved all the residents of Petropavlovsk.

[12] Throughout his diaries as a priest in Unalaska, Innocent complained of seasickness on every voyage. On one occasion he recommends holding a new onion inside the cheek as a trick to avoid this discomfort.

Finally, there arrived what we then thought would
be the last moments we would have to speak together
face-to-face on this earth. The bishop kissed me with
fatherly love, wished me all earthly and heavenly
blessings, and then his ship raised anchor. We went
ashore and with our eyes followed our departing
archpastor until finally his ship disappeared beyond
Cape Cancer. Soon signals announced the ship's safe
passage through Avacha Inlet into the open sea.
Parting forever with this best of all possible arch-
pastors lay like a stone upon my heart.

The *Kamchadal* arrived in Nizhne-Kamchatsk on
August 31, and after a short visit there the bishop began his
trip upstream. He passed through all of the major villages
lying along the course of the Kamchatka River up to its headwaters at Milkovo, just over half-way back to Petropavlovsk.
From Milkovo he was forced to ride some 93 miles on horseback—a much more difficult mode of transportation during
the summer—through three villages to the Bystraia River,
which he then followed as far as Malkinsk. After two more
days on horseback, he reached the Avacha River, which empties
into the bay near Petropavlovsk, and on the evening of September 25—ten days earlier than anyone thought possible—
Bp. Innocent reappeared in the port city, having visited the
whole interior of the peninsula.

There was no time to rest, however. The winter road
would soon be ready, and all around people were readying
their dogs and sleds which had been idle for several months.
The bishop, too, had preparations to make, among other
things ordaining two priests and a deacon for parishes along
his next path. By November 10 he was ready to bid farewell
for a second time to the kind people of Petropavlovsk, and
after a final liturgy in the cathedral, at which he thanked the
parishioners for the vestments they had given him—whose
spiritual value as an expression of unity and love far exceeded
even their considerable monetary value—he set off by dog sled
into the mountains to the northwest towards Bolsheretsk.

Bp. Innocent pressed forward rapidly, pausing in Bolsheretsk, Icha and Tigil only long enough to review parish records and speak a word of exhortation to both clergy and laity before moving on. By December 19 he was in Pallan, where he planned to celebrate the Feast of the Nativity. His brother Stephen had finished work on the church in Lesnov and had moved to his new assignment in this small village where, in addition to his pastoral work, he was serving—at the governor's request and after proper training—as a medical assistant. His services, however, were, in Bp. Innocent's opinion, more badly needed in Gizhiga, and so after being elevated to the rank of archpriest, he rather reluctantly left Pallan, accompanying his brother a second time as guide through the difficult terrain to his new assignment. Gizhiga was reached by mid-February and Okhotsk on March 12. En route, in both Yamsk and Tauisk, Bp. Innocent with full hierarchical ceremony consecrated recently-completed church buildings.

In Okhotsk the bishop succumbed to a disease which since autumn had been epidemic in the region and was laid up until the middle of Holy Week. By Holy Thursday he was sufficiently recovered to celebrate all the services through Bright Monday, and then he prepared to press on to Ayan. On Bright Tuesday—also the Feast of the Annunciation—Innocent was presented with yet another set of episcopal vestments purchased for him in Moscow by the local parishioners. That day he ordained a second deacon for the parish, fearing that should their aged deacon die or become incapacitated, it could easily be two years or more before he would hear of it in America and be able to send a replacement.

Preparing to leave Okhotsk, Bp. Innocent was faced with a dilemma. All Russian-American Company ships now sailed exclusively out of Ayan. The only vessels still visiting the old port were naval ones upon which he had no right at all to make demands. The governor offered to provide him free passage down the coast aboard one of these, but Innocent was afraid to accept this kind gesture. Once in Ayan he might well find no Company ships bound for America, which would force upon him a most unpleasant decision, either of imposing further upon the navy to take him on to Sitka (where the ship would be forced to winter most unprofitably for everyone concerned), or of himself wasting an entire year in Ayan, where there was still insufficient work to occupy him usefully. Faced with such a prospect, Innocent decided to utilize what remained of the winter land route in order to reach Ayan as early as possible before any ships could succeed in leaving port.

Once again a choice had to be made, between two land routes. The first had the advantages of being shorter and more convenient, following post roads and the Maia River on reindeer. Its disadvantage was that, following a river's course, it could be quite dangerous once spring flooding began. The second route, arching northward almost to Yakutsk before returning south, was over twice as long (some 1452 miles) and lay partially within the Diocese of Irkutsk. It was, however, safe in the event of an early thaw, and this proved to be the deciding factor.

On March 27 Bp. Innocent's dog sleds left Okhotsk along the old post road. Five days later he reached the northernmost point of his journey at Churopcha Station, just 93 miles from Yakutsk. Two days later he stopped in the village of Amginsk, still well within the Diocese of Irkutsk, but as it was a Sunday and as there was even a church building (an extreme rarity in that region) and as he had three priests in attendance, the bishop decided to stretch canonical rules a bit and celebrate the Divine Liturgy. Later that same day Bp. Innocent fell ill for the second time on this trip, and lost two days in bed with fever and chills before he felt up to setting out again. Even then he suffered a bad cough for a full week. Fortunately, soon afterwards he reached the Ayan Road, which was still under construction by the Russian-American Company. Its chain of way stations made the going much easier for a time. But one hundred and fifty miles out of Ayan this road came to an abrupt end, and it was through still-virgin forests and deep snows that the bishop had to press on by reindeer and dog to reach the port, arriving on May 5.

Even so, his travels were not yet over, for in Ayan he learned that it was now considered safe to visit yet another Russian settlement some 250 miles further south on the very border of China. Reasoning that the roundtrip could easily be

completed in time to catch the first ship to America, he decided
to go.

On June 6, Innocent and his retinue set out in large,
multi-seat kayaks (or umiaks) laden with Company cargo to
supply that isolated region. In six days' travel they encountered no particular difficulties, but on June 11, with heavy
iceflows near shore and in unfamiliar waters, they were forced
to seek refuge on land. Strong onshore winds lashed them for
four days, preventing them from pushing on even to search
for more convenient shelter. Only towards evening on June 15
did the tide carry the ice out and allow the party to resume
its way. "The Lord helped us," Bp. Innocent declares. "And
this I say in the literal sense, for as we passed a certain cape
our umiak was in grave danger of being dashed against the
ice by a strong current." One smaller kayak in their flotilla,
however, somehow unhampered by the ice, managed to forge
ahead to bring to the people of Udsk news of their bishop's
coming. Hearing this, the priest and a Cossack sergeant immediately set out to meet him and accompany him in. On
June 17 the bishop's entourage reached the mouth of the Uda
River and at floodtide was able to enter the estuary to begin
the trip upstream, aided by winds which happily turned
favorable about that time. Towards dusk on June 19 Bp. Innocent reached his destination, almost twenty-four hours later
than expected.

The scene which greeted him as he stepped ashore at
Udsk would scarcely have seemed to justify the efforts this
trip had required. A handful of wretched huts dominated the
backdrop for a welcoming party of thirty-five, many of whom
were not inhabitants of the village at all but migrant Yakuts
newly-arrived to trade their wares. Nevertheless, the bishop
blessed them all and greeted them as warmly as he could
through an interpreter—for it was evident that even the Russians had lived here so long that they could not understand
even simple words addressed to them in their native tongue.
Indeed, nothing about these people or this place seemed note-
worthy, yet tradition held that this village's roots went back
almost two centuries.

Confirmation of the historic significance of Udsk came

in its St. Nicholas Church. There Bp. Innocent venerated three icons—one of Christ "the All-Merciful," one of the Virgin Mary, and one of the patron saint himself—all evidently quite old yet only recently discovered in the process of constructing a new church building near-by. With this discovery was found the link to the region's past. These icons had accompanied the flight from China of the village's forefathers, driven from their home in Albasin in the Amur River valley by the Manchus in the 1680's.

For now, time would not permit Bp. Innocent to investigate at any length the history of this region, but seeing the workers determined to finish work before his departure, he remained long enough to consecrate with the full splendor of the hierarchical Liturgy the re-named Church of the All-Merciful Savior and St. Nicholas on June 22. Soon afterwards his party paddled off down the Uda River to the sea.

The return voyage was only slightly shorter than the trip out, heavy rains and adverse winds constantly whipping up the surf to hinder progress. Nevertheless, on July 15, Bp. Innocent reached Ayan to complete his second visitation of his Asian flock, having covered some 6000 miles on land and by river, utilizing—in addition to his own two feet—dogs, reindeer, horses and in one place even a bull. This, on top of 4600 miles of ocean voyages on the way out and the 495-mile roundtrip to Udsk, would ensure that by the time he again saw Sitka he would have traveled over 14,850 miles in fourteen months. Even so he still had the energy and enthusiasm to write in his report to the Holy Synod:

> Glory and thanks be to the Lord my God!
> No matter how long or how hard my travels may have been in a variety of seasons, in a variety of places, among a variety of peoples, in a variety of vehicles, under a variety of conditions, means etc., I can state that I was always perfectly healthy—for the three times I suffered a cough as a result of infection can scarcely be considered a true sickness, given the exertions and difficulties we could have experienced during such a journey (and in part,

did). Those who were with me were just as healthy.
Not one of us endured anything too unpleasant or
harmful to the health . . .

The external condition of the churches and
cathedrals was, in comparison with what I saw on
my first visit, generally speaking greatly improved . . .
For the fifteen churches there are legally allotted
two deacons, and thirty-eight lesser ecclesiastics. Of
this allotment we presently lack two priests (in Kamchatka) and six ecclesiastics. Ecclesiastics are very
easily found, but at present we have no one to
occupy the priestly positions, except the oldest students in the New Archangel Seminary.[14]

The flock of the churches in Kamchatka and
Okhotia has improved (generally speaking) spiritually in comparison with its condition four years
ago. There are very few people who avoid fulfilling
their Christian duties. My orders not to give Communion to manifest sinners has had great influence,
particularly on those with concubines or living together unmarried . . . *Even the Yakuts* are obviously
improving, as can be determined from the fact that
shamanism is now unheard of, and many of them
request prayer-services. Only the *Koryaks* remain
as before deaf to the preaching of the Word of God.
In the past four years only one of them has been
baptized.

[14] "I do not wish," he adds, "to ordain seminarians to the priesthood
for two or three years after graduation, and no younger than twenty-five;
however, I do not know if circumstances will allow this."

CHAPTER 6

THE VERDICT

By August 23, 1847, Bp. Innocent was safely back in Sitka, where he quickly busied himself investigating reports submitted in his absence by missionaries throughout the Aleutian Islands and on the American continent. These showed clearly that in most places the Gospel had taken root. Every year hundreds of adults were being baptized—and this was increasingly a result not of the clergy's formal preaching but of the witness and example of natives previously baptized, and of observing the good effects of Christianity upon the children who day after day were being taught by the missionaries. Texts were being prepared in more and more local languages, making participation in the worship of the Church easier and more meaningful for these new Christians. People were accepting the Gospel with joy, as demonstrated year after year by the records of those confessing their sins and receiving Holy Communion. The seed had indeed been well planted in good soil.

On May 1, 1850, Bp. Innocent submitted to the Holy Synod a lengthy report covering the first ten years of his episcopal ministry in America. We present here only its general conclusions, entitled, "A General View of the Condition of the Diocese." [15]

> ... we can conclude that at present, with the cooperation of the grace of God the condition of the Diocese of Kamchatka is gradually—but percept-

[15] Additional data from throughout the report are included where relevant in the form of footnotes to the text.

ibly—improving in all areas (except the composition
of the central diocesan administration, which needs
considerable change).[16]

Despite the size of the diocese and difficulty
of communication,[17] all locations within the Diocese
of Kamchatka (except the most isolated) are visited
from time-to-time either by the deans or by the bishop
himself. Despite a paucity of local funds and quite
adverse circumstances, the number of churches is
gradually increasing,[18] and they are improving outwardly for the most part without placing any demands on the State. For the most part, the clergy
attempt, insofar as possible, to fulfill the duties
assigned them. Very few of them require special
supervision of how they conduct their lives or correction through harsh constructive measures.[19] Many of
the priests, either personally or with the help of
lesser ecclesiastics, teach the children reading, writing
and catechism. Almost all are scrupulous about how
they perform the services and rites, despite the fact
that for the latter one must undertake real journeys
(so to speak) rather than simple visits. In terms of
education the local clergy will not soon equal that of
other dioceses. With the establishment of a seminary,

[16] The chancery consisted of three staff members (two priests and a
secretary/deacon) in Sitka and four (two priests, a chief clerk and one assistant) in Petropavlovsk. The latter staff Innocent pronounced adequate to
its task, but the one in America needed augmenting by a third priest, a full-time
secretary, a chief clerk and two assistants just in order to keep up with the
paperwork.

[17] "There is no place in the entire diocese where travel by normal carriage is possible." (Footnote in the original report.)

[18] There were in existence then 24 established churches (eight in America, including the bishop's chapel) and 37 "prayer-houses." An additional three
churches were then under construction and four more were authorized to begin.
Nineteen more prayer-houses were also either under construction or so
authorized.

[19] Bp. Innocent cites as a major factor in this the fact that vodka was not
as readily available in his diocese as in Russia. The people, too, were less
of a pastoral problem than in other places. He remarks repeatedly that most
of the problems in his diocese were caused by the Russians living there rather
than by the native populations (cf. below).

however, the number of clergy who have not completed seminary should in five to ten years be quite small.[20]

The spiritual condition of the flock in the Diocese of Kamchatka, which consists primarily of recently- and newly-converted peoples (of a total number of 23,130 persons only 5,820 are Russians or creoles, including clergy), is comforting now as in the past. The following serves to demonstrate this fact:

(1) Last year there were only 226 people who by omission failed to fulfill their duty of cleansing their consciences. Of this number 126 were Russians, 73 Kamchadals, and the remaining 27 belonged to various nationalities.

(2) For some time now there have been no crimes (whether felony or misdemeanor) despite the fact that they (the natives) are, so to speak, self-governing.

(3) Very few of them are unwilling to endure wrongs or insults rather than to complain of these. In large measure this is a function of their character, but many can be found who act this way precisely in the spirit of Christianity. One must also note their innate virtue of charity, which under the influence of Christianity cannot help but be perfected to a greater or lesser degree, in a few of them at least.

Catechetical instruction—or more accurately put, teaching the children their Christian duties—has been instituted in seventeen parishes as of January 1849 (excluding my personal chapel).[21] There were only six in which this has not been instituted, and in only two of these (both in Kamchatka) will it perhaps

[20] Of a total number of 89 clerics (29 priests, five deacons, and 55 minor ecclesiastics) only seven were seminary graduates. Another fifteen had attended some seminary but had never completed the course, while the rest (67) had only an elementary education or less.

[21] He states elsewhere that with so few clergy trained properly to teach children, "I thank God that at least the priests have begun this task."

ever become possible to do so; in the other four churches it is presently quite inopportune. Reading was being taught to the children of parishioners in fourteen parishes in 1849 (excluding New Archangel), this being over half the parishes. Of course, the total number of students being taught by the clergy is quite small (no more than 100 in all), but this is the fault not so much of the clergy as of local conditions. Literacy is, however, spreading in the parishes of Unalaska and Atkha quite successfully, and not without the participation of the priests. One can hope that soon more people will become literate in other areas as well.

Finally, one can say that through the grace of God, gradually and according to our means, we are nearing the chief goals with which the Diocese of Kamchatka was established, *viz.* the conversion of non-believers to Christianity. By human calculations, it would seem, based on local circumstances, that were we to have greater means, we would also enjoy greater success in our work. Doubtless, this only *seems* so to us, otherwise—had the time come for the conversion to the path of truth of each and every pagan living near us—the Lord would not have failed to send us workers and to have given them the full possibility of working and supporting themselves. Therefore, we have only to pray to Him concerning this and to work as hard as we can. Our major goal in this work should at present be to support our present missions and gradually to build new ones near them according to our means.

To improve the operation of the diocese, Bp. Innocent offered one concrete suggestion which would have quite an impact on his own future life and ministry. In reporting that it would be necessary to add to the chancery staff another five persons in order for it to function smoothly, he noted that adequate financial support of such an enlarged staff in Alaska would be unfeasible. Profits of the Russian-American Company had fallen off and internal politics were weakening its operation, forcing cut-backs whose effects were already being felt in the Church in America and could only be expected to become more serious. Housing in Sitka was already inadequate for the number of clergy assigned there, and only the use of the seminary's facilities had prevented a crisis. Obviously no expansion in this area was possible. Salaries had not yet reached the levels agreed upon in 1840 at the founding of the diocese. Furthermore, as Bp. Innocent had already recognized several years before:

> ... the goal in establishing the episcopal see of the Diocese of Kamchatka in America rather than in Asia has been fully realized. For Christianity is, with the cooperation of the grace of God, spreading successfully. Missions have been established in all major locations (which would, of course, have been scarcely possible without having a bishop in New Archangel) with the sole exception of New Archangel itself ... for the Tlingits themselves still have no preacher.

A bishop's continued presence in America was not only far less essential now than in 1840; in many respects it had become superfluous. The missionary priests had begun to penetrate so far into the hinterlands that Russian-American Company vessels rarely made contact with them, and hence the bishop could not reasonably visit these missions even if he so desired.

Conversely, the Asian portions of the diocese were in a constant state of flux. China's might was on the wane, and the oppressive trade restrictions that she had placed upon Russia at the height of her power were fast being removed. A young and energetic man had recently been named Governor-General of Eastern Siberia and was known to favor re-annexation of the Amur River basin, by which, as he would write to Bp. Innocent, "Siberia's appearance will change completely. Kamchatka and America will be brought closer together." Russian settlers were being sent into the coastal regions that he had just visited between Udsk and Ayan and, as Innocent was assured with great enthusiasm, "a great field is being opened for a special mission. I speak of the land of the Gilyaks, of which you know. Christianity could advance tremendously the future of Russia." Taking all of this into consideration one conclusion became virtually inescapable: the time had come for Bp. Innocent to be located more centrally within his vast diocese. The time had come for the Orthodox Church in America to be deprived of the physical presence—although never the spiritual concern—of her first hierarch and greatest missionary.

PART FIVE

THE VENIAMINOVS

THE VENIAMINOVS

It was in this same period, the late 1840's and the decade of the 1850's, that the Veniaminov children began to come of age and to make their own way in the world. With this there returned to Bp. Innocent—albeit for the most part and of necessity by "long-distance"—the joys and sorrows of parenthood. We will, therefore, interrupt our chronological approach to look at another side of this great hierarch and missionary.

We have already seen how in 1839, with the death of Catherine Veniaminov, her seven children were stranded in Irkutsk, virtual orphans, and it appeared as though their father's days of active missionary work were numbered. The Russian imperial family intervened, however, guaranteeing their education and thereby freeing Fr. John to continue the ministry for which he felt himself best suited "by education and talents," to use his own words. The boys, as we have seen, transferred from the seminary in Irkutsk to that in St. Petersburg while their sisters were enrolled in fine girls' schools in the northern capital.

We begin our story in the year 1845, which brought the bishop disturbing news that his eldest son Innocent had been expelled first from the St. Petersburg Seminary and then from Bethany in Moscow. Declaring himself uninterested in remaining in the clerical caste, he vanished despite all that Metr. Philaret and others might do to return him to the "good path." "This unfortunate son of mine," Bp. Innocent writes,

> was the fourth child to be born. Those born before him all died at an early age, and he too would have died—indeed he *did* die—but I snatched him back by

force from the hands of Death (or from the hands of God—the two are the same). And God in His mercy gave him to me, but has used him at the same time to punish me—a punishment which I humbly accept. Had he died then he would now be in school in heaven with the other children, and I would long ago have forgotten him. Now only God knows what will happen to him! May God's will be done!

The bishop made repeated attempts to learn of his son's whereabouts and affairs and to offer him his help. "May God bless him in his new endeavors," he wrote to his friend Nicholas Lozhechnikov[1] in St. Petersburg. "Be sure to tell him that no matter what grief his behavior may have caused me, I haven't stopped loving him." And to the seminary's rector, Archimandrite Mitrophanes, he wrote, "No matter where he is or what is he—even if he embarrasses me—I'll always call him my son and be ready to look after him if necessary (and that's quite possible). For God's sake, I beg you, do not abandon him. If he needs it, feed him on my account and I'll pay for everything."

Despite this loyalty to his son, Bp. Innocent did not shrink back in the least from the words he had written in 1841 to Andrew Muravev, when he entrusted Innocent and Gabriel to his care. "My sole desire," he stated then, "is that they be of use to the Church. Otherwise it is better that I lose them." So now, he writes to Archimandrite Mitrophanes asking him not to allow Innocent's ordination: "If it were up to me, I wouldn't lay so much as a *finger* on him—much less *hands!* There's no reason for him to come to me—I'll give him no responsibilities of any sort, and he'd only be in my way here."

In 1846 it was learned that this "unfortunate son" had joined the army and was en route to duty in the Caucasus Mountains. Two years later he married. All of this could have been a sign of maturity long overdue, but it proved otherwise, for in 1852 word came from a certain Fr. Jerome in Tomsk

[1] An official of the head office of the Russian-American Company whom he met during his trip to Russia.

that Innocent Veniaminov had been sentenced to two years
in prison. It was the cleric's opinion that this would surely
be enough to bring the young man to his senses.

Pain is by no means the only emotion destined to fill a
parent's heart. In 1848 we read:

> Though my first-born and beloved son is sadness and
> grief to me, I have no right to grumble—or even
> sigh—under their weight, for the Lord has been im-
> measurably merciful to me. My second son (glory
> and praise be to God!) has arrived in New Archangel
> and brings me comfort and great joy—not at his eru-
> dition, but by his love and obedience to me and his
> devotion and piety. I will appoint him to minister
> to the Tlingits. Next year I'll send him on leave to
> Russia to be married.

Gabriel Veniaminov was thus tonsured a reader by his
father and appointed to serve as subdeacon in St. Michael's
Cathedral and in the seminary as teacher, secretary, librarian
and assistant dean. His arrival freed a priest for full-time
missionary work while not requiring that the staff of five be
reduced. Gabriel was the only full-time instructor in the
seminary, for the other four teachers were all members of
the cathedral staff and had to divide their time and energies.
Gabriel worked ably in this capacity not one but three years
before departing for Moscow in July of 1850 in search of a
bride. Bp. Innocent asked the boys' old benefactress in the
capital, Barbara Sheremeteva, to be Gabriel's "mother" at
the wedding and Andrew Muravev to "please fulfill his
[Gabriel's] desire—and my own—not only during the wedding
but throughout his stay in the capitals and in Russia. To you
I yield and transfer my [parental] rights. *Be* his father in
all ways . . ." [3]

Another Barbara, Princess Golitsyna, aided by Metr. Philaret and the Archpriest Nicholas Lavrov, arranged a marriage
for the young Veniaminov. A clerical orphan named Catherine

[3] In the end, a stranger who was to become a great benefactor of Bp.
Innocent's missions, Platon Golubkov, stood in at the wedding.

Popova was chosen as his bride. Although neither particularly attractive nor well-educated, she was bright, pious and very kind and had an honest, open manner about her. It was explained to her in detail the kind of life that this marriage would bring her—hardships and deprivations as a missionary's wife in distant lands—and although she and Gabriel did not strike it off particularly well at first, she accepted and he concurred. "I *more* than rejoice," Bp. Innocent writes, "I am *amazed*—at his obedience to the will of God and my advice that he leave the choice of a wife up to God. Now I have only to pray continually that in moments of temptation (which are inevitable in family life) the Lord will not remove His grace from him."

Fr. Lavrov performed the Sacrament of Matrimony and then, in accordance with Bp. Innocent's plea that he not be required to advance his own son to Holy Orders, Metr. Philaret ordained the young man to the priesthood on February 25, 1851. The newlyweds departed immediately on their rigorous trek across Siberia to the Diocese of Kamchatka, and in the course of this journey, sharing its hardships, the two began to fall in love.

Fr. Gabriel and Catherine arrived in Ayan in July of 1851, bringing Bp. Innocent news of his other children as well. The impression Catherine made initially upon her new father-in-law was much the same as on her husband, but as the two found time to talk she won him over as well by her genuine kindness and openness. Perhaps, the bishop felt, it was her name—Catherine—which she shared with both his late wife and his eldest daughter which more than anything else began the process. At any rate, in time he was to write, "I shall remain eternally grateful to Moscow for giving me such a daughter-in-law!"

And Catherine for her part proved worthy of such high praise. At the very start of her new life in the easternmost parts of the Russian Empire, she demonstrated her own missionary spirit, vowing to learn the local languages in order to help her husband convert the people to Christ by teaching the children.

As she and Fr. Gabriel will remain prominent characters throughout the rest of our narrative, we will leave them here in order to turn our attention to the rest of the Veniaminov children.

Bp. Innocent's eldest daughter, Catherine, was too old in 1839 to be sent to St. Petersburg to begin an education. Instead she married her childhood friend, Elijah Petelin, who in 1841 was, as we have seen, ordained to the priesthood in Sitka by his father-in-law and sent to Nushegak. After working in American missions for some time they were transferred to the Amur region and settled for good in Mariinsk.

The younger Veniaminov girls, who did go to the Russian capital, soon found that their father's fame opened many doors to them. Olga, the eldest, married into one of the most prominent clerical families in St. Petersburg and soon bore a child, Natalia. Her destiny we will see detailed below.

The youngest girl, Thekla (or Kushenka as Bp. Innocent calls her) was already a seasoned world traveler by the time she enrolled in school. This adventure, on top of the attention shown her by famous people in St. Petersburg, seems to have turned her young head, and in 1849 she received this bit of fatherly advice:

> My dear Kushenka,
>   Thanks for the letter which you sent with Gania.[3] You're all alone in the Institute now, and probably bored, but you'll find it even more boring out in the world, my dear. You'll recall your school days a hundred times over but will never be able to return to them. Your present state is the happiest. Now you see everything through rose-colored glasses and dream of eternal, continual happiness. Alas, it's all deceit! God's Word says that the world lies in evil, and we reach the goal before us only through much grief. All of this is real, unchangeable, eternal truth.
>   Gania has told me about all of you children. He says that you, Kushenka, aren't studying too well and are putting on airs—that you're acting like a

---

[3] Fr. Gabriel Veniaminov.

baroness. I'm not *angry* with you over this, because everyone likes to act proudly and put on airs in front of anyone they can—but I advise and ask you not to do so. Behave more simply and be kind to all. The proud only show their stupidity. Wise men are never proud, never put on airs. And God only knows what you'll be in the world. One thing you *won't* be, though, is a countess or rich, because I can't give you a dowry.

Kushenka, my dear, comfort me! Study hard. Pray more fervently to God, and stop putting on airs and being proud. Don't be angry so often. Hold your temper. Otherwise it won't go well with you.

Kushenka heeded this paternal plea, finished school, and like Olga married into a very good clerical family in Moscow. Constantine Molchanov, her husband, had a guaranteed position as a deacon as soon as he married—quite a rarity in Moscow at a time when competition for any clerical position was likely to be fierce. Eventually they moved to Petergof, where as a priest Fr. Constantine was assigned to the cathedral.

Like her sisters, Paraskovia (or Pasha as she was known) received a fine education in St. Petersburg and, enjoying many connections through her father's name, had every prospect of a very good life. She chose, however, a very different and unexpected path. She renounced the world and became a nun.

When Bp. Innocent learned of her decision he knew how difficult a path this would be for an attractive, educated young girl and so wrote many letters to strengthen and encourage her. These are among the warmest and most touching of all the documents he has left us—and most revealing of his own soul. Therefore we shall quote several of them here at length.

July 4, 1850

Dear Pashenka,

Thanks for your letters. I read them with pleasure. I praise, bless and approve your intention to enter the convent! You say that you want to go to a convent somewhere other than in Petersburg, but all convents are the same. There's not a convent in the world where you can find spiritual peace without prayer and effort. You say beautifully that you "want to go to a convent for no other reason than to save your soul," and that you want "to pray to God with a soul capable of burning with love for Him." It would be pleasant and comforting to hear you say such words even if they were someone else's rather than your own. But it's even *more* comforting for me that you say them on your own! Let me tell you, though, that to fulfill this desire goes beyond Christian perfection, and very, very few attain it. Oh! if you could attain half—even one percent—of your desire, how happy you would be! And if you keep this goal in mind and pray fervently, God is faithful and powerful, and you *will* attain it. *You will!* But first, learn to pray.

You say you want to see me. I don't know if we'll ever see one another again on this earth—and what would there be in such an earthly meeting? A few moments of joy—and then indifference. We must strive instead to see one another in heaven! And may God help us!

Good-bye, my dear. God be with you. My greetings to all who love you.

Pashenka made her decision to enter the convent on July 18, 1851, and we read her father's loving advice:

Peace and blessings to you, my dear and beloved daughter, Paraskovia Ivanovna,

I rejoice and thank God that you have chosen that right thing which will not be taken away from you [4] — if only you do not yourself decide to deprive yourself of it. Of course, for a very young girl the convent is like a grave—but a grave which can become the source of life and incorruption. I haven't received

[4] Lk. 10:41.

your letters because Gania hasn't yet arrived. But
it doesn't matter whether or not I receive any letters
from you. Nicholas Emelianovich [5] wrote me that
you are not sorry that you left the world. Oh! may the
Lord strengthen you in this resolve! Indeed, there's
not much in this world to be envied. Just look at
others: are they so greatly happy in their lot as
women? Only 'til the first child is born are they
happy and blessed—afterwards there's almost continual trouble and worries, sadness and grief! Of
course, life in the convent promises no vain joys or
pleasures, but you will be delivered from much fuss,
worry, sadness and grief. To anyone who is careful
about her vocation, convent life promises — and
delivers—much true comfort. If you decide to be tonsured, I wish only that you go outside of the convent
as little as possible—and then only in obedience to
some order. But don't think that you'll never have
any temptations from one side or another. No! Life
without temptations is impossible. Just believe that
our merciful Father in heaven will not allow you to
be tempted beyond your power to remain firm. [6] Don't
be careless. Pray as much as you can—more frequently
and more fervently. Prod youself—*force* yourself—
to do so, for the Kingdom is *taken by force*,[7] and
you'll never attain it without forcing yourself! When
you are disheartened or tempted, write me. Write
to me—every day if you can—the whole history of
your soul . . . I will receive and read your letters
with love and joy and will answer them as best I
can. (Just write clearly and with large letters.)

Your sister Katia rejoices over you and envies
your entering the convent because now you have to
worry only about your own soul, while she has to
worry about her own soul plus those of her children
and eventually of her grandchildren. She says that

[5] Lozhechnikov.
[6] 1 Cor. 10:13.
[7] Mt. 11:12, Lk. 16:16.

had she known what it means to marry and have children she never would have.

Good-bye, my dear. God be with you. Be more patient and brave. Pray for yourself and for your father.

P. S. My blessing and greetings to the Reverend Mother of the convent in which you live and to all the elders close to you.

After less than a year of testing Pashenka was received as a novice in the Hermitage of St. Boris in the Kursk region. Again her father hurried to encourage her:

May 24, 1852

Today I received a letter stating that the Mother Superior of the hermitage in which you live has found you "by reason of your modest behavior and zeal for God's Church and monastic obedience" worthy of entering the novitiate, and that you wish to dwell permanently in this hermitage. I don't think I've ever rejoiced over you as I did—and do—today! Glory and thanks be to the Lord Who has given you this desire to enter the convent and has strengthened you in your service to the sisters. May the Lord God strengthen you 'til the end of your life in your intention to dedicate yourself to Him, the Heavenly Bridegroom! O Pashenka, my joy! You've chosen the good—the *exceedingly good*—thing which will not be taken away from you if only you do not foolishly remove from yourself Christ's yoke. Now you have just one concern—to please the Lord and to battle yourself. That's *all!*

I wrote you that your older sister envies your present life. Her husband is a gentle man and they have lived together thirteen years without a single harsh word between them; their children are very intelligent and healthy, and yet she considers *you* happier than herself. She is worried about her

husband, about the children, about the house, about
the future, *and* about her soul. And the longer she
lives, the greater her cares become. Indeed, how she
should fear the future! But *you*, my little one, you
have none of this—and *can* have none of it. So stay
where you are now, my joy, for your entire life. Don't
desire—don't seek—to see your relatives. The Lord
is merciful, so pray to Him that we may all see one
another some day in the mansions of our Father in
heaven; there we shall see one another in eternal,
indescribable joy. We'll see one another not for just
a month or even a year—but *for all eternity*. So what
kind of meeting could we have on earth? Pray, my
friend, pray as much as you can. Force yourself to
pray. The desire to pray is a gift from God and isn't
always given. It is, however, inevitably to those who
force themselves to pray that it is given. At first it
seems burdensome and difficult, but becomes lighter
and lighter as you go. Then, when you receive the
gift of prayer you'll never desire anything greater.
May the Lord God strengthen you! My greetings to
Reverend Mother Arsenia and my blessings to the
sisters. May the Lord our God help you all to attain
to His eternal kingdom. Good-bye. The Lord be
with you always.

In another letter to Pashenka, dated August 3, 1853,
Innocent develops further the theme of the "heavenly Bridegroom," and we learn further about his daughter Olga:

> ... *your* Husband will never get sick or die; your
> Heavenly Bridegroom is immortal. You can have as
> many children as you wish (by this I mean your good
> deeds and feats of prayer) and they will never
> cause you worry. On the contrary, they will com-
> fort you and bring you joy. They will never be sick,
> never die, nor will they be left orphans without you.
> They will accompany you into the grave. And so,
> my friend, try to multiply these children—your good

deeds and feats of prayer. Of course, you'll never be free from attacks by your enemies: the flesh, the world and the devil. But then, are girls and women living in the world free from them? Don't these same enemies attack them too? No, my friend, there's no peace from these anywhere, but to tell the truth the convent is a better place than anywhere else to find peace. There if you are attacked by (let's say) the flesh with its passions, you have only to avoid being lazy in prayer—lift up your hands to Him Who was crucified for us and to His most pure Mother—and you will find peace. And living in the convent, in your cell, you can *always* pray. So, my happy Pashenka, live, pray and thank God for the lot He has given you.

Olinka was married—a happy woman, right? Her in-laws loved her. But now? She's a widow, an orphan. Her in-laws may well have loved her and been kind to her, but now this will end, and they'll even perhaps begin quarreling over the inheritance. But you—you have nothing to divide, no one with whom to quarrel . . .

Bp. Innocent's next letter to Pashenka, dated November 3, 1853, provides the final chapter on Olga's earthly life:

. . . our Olinka is no more. I rejoice and thank God that He granted her the kind of death which Tatiana Borisovna [*] describes. May the Lord grant us all such a death!

Olga left her sister Paraskovia 1000 rubles which, when added to her other assets gave her over 2500 rubles to her name. "Why would *you* need such money?" her father chides her, trying to remind her of her monastic calling.

Your sister Katia is burdened with a family and her husband is sick. He has no money, and she has very

[*] Potemkina.

little. Should she be left a widow she'd be in dire
distress. I'd recommend that while you still have
control over your money you divide Olinka's money
between Katia and Innocent. (Gabriel, thank God,
has no need.)

He warned, however, that should she decide to do so, "it's
dangerous to put money into Innocent's hands," and recommended that she do as he always did: send it to Fr. Gabriel
in trust for his brother and his wife.[*]

Five years passed from the time that Pashenka entered
the convent to begin her testing in the monastic struggle until
the time came when she knew within herself that this was the
life for her. Finally, in October of 1854 she was tonsured and
renamed Polyxenia. This joyous event, however, took its toll
on her health, and Tatiana Potemkina wrote to her father
that "she walks about like a shadow." She was quick to add,
however, that "she loves her ill-health *in* the convent far
more than good health without it. She's a true ascetic war-
rior!"

"May the Lord grant that even half of this is true,"
Bp. Innocent wrote, describing the event to his other children.
"Glory and thanks be to God!"

The correspondence between father and daughter grew
less frequent as the years went by, but in content it remained
as warm and open as ever. Bp. Innocent continued to direct
her as best he could in the angelic life:

. . . your letter comforts me in particular in that you
speak openly of your weaknesses and sins—laziness
and disobedience. If you've begun to notice these
in yourself, it means you're becoming attentive to
yourself, and this is a great mercy from God. You
feel that you won't be saved—and that's an important
thought to have! It's bad *not* to have it, for without
it you can fall into self-esteem and false pride, and
so perish in spite of your good deeds. On the other
hand, it's also bad to indulge in this thought too

[*] This is the last reference to Innocent in his father's letters.

much, because you can fall into despair. Pray. Pray. Pray. That's all I can tell you in this regard, and the Lord will make you understand.

Fight your laziness at least. Don't give in to it. Fulfill your rule of prayer. Even if you don't feel like it, fulfill it without fail. In this way little by little you'll conquer your laziness. Your whole struggle consists in fighting your passions. Fight! Remember where you are . . .[10]

In 1856 Mother Polyxenia wrote her father asking him to "teach me how I can be saved." His reply is a model of humility:

O Pashenka! I could sooner ask *your* advice on how *I* can be saved. I began learning this a long time ago, but I'm still on the "A's." At times it seems as though I've begun to see the rhyme and reason, and then I look again and see I've forgotten all the old lessons and have to start all over with the "A's" again. When I'll be able actually to "read"—and whether I'll reach this at all—only God knows. But I'll gladly tell you what I know—or rather, what I can recall from other people's advice and thoughts on salvation.

You say that you have no humility, no obedience, that you're lazy about praying to God. True humility is a gift from God, my dear, so you can't just have it whenever you wish to. It has to be attained, but it *can* be only if you consider yourself never, no where and in nothing above anyone else. Hence, you must never dare to judge another, or grow angry with another, or consider yourself innocent or in the right before another. In a word, you must consider yourself dust and ashes over which no one is forbidden to walk. Having this kind of humility, obedience will follow naturally

You are lazy about prayer—remember where

[10] In the Russian this is a play on words: "fight" (*boris'*) resembles the name of the hermitage, *Borisova*.

you are ... *Fight* yourself and your laziness! Don't despair if it conquers you from time to time. It doesn't matter—just don't lie down; don't give in. At least use all your strength to arise, and the Lord will see your fervent desire to get up and will help you. By the way, don't think—don't even imagine—that here on earth you can ever reach the state where you won't have to fight yourself and the spirit of evil. No! The earth is not paradise. There's no eternal rest to be found here—just an arena, a school. You say that you can't conquer your temper. O my dear! That's your most ferocious enemy—the most tireless and persistent one, because it's part of your very character (that is, you're hot-tempered by nature). What can I say to you about this? Again—fight! As hard as you can! Take a pledge that after every fit of anger you will remain silent for a while, saying nothing other than that which your work requires. And, with the Mother Superior's permission, you could even remain silent at work for a time. More than anything else—pray. If you offend someone by your temper, ask forgiveness every time in the monastic manner. This roots out anger very efficiently ...

Finally, in one of his last [11] letters to Mother Polyxenia Bp. Innocent writes:

I cannot teach you the monastic life, for I have never been a "normal" monk myself. I don't know by experience what it means from the beginning, and only one who is experienced can teach such things ... What advice can I give you? Read the Gospels and pray. That's all ... May the Lord God forgive and have mercy on us all. May the Lord be with you unto ages of ages. Amen.

[11] In a rare letter preserved from daughter to father, we read the following most unusual incident:

One night in August of 1866 while I was sleeping before Nocturn, I suddenly heard a voice in my cell which said: *"Prepare now to*

receive Thekla." I awoke in amazement. I saw no one in my cell.
I began to think about the name which had been pronounced, and
recalled no one by the name of Thekla who might come to me.
Pensively and in confusion I went to Nocturn. Later, when I went
to early Liturgy I saw near the church a woman lying on a stretcher
with no one near her. I asked her why she didn't go to church. She
answered that she was unable to walk and that the women who had
brought her had gone to church to find a place where she could most
conveniently be placed during the service. I went into church. A
quarter of an hour later they brought in the woman whom I had seen
and placed her on the floor. "Oh!" I thought, "how I sinned! I
should have taken an interest in this sick woman and ordered the
novices to bring her inside earlier to spare her the cold." In thoughts
of compassion I summoned a novice and told her to go out and buy a
prosphora, ask the sick woman's name, have a particle removed in
prayer for her health, and to give the bread to her. I saw the novice
obey my order, and when they came to report to me on its being
carried out, I asked what the sick woman's name was. She answered,
"Thekla." I was greatly amazed and barely able to stand through
Liturgy. Then, with the permission of Mother Superior Macaria (in
whose cell I lived), I invited to visit me this sick woman lying on
her stretcher, scarcely able to move, who had been foretold to me in
a dream. In compassion for her I filled her with tea and learned
from her the history of her disease. She stayed in my cell for about
three hours, after which she was taken to the hostel on her stretcher.
The Mother Superior sent dinner to her there. Having spent two
days in the hostel, Thekla Adrianova and those who served her in
her sickness left on horseback bound on pilgrimage for Kiev.

Thekla's nine-year pilgrimage did not end there, but within the precincts
of the St. Sergius-Holy Trinity Lavra on September 1, 1869. There, in a
cave chapel in the Gethsemane Skete, at prayer before an icon of the Theotokos,
her legs were miraculously restored to health. A large crowd witnessed the
healing. Innocent, hearing this, ordered a prayer-service to be celebrated before
the icon, which he himself attended.

PART SIX

THE ASIAN YEARS

CHAPTER 1

THE BACKGROUND

In the 1850's, forces and events on a global level were at work setting the stage for Bp. Innocent's Asian years. In Palestine half a world away, quarrels—quite ordinary, even petty—between Greek and Roman Catholic monks over custody of the holy places—part of everyday life there—quite to the surprise of everyone struck a spark which ignited yet another war in Europe. Little pretext was needed and little was given, but soon Englishmen, Frenchmen and Russians were spilling their blood on the fields of the Crimea, and as we shall see these events touched the life of the Diocese of Kamchatka.

Closer to home, in Asia itself, turmoil at times less volatile (but considerably more substantial) was no less at work reshaping the region. Japan, a commercial market long coveted by all the Western powers (with the Russian-American Company being by no means last among them), was clinging to the last years of her own highly-cherished isolation, while in China the seeds of change had already been sown. The Manchus, who a century and a half before as mighty overlords had forced the Russians from their border-lands, were now themselves increasingly being forced to yield trade concessions along their southern coastline to England and other European nations, and to some Russians the time seemed right for their nation to do likewise in the north and reclaim lost lands.

The Amur Basin, prime object of Russian interest, was a land for which the endless expanses of northern Russian wilderness could offer no real substitute. Opened largely by

fur-hunters, Siberia had little left to offer once that industry
neared extinction other than perhaps its services as a vast
(and vastly effective) natural penal colony; with nineteenth-
century technology agriculture and industry were still largely
out of the question there. Therefore, it was natural and highly
tempting to look to the fertile land just to the south as a
source of salvation for the whole eastern part of the Empire.
Among those most vocally in favor of reclaiming these territories was Bp. Innocent, who writes:

> The Amur is for us what South America or the
> United States are for Europeans: let the entire sur-
> plus population of Russia go to the Amur and it will
> be capable of feeding and enriching millions.

His enthusiasm, so thoroughly understandable after many
years of experiencing first-hand the hardships which *not*
having access to this waterway wrought upon those living
on the Russian seaboard and beyond, had been bolstered in
1849 by a surprise meeting in Petropavlovsk with the young
and energetic new Governor-General of Eastern Siberia, Nicholas Muravev.

Muravev's reputation for honesty, firmness and energy
were well-established even before, in the third year of his
administration, he broke precedent by undertaking (with his
French-born wife beside him) the arduous trek to Kamchatka.
Never before had an official of his stature visited the region
and seen its plight first-hand. Long consultations with the
widely-experienced and now rather famous missionary hierarch first suggested some of the changes which would ultimately effect the transformation of the region which both
men desired. These were destined to come, however, only
after a period of frustrating conflict with St. Petersburg where,
faced with rising tides of war far closer to home, the tsar's
advisers understandably recommended that the peaceful
status quo in Asia be preserved. Such reasoning, while understandable to Bp. Innocent, was not at all acceptable.

As we have seen, he was faced with the immediate necessity of finding himself a central location for his residence, to

which, as he writes, "papers from all over [the diocese] can arrive in good time and in good order." From what he had seen, Ayan best fit this description, and he so reported to the Holy Synod. Early in 1851, however, he received from Andrew Muravev in St. Petersburg a letter which put this decision in question and offered new hopes, but was incapable as yet of offering anything concrete upon which to work:

That matter of transferring your See from America to our continent and of joining Yakutia [1] to your diocese has been submitted to the Holy Synod. Perhaps it will take some time. But this may itself prove propitious, for as it now looks, in a year or two it might be more expedient for you to transfer to the mouth of the Amur.

To this Bp. Innocent replies, "with both hands I will bless this new undertaking," and to Muravev's observation that "if your son [Gabriel] is there, the work will, of course, proceed more quickly," he says, "and I am ready with both hands to give to it my son."

There was, it would seem, full reason for optimism that all of this would soon come to pass. The influential Metr. Philaret was known to be enthusiastic about the project, and had offered personally to defray the costs of sending a missionary into the area. The only obstacle appeared to be the fact that the Gilyaks living between Udsk and Ayan whom he wished to evangelize were nominally Chinese subjects, and a mission to them could begin only with the personal political approval of the tsar in addition to the usual authorizations from the Holy Synod. Nevertheless, with full confidence that

[1] On August 7, 1854, Muravev filed a report on his travels throughout Eastern Siberia and Kamchatka. Paragraph five dealt with the Church:

The American episcopal See [is to] be transferred to Avacha Bay [Petropavlovsk], the Yakutia region joined to it, and it be made a second-class [diocese]; Bp. Innocent [is to be] named an archbishop. Everyone knows of his mind, his abilities and his Christian principles, even without my recommendation, but I can state what I know intimately—his high degree of love for the Emperor and this country, and his unusual labors and efforts in his assignment.

soon his son would be preaching to people whom he knew
to be thirsting to hear the Good News of Christ,[2] he requested
the needed authorizations.

As weeks and months passed without word from St. Petersburg (despite the fact that through Muravev the bishop
knew for a fact that his plans had been submitted) Innocent
began to give thought to how his plans could be initiated in
spite of the official silence. He knew that—in theory at least—
he had the perfect right to send a priest to minister to the
Russians who were settling the region in droves—and how
then could he in good conscience *prohibit* this man from talking
to the local natives whom he would meet? This question of
conscience he countered with another: "Can we, and ought
we to begin God's great work with cunning and non-spiritual
means?" His answer was a decisive *no*, and yet his missionary
spirit could not abide these delays. In time his patience indeed
wore thin as letter after letter, each more persistently worded
than the last, went unanswered, unacknowledged. It mattered
little to him, he says, whether by his persistence he should
become unpopular with the members of the Holy Synod. He
would simply not allow them to overlook his flock and his
missions.

As he anxiously awaited word from St. Petersburg,
Bp. Innocent decided in 1850 to set out on a third extended
visitation of the Asian portion of his diocese, going first to
Petropavlovsk. There, shortly after his arrival, he was surprised at being greeted by the Governor of Kamchatka with,
"Congratulations, *Your Eminence*". Then he was handed a
letter which explained these words. It was from Fr. Gromov
in Irkutsk and was sent to Kamchatka on a hunch that Innocent might be found there. It contained a copy he had made
of an ukase from the Holy Synod dated April 21, 1850,
elevating Bp. Innocent to the dignity of Archbishop, "for his
fruitful missionary activities."

[2] In 1850 while in Ayan, Innocent talked with a delegation of natives
from the region who had come to petition the governor for protection against
the Manchus and crews from foreign ships alike. "Did you come willingly,
freely to us?" Innocent inquired through an interpreter.
"Yes. We wanted to visit you and see your yurts."

"Didn't write much, did he?" remarked the bishop wryly, and for a while he remained sceptical about information obtained in such an irregular manner (as no official notification had reached him). It was only after considerable prodding by both the governor and the new priest of Petropavlovsk that Innocent was persuaded of its probable veracity and finally consented to be commemorated during services in his new rank.

Fr. Gromov's letter and later documents on other matters addressed from the Holy Synod to "Archbishop Innocent" were destined to be the only indications which ever reached him that he had indeed been given this honor. He was now truly a man without a home. He would spend some time in Alaska, some time in Kamchatka, some time in Gizhiga, Okhotsk, and Ayan, but nowhere did he maintain a fixed address. Mail still reached Kamchatka only twice a year, America only once. Furthermore, all Russian shipping was increasingly being menaced by hostile warships patrolling the Pacific Ocean in connection with the Crimean War. As the new archbishop remarked, "Only the Archpriest Gromov announced to me the Tsar's will that I be an archbishop. The actual ukase on this matter is now being read by the English monarch and Napoleon III!"

"You know, I've heard rumors that some people [Yakuts wishing to disrupt trade] are frightening you by saying that a priest is going to come and harm you. Is that so?"

"Yes."

"Whoever told you that is a bad person. I'm the chief of the priests here, and I assure you that if you ever see a priest he won't bother you. But if one of them should ever harm you, you just tell Dmitrii Ivanovich [Orlov, commander of the local Russian settlement] and he'll tell me, and I'll get rid of him."

"Good. That's what Dmitrii Ivanovich told us, too."

The discussion broke off there, for the interpreter was not up to continuing. It was clear, however, that the people wished to be baptized. This was confirmed a month later when three Gilyaks arrived aboard a Russian ship and after witnessing a celebration of the Divine Liturgy asked to be baptized. Characteristically, Innocent told them to think about this more carefully, and that if they still wished to receive the sacrament they would, at the hands of his son. They thanked him and assured him that if Fr. Gabriel were to live among them he would be well-loved and his work would be fruitful. Two days later he was dispatched on a preliminary short visit to Amuria in preparation for planned residency there in 1851.

Leaving Petropavlovsk, Abp. Innocent began a tour of Kamchatka at the conclusion of which he would head north-ward with the permission of the Bishop of Irkutsk into Yakutia to survey that region in preparation for its transfer into his jurisdiction. During his travels Innocent prepared to celebrate the tenth anniversary of his elevation to the episcopacy, once again on the tortuous path to Drainka. "I held no hope," he writes,

> of reaching Drainka by this date, but the Lord Who by His mercy has always amazed me, a sinner, was pleased to show me this mercy as well. Beyond all calculation I arrived in Drainka on the morning of the thirteenth [of December]—that is, precisely on time—and on the fifteenth the Lord enabled me to consecrate a new church in honor of my patron saint. At the same time, the chiefs and elders of all the villages in Oliutorsk also arrived, and none of them had ever seen a pontifical liturgy before, as they but rarely can come to church because of the distances involved. I consider this a tremendous reward for my travels.

Heading north into Yakutia, he found it to be "a world all its own. Local conditions differ from those in all other Russian dioceses, including those in Irkutsk." Thus he was convinced that its transfer to his own atypical diocese was a wise move. Yet he could not help but be overwhelmed by the pastoral problems this would present. Virtually all of its 200,000 inhabitants were migrant animal herders, neither maintaining permanent homes nor even living in reasonably-sized groups. "Parishes" counted up to 14,500 persons on the rolls, but so few people could be found living within miles of the church that the average attendance at Liturgy was ten. "I ask you," he writes,

> is it at all possible to exhort or teach the parishioners, much less confess them adequately when the priests can get around their parishes only during the spring

and autumn—just four or five months? And can one then be amazed that many Yakuts have never in their lives been to confession, or that some have never even *seen* a priest—in cassock, in vestments or even simply *at all?*

At the end of his visit, Abp. Innocent met with some of the clergy to discuss plans for future work, and then, leaving them detailed orders under seal in the event that the ukase of incorporation should arrive in Yakutsk during his absence, he took leave in May of 1852 to return to America.

Innocent's route took him to Ayan, where he would catch a ship to Sitka, for a joyful reunion with the oldest part of his flock. Instead he had to leave disheartened by news that on January 24, 1852, the tsar had officially denied him permission to open a mission in the Amur and had ordered him, furthermore, to leave off writing on this sensitive matter. This meant that a whole year had been spent needlessly in Asia, and that he would have to do something he really wished not to do: send a priest to the region to minister strictly to the Russians. Such was the beginning of what turned out to be Innocent's last visit to America.

With his son and daughter-in-law, whose talents he would not waste on Amuria under such conditions, the archbishop set sail for Sitka where he wintered and then began an extensive visitation of Kodiak and the Unalaskan chain. We have a first-hand account of his work in a testimony from a Russian Jew, Moshe Silverberg, written in 1882: [a]

... I arrived in Sitka from California aboard the frigate *Aurora* and there had the pleasure of meeting the great preacher and enlightener of idolatrous

[a] The placement of this account in the chronology is questionable. Silverberg opens it by saying specifically, "At the end of 1859 (or the beginning of 1860) I arrived in Sitka..." Such a date, however, is impossible. Innocent's presence in Yakutsk and Irkutsk at the time can be clearly documented. Furthermore, while the reference to Nikolaevsk and to a meeting there with Fr. Gabriel Veniaminov would not rule out the year 1852, Innocent himself states that on this trip his son and daughter-in-law were in Alaska with him. The difficulty cannot be authoritatively resolved.

savages, Abp. Innocent of Kamchatka. And he, knowing that I knew well the language of the natives, suggested that I accompany him on his tour of the Aleutian Islands, at a salary of 35 rubles per month.

It is difficult to describe in full the labors which this great worker took upon himself! Travel on reindeer, sometimes lack of food, inclement weather—even foul weather—hostile natives, and insults all around—all of this the old man endured patiently and in good humor. Often, when I would mention his incredible labors to him, he would tell me about patience and the rewards in heaven which await those who do good for God and their neighbor. Without rest for nine months the great old man preached the true God before hundreds of savages. With animation, zeal, and often tears in his eyes he taught them the truths of the Gospel, and his labors did not prove in vain. Some 1800 savages of both sexes were baptized during this period.

Such a life of privations of all sorts, however, was beyond my strength to endure. Exhausted from the tortuous travels and the inadequate food, and longing also for my homeland, I asked Abp. Innocent to excuse me from my duties as translator and allow me to go to my aged mother. "Go," he said, "and comfort your mother by the sight of you. Your path is good, my son, and true. God will reward you for your labors, and I am sure that your Lord Jesus Christ will call you to be one of His followers, and you will become a true Christian."

Tearfully I kissed the hand of this distinguished old man and left aboard the *St. Nicholas* bound for Nikolaevsk . . . Thus fate brought me together with one of those people whom one finds but rarely, and it was perhaps the company of this great worker during our nine months of traveling together which ignited in me the first sparks of faith in Christ the Savior.

In July of 1853 Abp. Innocent was back in Ayan, where the joy he must have felt at having completed such a mission was increased by the news that as of July 26, 1852, Yakutia was part of his diocese. On September 11, the archbishop took up permanent residence in the Monastery of the Savior in Yakutsk⁴ and set to work immediately with this newest part of his flock.

⁴ Archimandrite Samuel, its superior, died on March 29, 1853. Since there was no candidate to succeed him, the archbishop personally assumed the position. This was most convenient for two reasons: first, it gave him the archimandrite's salary, which was absolutely vital since the scrip he received in salary from the Russian-American Company was worthless outside the colonies.

CHAPTER 2

EXPANSION

Christianity was two centuries old in Yakutia, and while the missionaries had consistently done their best to explain the Orthodox faith to the people, they had met with little tangible success. The people readily accepted baptism, but not as much for the sake of the Truth as in order to obtain the lucrative material incentives offered by the State to those who converted. The Yakuts thus remained at best nominal Christians, but were in reality semi-pagans.

As can well be expected under such circumstances, Abp. Innocent launched into his work with all the diligence and care which had characterized his ministry everywhere. In January of 1854 he set out on an initial visitation of the region in which he did not, as others might well be tempted, visit just those settlements lying conveniently along the banks of the Lena River, but penetrated the interior, covering some 2640 miles in six weeks, studying the populations to determine their religious needs.

The most obvious need was for more clergy. Of the fifteen priests assigned to the region only nine could function with all the traveling this entailed, and even if all of them could be mustered this would leave something like one priest for every 6000 people. Writing to the Procurator of the Holy Synod that

> the difficulty in meeting ... the needs of the local Yakuts will increase more and more, until it becomes impossible to meet them at all—and this could destroy the entire effort, even among those who—unlike the Yakuts—are not babes in the faith.

Abp. Innocent requested that additional clerics be recruited from surrounding dioceses to make the ratio more "manageable" (at something like 2000 or 3200 to one, he says!). Otherwise, he was fully pleased with his new flock. "The zeal of the Yakuts for me," he writes,

> and, one might say, their flaming desire to see me in order through me to receive a blessing, has comforted me greatly. Proof of the former is that they cleared for me a road almost 200 miles long, and of the latter that long before my arrival they gathered from great distances at the various stations where I was scheduled to stop for a change of horses, precisely in order to receive my blessing. And having received it, they made the sign of the cross and thanked God for it . . .

Despite all the work which needed to be done there, Yakutia was not Abp. Innocent's only concern in Asia. He still longed to visit the Amur, and though permission for such a trip had not yet come from St. Petersburg, he made up his mind all the same to go. The danger of such a trip, however was increasing daily, since an Anglo-French fleet was expected to arrive in the Sea of Okhotsk by July of 1855. In spite of this the archbishop set out. His pastoral concern—that the severely limited, unofficial missionary work in the region would be harmed as Russian immigration accelerated—outweighed such dangers. He describes his fears in this way:

> One cannot doubt that there will be success. Of course, everything comes from the Lord. God Himself—and not the preachers—converts people to the path of Truth; these are only His "weapons."
> From my vantage point I can see only one obstacle—but it is a rather weighty one. I will explain by means of an example. Three times have I traveled among the Koryaks, and of course, at least that many times I have spoken to them about accepting Chris-

tianity. Each time I heard from them, "Why should we be baptized? To become like the Russians: deceivers, profligates?" etc. Of course, it's hard to answer such objections, but I told them not even to look at the Russians with whom they have dealings; these Russians are worse than all the rest. We give this same answer to the objections raised by our neighbors, the Tlingits, and while such an answer might be possible in Gizhiga or New Archangel, how can we answer the Gilyaks if *they* say the same thing? Indeed, although it is painful and shameful to admit it, holy truth demands we say that the present Russian Orthodox are themselves an obstacle to spreading and confirming Christianity. Our exhortations here are useless . . .

Muddy roads and insufficient drivers slowed Innocent's trip from Yakutsk to Ayan, and so it came as little surprise to learn while still a good way from that town that already several weeks before his ship, the *Okhotsk*, had set sail for the Amur without him.[5] Of greater and more immediate concern was the rumor that the enemy had seized Ayan on June 27. Leaving his retinue behind, the archbishop went on to investigate, accompanied only by his cell attendant Gavrilo and a Russian official.

Some fifteen miles out of Ayan, they met refugees who told wild tales of destruction and desecration as the troops pulled out the day before. Full of trepidation, therefore, Innocent and a very few companions entered the town on July 9. There they found only a few American whalers, leisurely helping themselves to some spoils. The archbishop's first concern was for the church. He found posted on its doors proclamations from the English commander warning against attempts at resistance, and although there was evidence that the church had been searched, nothing had been destroyed or stolen. Indeed, all of the rumors he had heard proved un-

[5] The delay thus proved providential, for while trying to evade pursuing warships the *Okhotsk* ran aground and her crew was captured.

founded. During their stay the British had, in fact, taken pains to prevent looting and vandalism altogether.

As the people returned from their hiding places in the forests, Abp. Innocent set about ministering to them, since the local priest had been away on visitations during the entire crisis. He baptized newborns, heard confessions and on July 22 celebrated Liturgy. He was about to admit defeat and return home to Yakutsk when an English frigate appeared unexpectedly in the harbor. As first the *Sibyl*, then the *Baracuda*, then several other English men-of-war sailed in and anchored, most of the locals panicked and returned to their former sanctuaries. Innocent, however, decided to remain, taking at face value the British proclamations of respect for both persons and property and reasoning that his flight would at any rate be pointless, for the Americans would doubtless inform the invaders that a Russian bishop had been there, and if they were really minded to capture him, they would certainly do so. In this case his flight would be not only pointless, but would place everyone else in even greater jeopardy.

In the evening while the Russians were in church, the English second-in-command came ashore at the head of his troops. As expected the Americans made haste to inform them of the presence of a bishop, and off they went in search of him. Not finding him in the parish house they turned to the church itself. Entering with a great deal of tumult, they found Abp. Innocent on his knees, conducting a prayer-service. Despite all the commotion he never paused, neither arose nor even looked around, but continued reading the prayers in a loud, clear voice. Though unable to understand his words, the invaders were confounded by the archbishop's poise and the reverent expression on his face and in silence more or less patiently awaited the conclusion of the service. When later recalling the incident, Innocent quipped: "Had the British known what I was praying for, they probably would have torn me to pieces on the spot!"

When the service was over, the soldiers approached the Russian hierarch with great courtesy and respect, and asked in amazement how he happened to be in Ayan. "It is our duty," they went on to inform him (through an interpreter) "to take you prisoner." Innocent could only laugh, for before his departure his daughter Catherine had tried to warn him against going, fearing that just this would happen. But he told them the same thing he had told her, "You have no need of me. I'm not a soldier, so I'm of no use to you. It'll be your loss: you'll just have to feed me." He then invited them to his house for tea, and they chatted pleasantly for hours. In the end the archbishop not only convinced them that he should remain free, but also gained provisional release of a certain Fr. Makhov, a missionary priest whom they had seized earlier on one of the nearby islands.

Next day after Vespers the British returned for a second visit with the archbishop, bringing word that their commander, Lord Charles Elliot, had authorized his release and wished very much to meet him. The two first met that evening over champagne aboard the firigate *Peake*, then, as in the weeks that followed, spending many a pleasant hour in conversation. Innocent also played cordial host to the many curious officers and crewmen who wished to see inside a Russian church. Before he left, Lord Elliot had gained such respect for this daring hierarch that he ordered his portrait taken.

With the invaders finally gone in early August, Abp. Innocent found he had no choice but to return to Yakutsk. The whalers, who being Americans were officially neutral in the hostilities and thus free to come and go anywhere in the Sea of Okhotsk, would doubtless for a price have tried to run him down the coast to Amuria, but word from other Russian coastal towns left little hope that their efforts would prove successful. Okhotsk had been raided, and the abandoned port of Petropavlovsk had been burned to the ground. No, even with the enemy forces cut by ten vessels (as the French dispatched a flotilla to patrol the waters off Sitka), there were still 46 warships cruising offshore, and the chances were not good that these would fail to detect him. Even though he was rather confident that if taken he could talk his way once more out of being arrested, it was virtually certain that his entourage and the supplies so badly needed in Amuria would not share his good fortune but be lost. Therefore, he decided not to take the chance. Even the surer strategy of rowing himself alone down the coastline sufficiently close in to shore to avoid detection (or at least, successful apprehension) was closed to him for want in Ayan of even one of those reliable craft of his younger days, the kayak.

In September of 1855 Innocent was back in Yakutsk, but a visitation of the Amur region remained never far from his mind. It had been five years since the Russian flag was first hoisted over Nikolevsk, a fort established some 65 miles up river from the coast. It had been two since Fr. Gabriel Veniaminov had been dispatched there. It had been over a year since the strategic value of the waterway had been graphically demonstrated as a force of 80 barges floated down its course to deliver to waiting ships the reinforcements which alone made possible the heroic eight-day defense of Petropavlovsk in August of 1854.[*] Innocent had been in Irkutsk at Pascha that year. He had felt the electricity as preparations were being made for that historic expedition, and now he was more determined than ever to visit his flock there. The previous spring a second massive movement of military hardware had been accomplished to arm the mouth of the river against attack, and in its wake five new agricultural settlements had been established along the route. There were now over 500 Russians living along the river, with another 5000 scattered throughout the surrounding countryside, and even with negotiations with China floundering, it was clear that annexation was inevitable. The lone missionary reported that given extra clergy another one or two missions could be opened right away. The people were eager for their archpastor to pay them a visit, and realizing all the work which had to be done if the mission to the Gilyaks was to begin successfully, he was just as eager to oblige them. Early in 1856, therefore, Abp. Innocent decided to make another attempt to reach the Amur, this time taking the precaution of approaching it from the long—but safe—inland route around Lake Baykal.

He left Yakutsk on February 11 and reached Irkutsk

[*] The port was subsequently abandoned in an all-out effort to arm the strategically more important Amur River mouth.

nineteen days later. There he recruited a priest, two deacons
(all seminary graduates) and three churchmen for new missions and with them crossed the still-frozen waters of Lake
Baykal on April 5 to arrive in Kiakhta in time to celebrate
Holy Week and Pascha. Reaching the headwaters of the
Amur they boarded government barges for the trip to their
final destination. On May 27 the archbishop met with the
governor of Trans-Baykalia, who had recently been engaged
in negotiations with the Chinese over Russian rights of passage
on the river. He was comforted to hear that, contrary to rumors
in Irkutsk, there was apparently no massive effort being
mounted to prevent them.

Two days later Abp. Innocent enjoyed his own first opportunity to speak with the Chinese personally. On May 29
his barges dropped anchor in mid-stream at the town of
Aigun, and Innocent sent word ashore that he would be
honored to receive the Chinese *amban* (or governor) on board.
An officer was dispatched ashore, met by a host of officials,
and with them returned to ask the hierarch if he would not
instead accept the amban's hospitality ashore. From mid-river
it was clear that this visit had been anticipated. Tables and
benches appeared on the dock, water was set to boil for tea,
and all the accoutrements of a reception were rapidly made
ready. Innocent accepted the invitation and again sent an
officer ashore, this time with a gift of wine and canapes, before himself disembarking. He was met on the bank by dignitaries and ushered in to meet not one, but two ambans. The
three sat together, sipping tea from Chinese cups and ex-
changing pleasantries until dusk through a team of two interpreters (one from Russian into Mongolian and another from
Mongolian into Manchurian). When the archbishop repeated
his invitation to visit his craft, the chief amban again declined,
not wishing, he said, to detain his honored guest any longer,
and Innocent, alone, resumed his voyage to the sea.

That at least one perennial question in Abp. Innocent's
mind was settled by this trip we can see in a letter to the acting
Ober-Procurator, Alexander Karasevskii:

Present circumstances make it quite clear that the

> See of the Diocese of Kamchatka ought to be located
> on the Amur, where there are already more than
> 5000 inhabitants in addition to locals who, some say,
> number from 30,000 to 70,000.

That it also raised many new questions can be seen from the
many projects he began planning for the coming year. For
one thing, the proper site within Amuria for his see had yet
to be determined. Nikolaevsk was too close to the sea—and
enemy guns—as a recent attack had clearly demonstrated.
Furthermore, building supplies—especially the availability of
quality lumber—would limit the number of acceptable locations.

For another thing, the size of his diocese seems for the
first time really to have struck him, and he began giving serious
thought to obtaining vicar bishops for Yakutsk and Sitka.
Fortunately, with a monastery in one and a soon-to-be vacant
seminary building in the other, both of these two most isolated
centers were blessed with facilities adequate to support a
bishop. The only obstacle was finding candidates to fill them.
At any rate, he writes, "the affairs of the Diocese of Kamchatka
cannot remain as they were in the past. Something definitely
must be done."

CHAPTER 3

CONFLICT IN ST. PETERSBURG

In order better to assess the situation in his diocese, Abp. Innocent intended to make 1857 another year of extensive travel and outlined these and other plans in a letter, dated February 5, 1857, to the new Ober-Procurator of the Holy Synod, Constantine Serbinovich:

Once again I prepare to take to the road: to Vilai, Olekma and throughout the churches of Yakutia. If God so grants, I shall be home in time for Pascha (by April 1 even). Then I plan to go to America—for the last time. (I have at present no thoughts at all of travelling through Kamchatka.) I still feel only very slightly the effects of my age, but I do feel some, and in two or three years these will make themselves even more evident. In your letter [of September 12, 1856] you stated that I need helpers, and you were right. But where can I get them? Indeed, I did take note of two men (should anyone have happened to ask me if I had anyone in mind as a vicar) but nothing came of either of them. Both are sick, and so I have absolutely no one in mind. (You will probably be amazed if I tell you this, but pay attention to the bearer of

---

[7] Dmitrii Khitrov (1818-1896). A native of the Riazan region, he graduated from seminary there in 1840. On April 6, 1841, he was ordained to the priesthood by St. Innocent in Irkutsk and was sent by Bp. Nilus to Yakutia as a roving missionary. He made his own the methods of his mentor, traveling extensively throughout his career until rheumatism forced him to stop. He became in a real sense Innocent's successor in the apostolic ministry to Siberia's pagans, writing to him, very much in his spirit: "A monk has

244

this letter, the Archpriest D. Khitrov.' There are many
similarities between his work and my own. He is a
missionary as was I. He translated the holy books
into a native tongue, as did I. He compiled a grammar
for a language of illiterates, as did I. I went to St. Petersburg and Moscow to have my translations published—and now he does the same. Is this not an
indication that he should leave St. Petersburg as did
I? True, there is an important factor which thus far
has prevented this: his wife is alive. But as she is in-
sane, this is almost the same as being dead. Already
he has borne this heavy cross for a long time, but
thanks to God he has not been crushed by it or strayed
into worldly consolations. With regard to his character, his heart, his skill, his zeal, his diligence, his
knowledge of the local customs and languages—no
one better could be desired or found for the Diocese of Yakutsk ...) And now I say ... the same
thing I said before—that there ought to be an *independent* see for Yakutia ...

In July as he was about to set sail, Abp. Innocent was
forced to change all of his plans. A summons came for him to
go St. Petersburg and attend a session of the Holy Synod. He
left for Irkutsk in January of 1858, hopeful that by presenting
his case in person to his fellow bishops he would bring benefit
to his flock. Nevertheless, at the same time he lamented, "that
once more I must put off my trip to America," adding, as it
turns out prophetically, "perhaps forever."

Abp. Innocent departed Irkutsk after Pascha and reached
St. Petersburg in August, and almost from the moment he
set foot in the northern capital he had good reason to feel
uneasy about his visit. The fact that his arrival went utterly
unnoticed, the frugal accommodations and poor service he was
given, the shoddy vestments he was issued by the Synodal

---

nothing to lose. If death overtakes him as he is preaching, it is turned into
a sacrifice to God. I ask God for just one thing: that He send me a Christian
ending, blameless and peaceful." His end was indeed such, in Moscow, as
Bishop of Ufimsk and Menzelinsk in retirement.

sacristy, the haughty people on the narrow streets who over
and over again made it their business to inform him that
"*No* one wears a *black* cassock *here!*" (until finally he sent
his most faded one out to be dyed purple)—none of this
accounted for the feeling of suffocation which he suffered and
which made him yearn for the open spaces of his native Siberia.
No, such slights, such pettiness could not upset a man whose
whole ministry had been spent under conditions which he
himself freely admitted would in Russia be considered "strange
and unusual." There was something deeper: an "obliviousness
to the faith" which he perceived to be "now a general disease,
at its strongest in Petersburg" and which he feared might
"perhaps already be over the brink." It was this that gnawed
at him and caused him to write almost as soon as he arrived:

> I've decided definitely to leave here in the beginning
> of January, whether or not I've completed my busi-
> ness . . . If they want to accomplish something, they'll
> have time enough to do so, but if they don't, nothing
> will ever move them . . .

The theological academies (especially Kazan) he found
to be centers of free thought, where interest in monasticism
was nonexistent. Eloquence was acceptable for its own sake—
and not for exhortation or provocation to the truth. Bishops
were no longer "a rule, an image, a teacher,"but something
"needed in the cities for solemn services and practically
nothing more," while beyond the city walls they remained
isolated (if not aloof) from their flocks, giving opportunity
for sectarians to lure people in increasing numbers away from
the Orthodox Faith.

Worst of all, perhaps, was the condition of the one group
of men who could do something to arrest this decay, the Holy
Synod. Without the active participation of its most outstanding

---

[8] On May 15, 1842, at the height of the scandal involving the Russian
Bible Society, Philaret left St. Petersburg for Moscow without permission,
incensed that the tsar would believe the unjust accusations leveled against him
and this worthy project. Although he was to remain until his death a valued
consultant of the Synod, he never emerged from virtual exile in his diocese
and never again set foot in the northern capital.

member and once guiding-force, Metr. Philaret of Moscow,[8] its work, in Abp. Innocent's words, was "going along lazily (*lento graduo*)." The basic premise for its existence, "salvation in numbers," he found tenable only where all are "of one heart and soul in the Lord"—and this was certainly not the case here. Only in signing protocols could unity be observed in the Synod. "Perhaps to sketch out a detailed plan . . ." he wrote at this time to Philaret himself,

> many opinions and much advice are needed, but to move and direct this project requires, in my opinion, a single person (with many helpers and sub-helpers, of course)—otherwise you'll get what happened with the Isaac Cathedral [in St. Petersburg]: a lot of treasures and art, and a lot of work, but as it turns out there's probably no other church anywhere more inconvenient and inadequate for *serving* in (there's no sacristy; they forgot to build a place for the choir, etc.). At the present time who could direct the work . . . better than you? I am of the belief that the Lord is preserving you for just this . . .

Under such conditions it is scarcely any wonder that from the beginning Innocent virtually despaired of anything definitive coming of his projects. "I came alone and I'll leave alone," he says; and, not bothering to conceal his nostalgia for the "ancient simplicity in establishing dioceses," he set about trying to have Yakutia organized as a diocese at least *on paper*, even if practical considerations (such as finances) would preclude its immediate formation.

To this end he made some rough notes on the subject from which to deliver his scheduled report to the Holy Synod, but even before its formal presentation, storms of controversy could be seen brewing on the horizon. Innocent was spurred on by the knowledge that he enjoyed some support for his ideas. He had shown his notes privately to the Ober-Procurator and to Bp. Philotheos and both approved, but apparently precisely because of their approval, they began discussing the general theses with others, among whom was the fiery

Abp. Nilus of Yaroslavl (formerly of Irkutsk). When the two hierarchs met to discuss a completely unrelated matter, Nilus seized the opportunity to launch an utterly demoralizing attack on the subject of vicariates, the vehemence of this tirade being surpassed only by his subsequent reaction to Innocent's brief verbal outline during the Holy Synod's official consideration of the matter. After the session Nilus demanded to see the full text, and Innocent complied, but with reluctance and apprehension. The reaction was predictable. Next morning the Archbishop of Kamchatka received back his manuscript scribbled over with negative comments, and a heated dispute was underway between the two hierarchs.

At this point there remained little left for Abp. Innocent to do in St. Petersburg other than to nominate potential candidates for a non-existent see in hopes that some day his two vicariates might be established. His first choice was a certain Archimandrite Leonid, a church historian and teacher of patristics in Moscow. Metr. Philaret agreed that this was an excellent choice, a man capable some day of succeeding Innocent in the See of Kamchatka. And Leonid, despite his poor health, had nothing to say against this, having lost none of the zeal which as a student in 1841 had motivated him to volunteer to accompany the newly-consecrated Bp. Innocent to America. At the time he had been too young for his petition to be considered seriously, and now, at the suggestion of Andrew Muravev that it would be better for him to remain in the capital at his present important work, Leonid was once more spared this difficult lot of ministry. (The wisdom of this advise we will see below.)

Innocent's second choice was Archimandrite Savva, rector of the Moscow Theological Academy. He was naturally flattered at being offered the post, but when told what it would entail—"traveling throughout the Aleutian Islands all summer to supervise the work of missionary priests, and spending the winter in Sitka engaged in paper work"—he begged time to mull over his decision. Abp. Innocent offered him six months. The final candidate, Archimandrite Peter, rector of the seminary in Sitka, was Muravev's favored candidate, but Abp. Nilus again rose in opposition, saying he had not liked

Fr. Peter when he had served in the Diocese of Yaroslavl.

The time was fast approaching when he would have to begin his long trek home, and a discouraged Abp. Innocent obtained permission to leave the capital. "If I remain here later than the beginning of January," he writes,

> it will mean not being able to leave until summer [because of spring thaw], and if I travel during the summer and arrive in Yakutsk (where I simply *have* to go) I won't be able to get to America, and a whole year will have been for nothing. And my years may well by now be numbered. At any rate, my eyesight won't last much longer.

Before leaving, however, Innocent wrote his old friend Metr. Philaret to defend himself in the conflict with Abp. Nilus and to present the ideas which the latter found so objectionable. Central to these was the need for a "multiplication of vicars" whose prime concern would be maintaining closer contact with the people and the church schools in order to stem the tide of sectarianism. This, he writes,

> is not *primarily* necessary in order to convert the sectarians alone. No! God—and God alone—is able to convert them. It is necessary, rather, in order that through hierarchical ministry and the living Word we may keep in Orthodoxy those who are still considered ours.

Innocent's criticisms (and particularly those concerning the educational system, of which Philaret was the chief architect of reform) struck a sensitive nerve in the aging hierarch, and he responded in a letter dated November 25, 1857. "You would demand," he begins,

> that a vicar, bishop to 200 churches, should, without fail celebrate Liturgy in each and every parish at least once every year or two. In this way you would demand that he spend a third or more of each year traveling . . . Would this be very convenient?

Here we see the general theme of Philaret's critique: that Abp. Innocent erred by generalizing on the basis of his own extraordinary experience and practices. He makes precisely this point in regard to Innocent's comments concerning diocesan schools: "Do you not," he asks, "measure *all* pastoral schools by the measure of Irkutsk? I dare say this measure is untrue."

To this Abp. Innocent was willing to agree. He himself had once remarked that "not every bishop will want to ride around on horseback through grime and forests, or wander about in tents." He did not feel that all of his comments had been successfully refuted. Nevertheless, in the spirit of humility he vowed to mention these things no more if they were a source of trouble. Metr. Philaret's final—and wholly worthy—admonition was in his heart as he set off across the continent:

> It is easier to uncover and expose defects than to correct them. The misfortune of our time is that the number of errors and imprudences accumulated over more than a century are all but beyond our power and means of correction. Therefore, one must not oppose all defects at once, but take first those which are the most harmful. Likewise, one ought not to suggest all possible means of correction all at once, but rather, first put forward those which are both the most needful and the most practical.

As on his first trip across Siberia, so too now Abp. Innocent made a point of stopping to visit each of the eight diocesan bishops whose sees lay along his route. Everywhere he took pains to observe the condition of the church, and nowhere did he find his basic criticisms in error. To his great dismay (such tragedy could not cause joy, even if it marked his vindication) he found the Old Believers enjoying great success in luring the Orthodox away from the truth. The schools were in decay. Reality did indeed justify all that he had said in St. Petersburg, but this could not assuage Innocent's sadness over the fact that he and Metr. Philaret had quarreled. From deep in Siberia he penned to Moscow this apology:

> Every time I think . . . that I may have offended you greatly by my opinions and proposals (if not by all of them, then at least by many), it lies like a stone upon my heart. Forgive me, for God's sake. Of course, it would have been good for me never to have shown these notes to Your Eminence or to have spoken a word about them, but for me to have concealed from you anything of this sort would have been sinful and shameful for me. Better that your anger should fall upon me than that I should go against my conscience. This, though, will torment me, until of course, I receive a kind word from you.

CHAPTER 4

THE TRIUMPH

This forgiveness was, predictably, quick in coming. It was as welcome as the long-awaited triumph in Asia: on May 16, 1858, Governor-General Nicholas Muravev initialed the Treaty of Aigun, whereby China formally ceded to Russia the left bank of the Amur River. A week earlier, following celebration of the Paschal mystery in Irkutsk, Abp. Innocent had arrived in this Manchurian trading station located at the junction of the Zei River to lay the foundations of a church to be built there in honor of the Annunciation of the Theotokos. The governor ordered that the town itself be renamed "Blagoveshchensk" [9] in honor of this feast, and thereby in honor, too, of the archbishop, who forty years before began his ministry to the Church in Annunciation Church in Irkutsk.

For a long time this was the only honor to be bestowed upon Innocent in connection with the passing of this vital territory into Russian hands. Muravev was rightly hailed as a great national hero—and it was the archbishop who personally led the local celebration, offering a service of thanksgiving at which he addressed these words to his friend:

> Our Orthodox Church will never, never forget you, for she remembers those who have founded but a single church, while you, O chosen one of God, have opened the possibility, the hope, the prospects for thousands of churches to be built in this boundless Amur Basin.

[9] "Annunciation" in Russian. It is interesting to note that the city has retained this name through the revolution and down to the present day.

The new tsar, Alexander II, ennobled Muravev [10] for his efforts and bestowed upon the area's chief missionary, Fr. Gabriel Veniaminov, the Order of St. Vladimir, Fourth Class.
But the real moving force behind the entire project from its
inception went unheralded. Only posthumously would recognition come, when in 1881 Rear Admiral Zavoiko, the
former military governor of Kamchatka who had been in-
strumental in building up Russian strength on the Pacific,
would write:

> History has not yet made clear just who among those
> who labored during this period was the "Columbus"
> who first conceived the idea of surveying Amuria
> and petitioning for its settlement. [Nevertheless]
> nothing at all would have transpired in those regions
> without Abp. Innocent's fervent assistance through
> lively words, sincere encouragement and intercessions
> that all be done fairly—something so important in
> this distant and desolate land where "God is high
> above and the tsar far away." He, Innocent, by the
> astuteness of his mind and his practical under-
> standing, drew inferences, offered clear explanations,
> and helped tirelessly and energetically. Nor, as an
> excellent jointer, carpenter, and upholsterer, did he
> disdain working with his own hands. When there
> were churches to be built, he directed the work, and
> built the altars and iconostases personally. It was as
> though out of nothing the Church was adorned by
> him. Those who were required to perform some
> urgently-needed task—be they cashiers, accountants
> or store-keepers—he freed for their task by taking
> their place and performing their duties, even for a
> month or two if this would but advance the mission's
> success... He was a person of intelligence and
> action.

The second half of the year brought a return of disappointment, although the victory now lay just beyond the

[10] He is thus known in history as Count Nicholas Muravev-Amurskii.

horizon. Fr. Savva respectfully declined Innocent's invitation
to become his vicar in Alaska. The Russian-American Company's operations there were returning lower and lower profits (Innocent's own recommendations on conservation had
largely gone unheeded) and it appeared as through the un-
productive outer islands would soon be abandoned. Furthermore, as time approached for another charter renewal, the
complete collapse of the Company loomed as a distinct possibility. Without its help the Church's condition would soon
be as dismal (if not worse) as in the 1820's, when Innocent
was first called to serve in Unalaska.

Again Abp. Innocent pleaded with the Ober-Procurator
to find him a vicar and offered the names of four more pro-
spective candidates, even actively recommending, one of these
(Archimandrite Habakkuk, his companion on his most recent
travels in the Amur, an educated man conversant in Mandarin
Chinese). Yet because the most important consideration in
Alaska was that the situation be stabilized quickly, he hastened
to add that

> to me it is absolutely immaterial whom they send to
> be my helper. I leave that entirely up to the Lord.
> Let me ask only that Your Excellency expedite this
> matter, and especially that you inform me of the
> decision so that I can prepare my own instructions
> in good time. I have written some instructions for
> the Sitka vicar . . .

Then, receiving word that the faculty and students of the
diocesan seminary, headed by Archimandrite Peter, had arrived in Ayan from Sitka, Innocent hurried home to Yakutsk
to supervise its establishment in the monastery and the beginning of studies there.

With the new year came an end to Abp. Innocent's
greatest worry, as at long last authorization came from
St. Petersburg to proceed with the consecration of this same
Archimandrite Peter as Bishop of Sitka. The two left immediately for Irkutsk, where on March 29, 1859, the consecration took place. At the conclusion of the Divine Liturgy,

Abp. Innocent delivered the following instructions to his new vicar:

> Most Reverend Bishop Peter, accept this Pastoral Staff, and watch over the flock of Christ in Russian America which has been entrusted to your care. May it fortify those who heed your words and be wielded against those who fail to listen and submit themselves to you.
>
> I must say, however, to the spiritual joy both of yourself and of the many people who hear this— and moreso to the glory of God!— that few of our fellow bishops will obtain the joyous lot of ministry which is yours, for there are now but few locations where one can find children of the Church as obedient, as humble, as simple and as attentive to the Word of God as in the places where you are going. From my own experience I can say without exaggeration that even the most tireless and zealous preacher of the Word of God will grow tired before *their* zeal and attention will lag—all of them, from the least to the greatest. And that they listen not in vain or out of curiosity alone is clearly shown, one can state, by the fact that never has a single native believer refused to fulfill his duty of cleansing his conscience. For several decades now on end there has been no crime—not even the most minor. Indeed, one scarcely even hears of minor quarrels among them. I say this of the natives, and of the islanders in particular, who have been illumined by the light of the Gospel. But even the inhabitants of America's far north, still sitting in the darkness of paganism, are, as you yourself know, eager and attentive to hear the Gospel preached. Very many of them are ready to accept Christianity; it seems as though the work of converting them is hindered primarily by lack of funds. Therefore, by the grace of God, the Pastoral Staff which you have been handed will be used primarily (if not exclusively) to fortify, to strengthen,

and to guard the obedient—to clear and mark the
path into the Kingdom of Heaven for those who seek
it. Even Sitka's neighbors, no matter how coarse, undisciplined and stubborn they may be, are beginning
to bend their savage necks beneath the yoke of
Christ, and one can hope that with the help and the
grace of God your permanent presence among them
will have a positive effect upon their full conversion.
May the Lord help you, both in this work and in the
conversion and confirmation of the other inhabitants of our America. May the Almighty grant you
the strength and the power to fulfill your difficult
ministry and grant you wisdom in all your intentions,
undertakings and actions! May this Staff be for you
a sign of this. As you look at its top, adorned with
the symbol of wisdom,[11] may you recall the words
spoken by the Lord to those whom He sent on a ministry in some ways like the one which lies before
you: "Be as cautious as snakes and as gentle as
doves."[12]

The new bishop left for his see in America, and
Abp. Innocent returned to Yakutsk, relieved that soon the
most remote part of his flock would be enjoying the direct
care it required. The Holy Synod's response on this matter
filled him with new hope that like mercy would soon be shown
to the people of Yakutia, for whom he had submitted to
St. Petersburg the name of a candidate worthy of becoming
their bishop. This was Fr. Peter Popov, a widower whom
Innocent met on his recent trip across Russia, a man renowned
in Krasnoiarsk for his piety, simplicity and pastoral zeal.
Innocent therefore spent the winter months setting all local
affairs in good order in preparation for his departure to Blagoveshchensk, where he would at long last establish for himself
a permanent residence. Before making this move, however,
the archbishop was privileged to preside over one of the most
important events in the life of the Church of Yakutsk, the
first celebration of a Divine Liturgy entirely in the vernacular.

[11] The two-headed snake. Cf. Num. 21:6-9.
[12] Mt. 10:16.

CHAPTER 5

YAKUTSK

The task of translation into Yakut became one of Abp. Innocent's first priorities back in 1857, when the territory was originally added to his diocese. Only by allowing the people to worship God meaningfully in their own language could Christianity hope to root out persistent paganism. To this end, a committee was formed of whose operation we have a lively description provided by a most unlikely source. Ivan Goncharov,[13] a Russian novelist best known for his novel *Oblomov*, which deals with an indolent, pampered landowner (which in large part was an expression of his own way of life), found himself in 1857 in Yakutsk in the company of a truly indefatigable worker. Having first outlined, in his *Frigate Pallas*, the hierarch's past scholarly labors as a priest in America, the writer goes on:

> Abp. Innocent labors here in a wider field, leading a flock of some 200,000 Yakuts and several thousand Tungus and other tribes scattered over a territory covering some 440,000 square miles. Under his direction the Word of the Good News is being translated into their "dialect" (which in its poverty has no right even to claim citizenship among our languages). I happened to be on the committee which met in the quiet of his archpastoral cell, laboring at translating the Gospel. (All of the clergy here know

[13] (1812-1892). He found himself in Yakutsk as a result of a highly-uncharacteristic participation in the naval action which forced Japan to open its doors to Russian trade. The chronicle of this adventure, the *Frigate Pallas*, a portion of which is quoted here, unfortunately has never appeared in English.

the Yakut language.) A rough draft of the translation had already been completed, and while I was on the committee we conducted a final review of the *Gospel According to Matthew.* We compared the Greek, Slavonic and Russian texts with the translation into Yakut. Each word and expression was carefully weighed and verified by all the members.

The venerable fathers were frequently hampered by a lack of words adequate to express many things in Yakut — not just moral concepts, but material objects as well— because these things were wanting in their culture. For instance, the Yakuts have no word for "fruit," because they lack the concept. No fruit whatever—not even wild apples—grows under their skies, so there is nothing to which this name could be given. There are ashberries, cowberries, wild currants (or *"kislitsa"* as they are called here), and cloudberries—but all of these are *berries.* The Yakuts laboring to find names for the many objects introduced by the Russians call them by their Russian names, and so these have entered forever into the word stock of their language. Thus, because it was the Russians who taught them to eat bread, they simply refer to bread by its Russian name, *khleb.* There are many such examples.

When he translated the Gospel into Aleut, Abp. Innocent proceeded as the translators of the Holy Scriptures into Yakut are now doing (and incidentally the same procedure was used in translating the Gospel from Greek into Slavonic). One of the missionaries, namely the priest Khitrov, has been compiling a grammar of Yakut to guide those who will study the language. It is now completed.

You see the kind of work being contemplated here? I hear that all of the plans and labors of the local ecclesiastical authorities have already been approved by the government. In addition to Yakut, translation of the Gospel has already been completed into Tungus (which they say resembles Manchurian just as Yakut does Tatar). I have heard that a grammar of Tungus has also been compiled (again, entirely by churchmen; one of the local physicians has also compiled a Tungus-Russian dictionary several thousand words long). Since the Tungus are illiterate, the ecclesiastical authorities as an experiment intend for the time being to send out written copies of the Gospel in translation to priests serving the nomads in order to have it read to them, and thus gradually to spread among them an elementary knowledge of the truths of the faith. In this way they will also be preparing them to receive a more substantial knowledge of the Holy Scriptures when, hopefully, literacy becomes more widely-spread among them and printed translations can be provided.

Abp. Innocent tried to devote two evenings a week to this tedious work of polishing and revising the translations, and the difficulty of the task can be gathered from this additional, light-hearted excerpt from Goncharov:

What are the difficulties [of a Russian] learning to pronounce English in comparison with these sounds? To produce them one needs (it would seem) not only the participation of throat, tongue, lips and cheeks, but also of the eyebrows, the folds of the forehead and the hair on one's head as well! And what grammar! Case indications proceed the noun; the possessive pronoun collates with the noun, etc. And yet—all of this is overcome!

Soon interest in the translators' progress had been aroused in the Holy Synod, and when samples of their work were solicited by St. Petersburg, Fr. Dmitrii Khitrov was dispatched (as we have briefly seen) to make necessary corrections and supervise publication of the texts. In a letter to the Ober-Procurator Abp. Innocent states:

Finally, by the mercy and help of God I have the

comfort of presenting Your Excellency with a portion of our translations, for which you have waited
a long, long time. Please be assured that your long
wait was occasioned not by sloth or negligence on
our part but by circumstances—or rather, by the desire
that our translation be as good as possible. Perhaps
it will amaze Your Excellency if I tell you that we
reviewed the first Gospel several times and each time
made additional corrections and changes, required
primarily by the fact that in the past the members
of our committee had not known the Yakut language
as fully as they ought. Many of them speak Yakut
quite well, and know Russian as well as anyone could,
and yet when it came to translating from Russian
into Yakut—what nonsense at times resulted! In part
this was also caused by failure to understand the
Russian text sufficiently, but the prime cause was
their inability to transmit the message according to
the forms of the Yakut language.[14] All previous
translators (including the members of our committee) had tried to keep the Russian forms and sense
in translation. Taken in isolation, all the words
seemed correct in every way and correctly positioned—
making the translators think that their work was as
clear and good as possible. But for the native Yakut
the result was the same as with our liturgical heir-
moi: while the words might be ours, they cannot be
easily understood because the form isn't Russian but
Greek. Finally, however, the Lord gave our priests

[14] In his instructions to Fr. Khitrov, Abp. Innocent cautions him to exercise due caution in making unilateral editorial changes not sanctioned by the
entire committee. "It is better —incomparably better—, as sad experience has
shown, to sin against grammar (for instance) rather than destroy peace with our
brothers and lose spiritual unity with them by stringently observing grammar's requirements, even when these are most correct and obvious." From
experience he then goes on to note that "the time *will* come when grammar
will take its own, insofar as this is possible." Clearly the goal and governing
principle, however, is clarity in the Yakut text, for he tells the priest to refer
for exegesis to Metr. Philaret (or the Holy Synod) whenever "paraphrase" is
necessary, and to explain the use of non-equivalent words quite carefully in a
bilingual preface.

to understand how they should transmit Russian speech to the Yakuts, and now our work is moving along more rapidly . . .

In accordance with Abp. Innocent's instructions, Fr. Khitrov supervised the printing of the books, returned home with them to Yakutsk, and by the summer of 1859 preparations were completed to begin using them in the Liturgy.

The Cathedral of the Holy Trinity in Yakutsk was overflowing on the morning of July 19, 1859, as the people gathered from miles around to witness the great festivities. Before Liturgy began, Fr. Khitrov led the clergy in solemn procession to the center of the church where they presented the new service books to the archbishop for his blessing. From that moment their use was authorized wherever Yakut was understood.

Throughout the long service people stood in rapt attention. Some wept. Many kneeled spontaneously. At its conclusion people flocked up to the archbishop to express their joy. Some tribal leaders requested that that day, July 19, be henceforth designated a feastday throughout Yakutia in commemoration of the first hearing of their native language in the church. One Russian born and raised in this region told of his own joy that day, of how he had been amazed during the Hours, for although he had heard them innumerable times before read in Church Slavonic (and just as carefully by the very man who read that day in Yakut) he had never before understood their meaning.

No less gratifying was the occasion for those who so long had borne the burden of this project so pleasing in the sight of God, for it offered them real hope that their ministries would begin to bear fruit as a new era began in the spiritual life of the flock. As they listened to their native tongue being used in solemn communal worship—and particularly as they heard the Sermon on the Mount being read during the communion of the clergy—the people began for the first time to realize, to sense, the close bonds between themselves and all other nations who were children of their Mother, the Holy

Orthodox Church. Their former, meager knowledge of God—as a Being Who only punishes—produced in them nothing more than a boundless, instinctive fear which could bear little fruit. Now, gradually this could begin to be replaced by knowledge of "the only true God" and Jesus Christ Whom He sent in His love for the human race, and its result: a new religious and ethical life overflowing with that love of God—Judge certainly, but Creator, Provider and Savior as well—which is found in the Gospels. Within a month the sounds of Yakut began filling all the chapels of this vast territory.

Less than a year later, on February 10, 1860, the second half of Abp. Innocent's plan for the people of Yakutia was realized, as authorization came from the Holy Synod to proceed with the consecration of a vicar bishop for the region. The candidate, Fr. Peter Popov, was already on his way to Irkutsk, and Abp. Innocent left immediately to meet him there. Fr. Peter was tonsured into monasticism with the name Paul, canonically elected to his see, and on March 6 consecrated to the episcopacy. After a week of intensive instruction the new bishop left for Yakutsk, where he set to work with great zeal in the difficult task before him. "Glory to the Lord," Innocent writes to Metr. Philaret, "Who has sent to the flock of Yakutia the kind of pastor for which I had hoped!"

In the brief time he had known his new vicar, Abp. Innocent had come to appreciate him as an excellent man and already a real monk at heart. But he also saw in him a lack of liturgical finesse and administrative experience which, coupled with his unfamiliarity with the truly unique region of Yakutia, could prove a source of problems. Fortunately, however, there was in Yakutsk someone to whose care Innocent could entrust the new bishop until he was able to grow more familiar with his flock, the very man whom the archbishop had hoped—and still hoped and prayed—would some day himself occupy the episcopal throne of that diocese: Fr. Dmitrii Khitrov. For now, his wife's lingering and painful illness still prevented him from assuming this office, but as the archbishop wrote to him: "You see, the burden of governing the flock of Yakutia has not escaped you. In fact, it is upon *you* that it now lies *primarily.* I am sure that you will vindicate the trust put in you by him and moreso by me."

As an experienced pastor and observer of human foibles, Innocent realized full well the temptations this assignment would place in his friend's path. Therefore he penned him this warning:

> In name alone are you a master of trickery [15]—for everything is written on your face. (And quite often what's on your mind is on your tongue as well!) For those who don't know you well, your answers and manners can seem impolite (while for those prone to suspicion, they seem even worse than that!) So mull this over really well: *never* contradict the bishop's opinions publicly. Be polite to him. During services, never make sloppy bows (as you frequently do). Do not give anyone the *slightest* reason to think that you are *directing* him. In private be careful never to give him reason to suspect that you want to rule him. Even when he summons you in, be completely open. Try to make your thoughts and comments a sugar-coated pill. But *sat sapienti! . . .*

With the northern and easternmost portions of his flock now well provided for, Abp. Innocent was ready to turn his full attention to the southern regions, the Amur and Kamchatka proper. In the flurry of activity surrounding Bp. Paul's consecration, however, he was unable to care properly for a cold caught on the way in to Irkutsk, and shortly afterwards he was forced to take to his bed for a week. Feeling better on March 2, he got up for Liturgy and dinner but that evening suffered a relapse, and high fever and chills ushered in a disease which Innocent called "unprecedented" for himself. The painful red lesions of *erysipelas,* an ailment potentially fatal to the elderly, soon spread over his cheeks. His appetite and energy vanished. Each morning he awoke feeling somewhat better and would try to do something useful with

[15] *Khitryi* in Russian means "tricky."

ST. INNOCENT

his time, but inevitably the pain and fever would soon return, and the infection quickly spread to cover his whole head.

It was April 10 before he felt up to traveling again, but then, despite the fact he had no definite plans in mind, he lost no time in setting off across Lake Baykal bound for the Amur. Cold weather produced new erruptions continually, and ten days out the swelling and pain grew so intense that he was forced to rest again. As soon as his strength returned, however, Innocent was relentlessly on his way, resigned if need be to live in pain the rest of his days rather than give in to the affliction. His comfort mattered little to him in the face of the needs of this newly-opened vineyard, and he was determined that each village and station would see its archpastor (and he, in turn, would examine their way of life).

Materially, Innocent found Amuria quite prosperous indeed. The climate was fair, the soil rich, the harvests plentiful (considering the limited acreage tilled that first year). Spiritually, however, the situation was less encouraging. Most of the Russians settling the region were, in the archbishop's words, "modernistic," doing whatever pleased them despite anything the canons of the Church—or the local priest—might say. "How can one justify," he asks Metr. Philaret,

> one's own people while telling others something else concerning such things? I must admit I am beginning to grow fainthearted as I think about the chances of the natives seeing anything better than this among our other immigrants to Amuria.

To make matters worse, he lacked the resources even to begin doing an adequate job. The Goldi, a good, humble, quiet and honest people inhabiting the region in numbers estimated at up to 5000, wished to have a church and a priest who could speak their language. They were open to the Word of God, as the missionary hierarch saw:

> In a word, we could baptize several hundred of them immediately. The matter of their conversion is now completely up to us, but I am hindered—not so much

by finances to build a church as by lack of person or persons capable of undertaking such work. The young, by reason of their inexperience and unformed characters, would ruin the project from its outset, while to supervise them from afar—what kind of missionaries would they be if they had to be watched at every step?! I have no middle-aged, experienced men . . .

From Khabarovska and vicinity Abp. Innocent went to Blagoveshchensk, where he spent some two months observing work on the cathedral and bishop's residence being built on a choice site several miles outside the city. A monastery consisting initially of six buildings and a chapel were also going up, all carefully designed by Innocent himself with a view to his eventual successor's comfort. "It seems to me," he writes at this time, "that I'll not live much longer."

CHAPTER 6

SHIPWRECK AND A SAINT

Comfort — whether present or future — still remained foreign to Abp. Innocent's mind. In Blagoveshchensk he soon formulated plans to pay a visit to Kamchatka, his first in a decade. In order to time his arrival to coincide with winter's optimal traveling conditions, he set out in July for the port of Nikolaevsk where he would briefly visit his family until a ship could be arranged to take him on his way.

The first craft to appear was a steamship of rather doubtful seaworthiness, but the archbishop's determination was such that he overlooked its condition and allowed it to conduct him out of port. They limped along for hours in calm coastal waters, constantly veering off course until finally their supply of coal ran out and they were forced to turn back to Nikolaevsk. Innocent, although unhappy at the prospects of wasting the winter there, was not disappointed to be back on dry land. "I am of the opinion," he writes, "that the Lord saved us and the ship by not allowing us out to sea—otherwise we should surely have perished."

Next autumn plans once again called for a visitation of Kamchatka. This time passage aboard a very able craft, the naval steamship *Gaidamak*, seemed to portend success. Nonetheless the archbishop reminded himself that "none of this will help if the Lord does not wish me in Kamchatka."

The *Gaidamak* left port on August 22, 1861, bound for stops in Sakhalin and Japan before going on to Kamchatka. The first leg of the voyage was quiet and uneventful. They reached Sakhalin and as planned laid over there several days. They were still standing peacefully at anchor at mid-day when a gale suddenly began to howl around them and in its fury tore the ship free from its moorings. For the next eight hours the wind did not relent and giant waves crashed violently across the deck. The pumps could not keep up with the flood of water entering the hold, and with no anchor the *Gaidamak* faced the twin danger of either being swept out to sea or being dashed against the rocks. Fear seized the passengers and crew. Abp. Innocent alone remained calm.

On his knees before the icons in his darkened cabin, he read the prayers for the departure of his soul. Then, fortified, he rose calmly and went up on deck to offer his services to the captain. In the middle of the night the winds in a last burst of fury drove the ship onto a sand bar where, as the storm then died down and passed, it settled above the tide line. The only casualties were the ship and its cargo, and as the sun came up the passengers were taken ashore, first the sick, then the bishop's retinue, and last of all, Innocent himself. "Not a single drop [of water] fell on me," he writes, "while I was on the ship, and as I stepped ashore it was with dry feet!" On the beach everyone kneeled with the archbishop to thank God for having spared their lives. "This was the first such experience in my life," he later recalled. "I've been in considerable danger before, but never on a ship breaking up. It's certainly not cheery!"

Without a ship it was beginning to look as though the trip to Kamchatka would have to be put off again, but a few days later the chief of the Russian cadre arrived at the accident scene and offered Abp. Innocent and his retinue passage aboard the *America* as far as Japan, whence (he assured them) passage the rest of the way to Kamchatka would easily be arranged. The hierarch reminded himself that "man proposes, but God disposes," and stepped aboard.

Early in the morning of September 9, Abp. Innocent stood on the pier in Hakodate, watching the *America* disappear over the horizon. He settled in the home of the Russian consul to Japan, John Goshkevich, while his retinue was housed with the mission's chaplain, Fr. Nicholas Kasatkin.[16]

---

[16] Later elevated to the episcopate, he died in 1912 as an archbishop. In 1970 he was canonized by the Russian Orthodox Church as "Apostle to

This was the second meeting of the two missionaries, for the year before the young priest had spent the winter with the archbishop in Nikolaevsk, en route from St. Petersburg to Japan. There the old missionary had treated him with fatherly affection, doubtless appreciating the opportunity to do something more profitable than reading and re-reading badly dated Russian journals. And for Fr. Nicholas the time had been most rewarding. Despite the fact that he had graduated from the seminary in Smolensk near the top of his class and had gone on to St. Petersburg for work at the theological academy before accepting the call to work in Japan, he was still ill-prepared for the work which lay before him. No classes could provide the insights which Abp. Innocent had gained through long years in the mission field. By the time he left, Fr. Kasatkin looked upon the venerable hierarch as a new St. Stephen of Perm, Russia's foremost missionary to date. With his wide interests and diverse talents, it was not just the benefit of his vast experience which Abp. Innocent was able to give the young priest. As the day approached for Fr. Nicholas to be on his way, the archbishop asked him, "Do you have a good cassock?"

"Of course I do," he replied, showing him the one he had worn in his seminary days, but Innocent did not find it to his liking. "If you go there like that, everyone will look at you and ask, 'What kind of a priest did we get?' You have to inspire *respect* in them from the very start. Go buy yourself some velvet."

Fr. Nicholas did as he was told, and Abp. Innocent, arming himself with a pair of scissors, proceeded to cut out a new garment for him.

"There, that's better," he said as the work was completed, "Now, do you have yourself a cross?" Fr. Nicholas did not. "Here, take this one," the archbishop said, placing around

Japan." The best study of his life (unfortunately available only in Russian) is by Abp. Anthony of Minsk and Belorussia, "Sviatoi ravnoapostol'nyi Arkhiepiskop Iaponskii Nikolai" [St. Nicholas, Abp. of Japan and Equal to the Apostles] in *Bogoslovskie trudy* [Theological Studies] 14 (Moscow, 1975) 4-61.

his neck the bronze cross he had been given in commemoration of the defense of Sebastopol. "It's not exactly right, but at least it's a cross. It wouldn't be right for you to go to the Japanese without one. (And not to the Japanese alone; even the Europeans would look at you strangely.)" [17]

Abp. Innocent now found that, although his young friend had indeed gathered sixteen Japanese pupils, his enthusiasm for his "bride," the Church of Japan, had cooled considerably by his initial experiences there. The Russians' disdain (he was too young and uncultured for their tastes) coupled with the Japanese' continued hostility to the Gospel reduced him to passing the time by reading some French and German books he had found there. "Throw those books away!" Innocent advised him. "They're of no use to you here. Instead study Japanese diligently."

Ultimately the archbishop's travel plans were only interrupted by eighteen days before a ship came to take him the rest of his way. In that time he celebrated Liturgy twice in the consulate chapel and was given a tour of the city. (Having very little money, this just frustrated him, for he was unable to buy anything of quality for his grandchildren in Nikolaevsk, and refused to send them anything cheap. In the end his retinue left Japan with little more than some silk for vestments.) The brief stay did, however, have lasting influence on the future of the Church of Japan. Fr. Kasatkin took the archbishop's advice to heart and began to apply himself so zealously to studying the language and culture of the people that within seven years he could speak and write fluently. He followed his mentor's example by beginning to translate the scriptures and service books into the vernacular, and also like him did everything he could to improve the quality of their everyday life, in health care, hygiene and other areas. And for his part, Abp. Innocent for the rest of his life held a special place in his heart for the young missionary and his flock, as we see from this remark made years later:

[17] Based upon St. Nicholas' own recollections as told to Archimandrite Sergius (Stratogorskii—later Patriarch of Moscow and All-Russia) on November 16, 1890, and recorded in his *Na Dal'nem Vostoke* [In the Far East] 2nd ed. (Arzamas: 1897) pp. 94ff.

When you go to Japan, you'll see for yourself that
this Church is under the direct guidance of the
Providence of God. The Lord has chosen the very
people whom He wants to serve there.[18]

On October 5, 1861, the government ship *Kalevala* delivered Abp. Innocent to the elusive port of Petropavlovsk,
and just over a month later he set out on a slow trip throughout the peninsula. Twice blizzards stopped his retinue in its
tracks, stranding them without provisions for over forty
hours in a row, while bad fishing, which meant starvation for
most of the dogteams, turned the archbishop into a vegeta-
rian. (He found his new diet so pleasing that he continued with
it after all necessity of doing so had passed.) The one thing
he could lament was the effects of age. The ground it had
taken eight days to cover on his second trip (at age fifty in
1846) now required 28 on the fourth. Remarkably, however,
his health *improved* on the arduous trip, chronic pains van-
ishing as he did the things which he had throughout his
life loved so much.

[18] St. Innocent remained even posthumously a constant inspiration to
Abp. Nicholas and the Church which he founded, through Barsukov's biography
published in 1883 and through reminders such as this one in the ukase of
Tsar Nicholas II of December 6, 1910, awarding the Enlightener of Japan the
order of St. Vladimir, First Class:

... We should keep eternal the memory of Innocent, the Enlightener
of Eastern Siberia, Bishop of Yakutsk and later Metropolitan of
Moscow, whose blessing you received when he arrived in Japan ...

Cf. P. Ushimaru, *Meiji bunka to Nikorai* [Meiji Culture and Nicholas]
(Tokyo: 1969) pp. 31, 122.

CHAPTER 7

NEW TIDES OF CHANGE

By the time he returned home to Blagoveshchensk, Abp. Innocent found the leaves beginning to fall, which was somehow fitting, for the reports and letters which he dutifully sat down to write (as he had after every trip throughout his ministry) reveal a man beginning to be preoccupied with the autumn of his own life. To say this of another man, one in whom the pettiness of pride and pessimism had taken root, would be but to point to the idle musings natural to this time of life. But in Innocent it reflected objective concerns raised by what he had just seen.

In two decades he had, out of the wilderness, gathered a flock, built for it churches and provided the necessary organization. In Kamchatka he found that, after not seeing his face in many years, "even the best people had weakened and changed," and the same was clearly revealed to him in Bp. Peter's preliminary reports from America. This, when contrasted with conditions in Yakutia (where the continued use of the vernacular and Bp. Paul's close supervision of the flock was bearing tremendous fruits), clearly vindicated his fundamental thesis, that "no matter how difficult or financially prohibitive it may be, it is imperative that a bishop visit his diocese (and every part thereof, if possible)". At the same time the situation was a source of genuine concern.

By no means an egotist, neither was the archbishop naïve about his own accomplishments. He was well aware of his abnormally central role in holding the diocese together. He was able to rule regions lying several thousand miles away because he was both intimately familiar with all the varied

territories under him and was himself willing to sacrifice his
own comfort in order to minister to their needs. Furthermore
he enjoyed a very special relationship with his vicars. They
had been given full freedom to act locally within the detailed
guidelines that he provided them (and had never cleared with
St. Petersburg, which was unlikely to have sanctioned them).
Given all these factors it was questionable whether his success-
sor would be able to keep such control. In this regard
his greatest concern was over Yakutia, which he felt would
likely be returned to the jurisdiction of somewhat-less-remote
Irkutsk and remain forever a vicariate ("just like all those
in Russia. . . , of little use or sense")—unless something were
done about it during his lifetime.

The magnitude of all these concerns can be seen in that
on September 22, 1864, the archbishop wrote a rare *confiden-
tial* letter to Adjutant-General Alexis Akhmatov to spell them
out. "The state of my health," he begins,

> and my age itself (67½ years) give me reason to
> think that I no longer have much time left to serve
> in my present ministry (or, perhaps, in the world).
> Under the circumstances, I cannot help but think
> about who my successor shall be.
>
> It is, without a doubt, a tremendous advantage
> to have as one's successor someone acquainted
> with local matters and circumstances. This would
> apply anywhere. But in a place as vast and diverse
> as the See of Kamchatka, is it not far *more* important
> to find someone familiar with local conditions in our
> American churches and missions? (This is what I
> had in mind when establishing the vicariates of this
> diocese.) As concerns Yakutia, however, my succes-
> sor need have no familiarity with this region at all,
> as it must *without fail* become an independent dio-
> cese. . . .
>
> It is no concern of mine—nor dare I assume
> even the slightest right—to indicate whom I should
> like to see as my successor. Yet, should it please
> Your Excellency (or the Holy Synod) to ask me

about this, I should immediately point to Peter, Bishop of New Archangel, who has been in America now continuously since *November of 1859* (in addition to the two years he served in New Archangel in the rank of archimandrite). Thus, even if we disregard the state of my own health (which demands, however, that I *not* put off thinking about a successor) and concentrate solely upon Bp. Peter, we will see that he deserves to be elevated to diocesan bishop. Unlike the heads of the colony who, receiving eight times his salary, are assigned for but a single five-year term, he has already served five years as a vicar and will in no case have served less than five and three-quarters years there—far away and with privations and needs unknown in the normal parts of Russia—before he can arrive home.

For this reason I dare impose upon Your Excellency my humble request that Vicar Bishop Peter be named a diocesan bishop, initially in one of the new Siberian sees (e.g., Tomsk or Enisei) in order that in the event of my death or retirement from ruling the diocese, he will be able to assume my position with a minimum of traveling expenses and time lost in transit.

Furthermore (if Your Excellency will deign to honor my humble request) could this not be done as quickly as possible, in order to allow Bp. Peter to leave New Archangel during the coming year? To do so it will be necessary to send him the ukase concerning his transfer through the chief board of directors of the Russian-American Company no later than mid-January.

Incidentally, Bp. Peter must leave as soon as possible in order to familiarize himself *directly* with the full variety of diocesan functions—something he will never be able to do in New Archangel. The more familiar he becomes the better, since with the Consistory in Blagoveshchensk not presently staffed as fully as it ought to be (nor likely to become so in the near future), it will take him a long time to master this.

Now, concerning myself. I will not request retirement from the diocese until the need is real. Nor do I have any desire whatsoever to be transferred to any other diocese. I plan and hope to continue serving still for as long as I am able.

It is still too early to speak about a successor to Bp. Peter in the See of New Archangel. That can be done after he has left America . . .

In time this letter had its desired effect, for, although he still had to pressure the authorities a bit more, by the spring of 1867 Abp. Innocent had at least secured the release of Bp. Peter from the tortures of Alaskan life ("the climate," he pleaded with the archbishop, "weakens one's spiritual and physical strength, and it becomes harder every year"). On September 29, 1867, in compliance with the archbishop's further plans, bishops Peter and Paul met in Yakutsk, the former to remain there temporarily pending his final assignment, the latter soon off to Sitka. Bp. Paul in a spirit of humility had accepted Innocent's plan for a simple exchange of vicars. He himself realized that with his ineptitude for administrative matters, Alaska—with its minimal bureaucracy—was an ideal place for him. (Yet already rumors had it that in the near future Alaska would be sold to the United States; Abp. Innocent immediately sought from St. Petersburg information as to what effects such action might have upon the good estate of the Orthodox mission there.)

With Bp. Paul on his way to America, the question of what to do with Bp. Peter remained a problem. During his brief stay in Yakutsk as rector of the seminary he had developed a dislike for the town (and it for him), with the result that the archbishop's plan of a simple "trade" was precluded. This, together with all the other problems facing Abp. Innocent, suddenly was resolved in the final month of 1867.

The first problem solved concerned Yakutia. News came from St. Petersburg that the Holy Synod had elected Fr. Khit-

rov to the See of Yakutsk, his wife's long sufferings having
finally ended, as he and Abp. Innocent both prayed, in a
peaceful death. An elated Abp. Innocent would have proceeded immediately with the consecration but was constrained
to wait by the fact that his co-consecrator, Bp. Benjamin of
Irkutsk, would be unavailable until May. When the spring
flooding was over, he and the bishop-elect would together
travel to Blagoveshchensk.

Next he found that, "the consecration to the episcopate
of Archimandrite Gurius (formerly of Peking) has completely changed my ideas concerning a successor." Having
made yet another visitation of the Asian coast during May of
that year, Abp. Innocent was anxious to find someone capable
of preaching to the Chinese, Mongols, Daurians and ex-
patriate Koreans now willing to hear the Gospel of Christ.
This new hierarch, he was convinced, was the man for the
job, as we read in this letter to the Ober-Procurator:

> Bp. Gurius, as one fully knowledgeable of the
> Chinese . . . would be infinitely more useful in my
> place than Bp. Peter of New Archangel (or even
> than myself). I indicated once that Bp. Peter was
> familiar both with America and with missionary
> work, but Bp. Gurius is just as familiar with the
> latter and would have only to read the journals of
> our American missionaries in order to become gen-
> erally familiar with the region and to know every-
> thing essential without having himself to visit
> America.

Finally, official reports received concerning the sale of
Alaska to the United States allayed the archbishop's fears and
gave him reason to believe that his grand visions for the Orthodox Church in America would yet come about. These he
recorded in a letter to the Ober-Procurator dated December 5, 1867:

> Rumor reaching me from Moscow purports that
> I wrote to someone of my great unhappiness about

the sale of our colonies to the Americans. This is utterly false. To the contrary, I see in this event one of the ways of Providence whereby Orthodoxy will penetrate the United States (where even now people have begun to pay serious attention to it). Were I to be asked about this, I would reply:

A. Do not close the American vicariate—even though the number of churches and missions there has been cut in half (i.e., to five).

B. Designate San Francisco rather than New Archangel the residence of the vicar. The climate is incomparably better there, and communications with the colonial churches are just as convenient from there as from New Archangel (if not more so).

C. Subordinate the vicariate to the Bishop of St. Petersburg or some other Baltic diocese, for once the colonies have been sold to the American Government, communications between the Amur and the colonies will end completely and all communications between the headquarters of the Diocese of Kamchatka and the colonies will have to be through St. Petersburg—which is completely unnatural.

D. Return to Russia the current vicar and all clergy in New Archangel (except churchmen) and appoint a new vicar from among those who know the English language. Likewise, his retinue ought to be composed of those who know English.

E. Allow the bishop to augment his retinue, transfer its members and ordain to the priesthood for our churches converts to Orthodoxy from among American citizens who accept all its institutions and customs.

F. Allow the vicar bishop and all clerics of the Orthodox Church in America to celebrate the Liturgy and other services in English (for which purpose, obviously, the service books must be translated into English).

G. To use English rather than Russian (which

must sooner or later be replaced by English) in all instruction in the schools to be established in San Francisco and elsewhere to prepare people for missionary and clerical positions.

With the prospect now good that his flock would be well-provided for, Abp. Innocent was able to give increasing thought to his own future. We have already seen the concern he felt as early as 1864. By the time he was notified of his nomination to membership in the Holy Synod (April 4, 1865) Innocent was losing confidence in his ability to function adequately much longer. In a letter to Metr. Philaret at this time we see him broach the question of his future in a first tentative way:

My health is still rather good (thank God!) despite my 69 years. But recently my eyesight began to dim noticeably, especially in the left eye. I don't know what will happen. My memory is growing weaker, too. No longer can I read something through just once and hope to retain it all as before. Sometimes even twice does not suffice. Hence, willingly or unwillingly, I am unable to keep up with other things. Therefore, in all fairness I must say that if I am still able to be of service at all, it is only here at home (and even then not without lapses). Elsewhere I would be absolutely useless. For this reason my recent elevation to membership in the Holy Synod was at first a source of considerable alarm to me, and even now I am not altogether tranquil about it. Your Holiness, I beg you, for God's sake, persuade the Ober-Procurator to forget about me entirely when assigning candidates to any and all dioceses. I would not (and *could* not) refuse one if it were to be assigned me, but my going anywhere else would serve absolutely no possible purpose and could cause quite a bit of damage and loss. One thing only do I wish, and I would consider this a reward: that you open the Diocese of Yakutsk.

A year later, in December of 1866 he wrote again, but more openly of his concerns over the future:

> Thank God, my health is fairly satisfactory. I must say that so far I do not feel the onslaught of senility. My eyesight, however, is weakening noticeably, but this is hereditary (by my age my uncle and older sister were already blind). Everything seems to be in a fog, especially on bright days. Judging by the rate at which my sight is weakening, I imagine it will not last much beyond 1868. Now, this is my concern: where shall I go then? Where shall I live out my remaining days? In addition to a church, a doctor and a pharmacy nearby, I would hope only to have my son (in a parish assignment, of course) with his children in order for me to educate my grandchildren. One need not even discuss this place —or the Diocese of Kamchatka as a whole—for with the exception of the monastery in Yakutsk there is not a single place for me in all of Eastern Siberia— and this is the only region I have known.
>
> The best and most convenient place to live would be, of course, Moscow,[19] but it is so far away —and wouldn't it be too sophisticated for my son? (He's not an academy graduate, you know.) He would be more than pleased, of course, if somehow he could obtain an assignment in Moscow. Then I would be more than satisfied if only I could have a cell near a church. More than this I would not re- quire. The pension which comes with the Order of St. Alexander (which I begin receiving on May 1 of this year) will suffice me.
>
> Holy Master! Show me your kindness and direct someone to write me (I would *never* dare trouble you personally with this) as to whether I can hope

---

[19] Local doctors, although divided in their opinions as to what might be causing this loss of sight (one felt it might be blocked tear ducts), agreed that if cataracts were diagnosed positively, treatment would be possible only in the capital city.

for a place in Moscow—but only if I can be with my
son. While I was strong, I didn't want him near me,
but now I need the help of relatives. Hirelings—
hirelings everywhere—especially for the blind!

In response to this request Metr. Philaret sent the following letter to Blagoveshchensk, and it perhaps better than
anything else summarizes the work to which Abp. Innocent
had dedicated his life, and stands as a memorial to his achievements.

You wish to have a place to rest in Moscow, and
you—more than any of us—deserve that when a place
shall become necessary, it be prepared in accordance
with your wishes. A residence will be found for you
in the monasteries of Moscow. It will not, however,
be as simple to arrange a place in Moscow for your
son. The parish churches cannot wait long to obtain
a rector, and openings in the cathedrals are few.
Furthermore, there are deserving local priests to
whom we must in all fairness give preference for
places of honor. We must also consider that any
promise I might give you will most likely fall to my
successor to fulfill, for I have not had the strength
for over two months now to celebrate Liturgy. How
my successor will view my promises I cannot say.

But then, there are even more important considerations than these. Unlike us, you did not build
upon another's foundations; like the Apostle [Paul]
you yourself laid foundations for churches, and they
would be strengthened anew were the remains of
your immense work to be laid atop them. Your son
is a precious servant of the Church there. He can
still minister greatly to the salvation of souls and
find great recompense. (To be sure, he could do the
same here in Moscow, but whether to the same degree or not is impossible to say, so very different are
the conditions here.) I have no intention of closing
Moscow to you, but in my inseparable love for you

and the Church, I do not wish your flock to suffer loss.

Take care of your eyes! May the Lord of Light preserve the light of your eyes! Yet, should their physical light fade, He is able nonetheless to illumine others through you, both through your word of instruction and by your administration. You have a son whose eyes can compensate for your own as they fade and who in all areas can fully complement your own tranquil presence. May the Lord show you what is pleasing to Himself and expedient for His Church. Pray for me.

PART SEVEN

METROPOLITAN OF MOSCOW

CHAPTER 1

THE CALL

Emerging in spiritual tranquility from an early-morning Liturgy in his private chapel, Abp. Innocent was handed an urgent dispatch from St. Petersburg.

IN HIS MERCY THE EMPEROR DEIGNS TO APPOINT YOUR EMINENCE METROPOLITAN OF MOSCOW. I HEARTILY CONGRATULATE YOU AND YOUR FLOCK IN MOSCOW. IT IS HOPED THAT YOU WILL COME TO MOSCOW AS QUICKLY AS POSSIBLE, HEALTH PERMITTING. PLEASE INFORM US BY TELEGRAM WHOM YOU WOULD HAVE SUCCEED YOURSELF IN AMURIA. I FOREWARN YOU THAT BP. GURIUS' HEALTH WILL NOT PERMIT HIM TO GO THERE.

Innocent was shocked. Just three weeks before, he had learned with profound grief of the death in Moscow on November 19, 1868, of that "pillar, light, and teacher of all Orthodoxy," Metr. Philaret. The numbness brought by that blow had just begun to pass when this news came. "The Emperor deigns to appoint YOUR EMINENCE Metropolitan of Moscow..." Reading and rereading the fateful words incredulously, oblivious to those around him, Innocent made his way to his room where, in strict seclusion for the remainder of the day and the long winter night which followed, he prayed fervently and contemplated what these words held in store for him.

In the morning a different man emerged. Fortified in

spirit by his vigil and confident of the course he should take, he sent his reply to St. Petersburg:

JANUARY 19, 1868

TO: THE OBER-PROCURATOR OF THE HOLY SYNOD.

WITH ALL DEVOTION TO THE LORD AND IN FULL OBEDIENCE TO THE EM-PEROR I ACCEPT HIS NEW ASSIGNMENT. I SINCERELY THANK YOUR EXCELLENCY FOR YOUR CONGRATULATIONS. I WOULD SUGGEST AS MY SUCCESSOR BP. BENJAMIN OF SELEGINSK, SOMEONE FAMILIAR WITH THE REGION, WITH MISSIONARY WORK, AND WITH ADMINISTRATIVE MATTERS. HE IS ACCUSTOMED TO TRAVELING AND WILLING TO DO SO. MY HEALTH IS SATIS-FACTORY, BUT MY EYE-SIGHT WEAK-ENING. SEASONAL BAD ROADS MAKE MY ARRIVAL ANY EARLIER THAN THE END OF MAY IMPOSSIBLE.

Moscow had a new archpastor. The first announcement of the choice had shocked the mourning city almost as much as the designee himself. Flames of speculation over who the successor would be had spread among the people and found its highest expression in one of the eulogies delivered over the fallen hierarch. Archimandrite Michael, rector of the of the theological academy, spoke on the text of 2 Kings 2:12, "Father! Father! the chariot of Israel and his horses!" He began:

Although deprived of great spiritual power when its Prophet was miraculously stolen away, the Church of Israel at least took comfort in seeing another prophet to fulfill their desire who cried, "May your spirit be increased in me." Dare we—standing at the

> tomb of the one who has been stolen from us—dare
> *we* now pray for such comfort? ... O Lord, if You
> wish to punish us for our sins, may Your will be
> done! We ask only that You not punish us greatly.
> If we have found grace before You (we boldly pray)
> may we not lack a man of power, a man of labors,
> wisdom and zeal for the faith! [1]

Most people in both capitals felt that the capable Bp. Leonid, the late hierarch's senior vicar and present *locum tenens* of the diocese, would succeed to the throne of Moscow. But then came the baffling—and electrifying—announcement that the great missionary of the East had been chosen: an "Elisha" to be sure, and as it turns out, one suggested by "Elijah" himself.

Just hours before his death Philaret had entertained his old friend Andrew Muravev in his Trinity Apartments. The metropolitan seemed cheerful and refreshed, stronger than he had been in months (he had even been up to celebrating Liturgy and preaching that morning). The two spoke for over an hour, dwelling on important church matters as had been their custom for almost forty years. Philaret mentioned receiving Abp. Innocent's letter asking to retire in Moscow, and told how he had advised instead that he "complete his apostolic labors in his See."

"What would you say if Abp. Innocent were to occupy your See after you?" Muravev asked suddenly, impulsively.

The normally staid old man smiled broadly and spoke the words which, when relayed posthumously to the tsar, by the former assistant Ober-Procurator proved decisive: "Why, I should be *very* pleased indeed, for I have a special love and respect for Abp. Innocent." [2]

[1] Meletii, Hieromonk, comp., *O blazhennoi konchinie prisnopamiatnago vysokopreosviashchennago Mitropolita moskovskago i kolomenskago i sviashchennago arkhimandrita Filareta* [On the Blessed Death of the Ever-Memorable ... Philaret] (Moscow: 1867) pp. 97-101.

[2] Philaret, Metr. of Moscow, *Pis'ma Mitropolita Filareta k A. N. M., 1832-1867* [Letters ... to A. N. M.—i.e., Andrew Nikolaevich Muravev] (Kiev: 1869) pp. 664-665. Also the epilogue: "Vpechatleniia konchiny i pogrebeniia Mitropolita moskovskago Filareta" [Impressions on the Death and Burial of Metr. Philaret of Moscow] by Muravev, pp. 669-692.

This same Andrew Muravev now warned from Moscow that the city was badly in need of its new archpastor as soon as possible. Factions were forming—the married clergy and aristocracy in favor of the new appointee; the monks, the merchants and the academies (which had never taken kindly to his proposals for their reform) against—and the Ober-Procurator was taking advantage of the interim to make changes according to his own liking. Planning, therefore, to set out as soon as possible, in April, Innocent began the task of putting his old diocese in good order for transfer to his successor.

To aid him in his travel plans, the Governor-General of Eastern Siberia had already dispatched an emissary to the Amur. The archbishop reasoned that since Irkutsk lay on his route to Moscow, he would meet Fr. Khitrov there for his consecration to the episcopate rather than forcing the bishop-elect to make the much longer journey to Blagoveshchensk. Therefore, he sent this telegram to Yakutsk:

CIRCUMSTANCES HAVE CHANGED. HURRY TO IRKUTSK. LEAVE OFF YOUR REVIEW OF THE CHURCHES. FROM IRKUTSK YOU WILL RETURN VIA THE SAME ROUTE; INSPECT EVERYTHING THEN. GIVE NO THOUGHT TO THE AYAN ROUTE OR TO STAYING OVER IN BLAGOVESHCHENSK. IF I AM NOT IN IRKUTSK ALREADY, YOU SHOULD WAIT FOR ME THERE. GOD BE WITH YOU. YOUR WELL-WISHING SERVANT,

INNOCENT, ABP. OF KAMCHATKA.

Shortly thereafter, independently of each other and much to the surprise of Abp. Innocent, two travelers arrived in Blagoveshchensk, Fr. Khitrov from Yakutia and Bp. Benjamin of Selenginsk from Baykalia. Neither had the slightest idea of all the things which had transpired during their travels. Plans were changed again, and on February 7 Fr. Khitrov received monastic tonsure and was given the name Dionysius.

Two days later, on the Feast of St. Innocent of Irkutsk, he was consecrated Bishop of Yakutsk.

Their providential coming allowed the metropolitan-elect to move up his departure to February 15. As the day approached, many a speaker sought to find words to express all that the people felt. Innocent was assured that as "the great apostle of the Word of Christ, founder of a flock and of churches of Christ throughout the land that you are leaving, a spiritual father and director unforgettable by all," he would occupy in history a "unique place, which no one else can share." Such rhetoric and all brave words of pride at his elevation and "most profound reverence, devotion and sorrow" at his leaving ultimately paled before the eloquence of the people's open tears. Fr. Gabriel and his oldest son, John, were with the archbishop as he gave his flock a final blessing and began his long journey to Moscow.

CHAPTER 2

THE COMING

On March 13 a long-awaited carriage approaching from the East brought all seventeen bell towers in the city of Irkutsk suddenly to life. Bp. Parthenius, the local clergy and the Governor-General stood at the head of a crowd overflowing the cathedral courtyard to welcome the metropolitan-elect on that sun-splashed spring day. Flooding farther to the west forced—or perhaps allowed—Abp. Innocent to spend one last celebration of Christ's passion and resurrection in his native land before continuing on. The sacred days were spent either in the Annunciation Church or in the near-by monastery, and after Bright Week had passed, Innocent made a last pilgrimage to Anga to say a truly final farewell to the mortal remains of his wife and parents interred in the parish cemetery there. This long-familiar trek and much of the rest of these days was spent together with Fr. Gromov. On April 17 the two old friends celebrated together a last Liturgy in the church where both had been ordained to the diaconate and the priesthood. For Fr. Gromov these days were particularly happy ones. He recalls:

> His gracious—one might almost say, brotherly and amiable—relations with me not only never changed, but grew stronger every time we met. I would frequently spend the evening at his house, or he would sit beneath my roof, talking in all simplicity until late at night. It was as though he was resting from the burdensome conventions of decorum which his rank demanded of him.

On April 19 Innocent left Irkutsk to spend one final night in the Monastery of the Ascension. There, in the morning, he celebrated the Divine Liturgy and at the relics of his heavenly protector heard Bp. Parthenius offer a prayer-service for his safe journey. The time of parting was at hand, and it was difficult both for the elderly hierarch and for the people who again turned out to receive his blessing and to say farewell. Tears came to the eyes of most of those who watched him squint to gaze as best he could upon the hills, the houses, the churches and the people that for him held so many fond memories. Providence, however, had called him to a new ministry, and Innocent remained as always obedient to its call. At 3 P.M. he left the monastery grounds. Beneath the arch of the main gates he paused and turned one last time to bless each of the monks and novices assembled there. Then, falling to his knees, he lay on the earth in a long moment of silent prayer to St. Innocent before arising, strengthened, to bid a final, emotional farewell. As the bells of the monastery pealed, Innocent's carriage disappeared down the path which led forever from the country of his birth.

Throngs of people, sounding bells, cheers and speeches, solemn receptions, tours, teas and dinners—all of these awaited the venerable hierarch as he made his way across Siberia. On feastdays he would stop to celebrate the Liturgy, but otherwise he politely declined all hospitality, in his determination to reach Moscow as quickly as possible. At Kazan the usual assembly stood on the shore of the Volga River as his ship pulled up to the dock, and although it was an "ordinary" day, Innocent came ashore, for he had been informed that at long last the official text of his appointment to the See of Moscow awaited him in the cathedral.

With Abp. Anthony accompanying him, the metropolitan-elect walked to the cathedral as every bell in the city rang a joyous welcome. With the customary solemnities the two hierarchs entered the church and venerated the icons and the relics of the city's first bishop, St. Gurius, who lay at rest there. Then the protopresbyter of the cathedral read the imperial ukase, dated April 16, 1868:

In view of your long episcopal ministry marked by tireless efforts and apostolic zeal in spreading and confirming the True Faith in the most remote territories of our country, and of your unremitting concern for satisfying the spiritual needs of your flock, I find it fitting to entrust to you the Diocese of Moscow and to elevate you to the rank of Metropolitan. Your fruitful labors and wholehearted loyalty to the Church give us full hope that following the example of the late Metropolitan Philaret of Moscow of Eternal Memory and of his illustrious predecessors, you will fulfill your new duties with the same selflessness and benefit to the Church which have marked your ministry heretofore.

May the Divine Chief-Pastor strengthen you in the new sacred tasks which lie before you. Imparting to you the white cowl with its cross of precious stones, and entrusting myself to your prayers, I remain every favorable towards you.

Alexander II.

As this symbol of his new office was brought to him from St. Gurius' reliquary, Innocent removed and set aside the old black cowl which he had worn in Asia and America. Then, while the choir sang "Many Years," the new metropolitan placed the white upon his head and without further ado pressed on.

Moscow was now drawing near. The outskirts, Nizhni-Novgorod, were reached on May 24, and a delegation came out to arrange the details of his triumphal entry into the ancient capital. The last leg of the journey was accomplished by rail, and on May 25, 1868, at 9:30 P.M., Moscow met its old friend now come as its spiritual father and archpastor.

The station platform was crowded with delegations from the theological academy, the seminaries and the diocesan consistory and trust-fund. At their head stood the metropolitan's two vicars, Bp. Leonid of Dmitrovskii and Bp. Ignatius of Mozhaisk. On behalf of the clergy and faithful of the diocese they presented Innocent with a copy of the Iberian icon of the Theotokos. A series of welcoming speeches by various civic dignitaries followed, and the clergy of the city assembled outside were presented to their new archpastor. Then, as the sound of church bells pierced the sleepless night, multitudes of people, from the greatest to the least, accompanied Innocent to his residence in the Trinity Apartments. There, after a short prayer-service offered on his behalf, he retired to the room where his predecessor had spent his final days on earth, while outside a choir sang the troparion to St. Sergius.

Next morning the festivities began anew. In the massive Kazan Cathedral Metr. Innocent was greeted with the following words:

"O Inhabitant of the deserts and angel in the flesh!" Rejoicing that the Lord has now established you as the Angel of our church, we joyfully greet you as a messenger from heaven and are inspired with the hope that now you will illumine *our* desert as well with the light of heaven, that you will warm it with the warmth of grace and make it fruitful by the spiritual dew of your prayers. By word and deed may you appeal to us and move us towards the divine life in imitation of Christ. "God bless him who comes in the Name of the Lord!"

A second speech, delivered by the rector of the Seminary, changed the image but continued to develop the basic theme:

In the fifty days just past, the Holy Church has offered us, from the Acts of the Apostles, readings about how, after journeys full of trouble, need and privation in preaching about God, Paul, first-enthroned among the apostles, completed a trip from the East to the West, to the capital of the then-known world. It had already been illumined by the light of Christ. During his trip, the Apostle to the Gentiles

was met lovingly and accompanied by those who believed in Jesus Christ, and he confirmed them in the
faith and with them offered prayers. Nearing Rome
he was met joyously by the Christians there who came
out of the city to meet him. Seeing them, the Apostle
thanked God and, strengthened, began in the capital
of the world to preach boldly the Kingdom of God
to the educated just as he had to foreigners and
ignorant men (Acts 28:31; Rom. 1:14-15).

This sacred narrative about the Apostle to the
Gentiles reminded us and turned our thoughts to
you and to your great apostolic labors, our Archpastor and our Father! Like the Apostle to the Gentiles, you went around vast territories preaching the
Gospel, proclaiming the true God, the Maker of
heaven and earth, and the Savior of mankind, Jesus
Christ, to tribes who had never heard of Him. In
this apostolic ministry, over many years you endured
much trouble and necessity, and now by the will of
God and of His Anointed One, after innumerable
declarations and demonstrations along your route
of the respect and love which all feel for you, you
have arrived at your hierarchical ministry in the ancient capital of the Russian Kingdom—to a city where
since ancient times the Name of Christ has been
named, and where all of us, your children, meet
and greet you with the same joy and love with which
the Christians of Rome met the great Apostle. We
believe and hope—and rejoice—that our Lord Jesus
Christ is, through your coming, through your prayers
and ministrations, through your hierarchical blessing,
through your word, deeds and example—opening
to the flock of Moscow new sources of grace, and that
by your ministry in this city the Name of Christ will
be glorified more and more. May your paternal heart
be comforted by the faith of its children who await
your presence and your blessing.

Immediately Innocent was vested to begin the solemn

procession across Red Square to the Dormition Cathedral, where he would for the first time officially meet his flock. "Grace to you and peace, from God the Father and our Lord Jesus Christ," he said, offering the people the apostolic benediction, and then with this speech responded to all the words which had thus far been addressed to him:

Who am I to dare take up the word and authority of my predecessors? A mere student from bygone days and far-off places, who spent over half his life in a country still farther off; no more than a humble worker in one of Christ's small fields, a teacher of children and babes in the faith—how can *I*, the least of all workers, work in this great and glorious and ancient vineyard of Christ? How can a teacher such as I instruct a flock from whose midst teachers and guides—indeed, teachers of teachers—have gone out to all parts of Russia? True, I could say these things, almost anywhere I might be sent, but *here* there is something quite particular. Look at whom I must follow. Who was my predecessor, then who am I? There can be no comparison (or rather, any comparison which might be drawn would be far from favorable to me, and would in fact be rather against me). I understood the full difficulty, the bitterness of such comparisons—comparisons wholly natural, unavoidable and just (and not at all of the same nature as gossip); I understood too how fully sublime and difficult it would be to minister here, and I ought to have (or at least *could* have) shirked it, having indeed reasons for doing so. But who am I to oppose God, the Heavenly King without Whose will not a hair falls from our heads? Or who am I to contradict our earthly king whose heart is in the hand of God? "No," I said to myself. "Let it be with me as the Lord wills. I will go wherever I am told!" And so, I have come. O Lord, bless me to begin my work. O Lord, I am Yours, and I wish to be Yours, everywhere and

always. Do with me as You wish in this life and
in the life to come. May I be here just a tool in Your
hands!

O Most Holy Lady, Theotokos, my Surety! Do
not take from me here your aid, your help, your intercessions, your prayers! O Hierarchs of Christ:
Peter, Alexis, Jonah and Philip [3]—and all of you who
lie at rest here—accept in your prayers me, your most
unworthy heir. Brothers and fathers—especially you
learned instructors and fathers—you do not deserve
an illiterate hierarch like me, but bear with me for
the love of Christ, and accept me in your daily prayers.
Pray even more that false doctrine and human philo-
sophizing may not creep into Orthodoxy by means of
my illiteracy. I ask all of you, my brethren and my
children, to pray for me, a sinner.

"Grace and peace to you, from God the Father
and from our Lord Jesus Christ!"

And the Liturgy began.

Surrounded by wave after wave of richly vested and
mitered clergy, facing a vast wall of ancient icons rising
through mists of incense to the great central vault of Moscow's
grandest church, its walls awash with brilliant frescos of the
saints gleaming in an ocean of gold, an old man raised his
hands and failing eyes to heaven in prayer: "O Heavenly King,
the Comforter, the Spirit of Truth. . . ," the same words which,
not so long before he had spoken so many times, alone, in
squalid native villages, in tiny chapels hung with sailcloth
and a few darkened, tattered icons. When the singing began
it was not a native cantor helping four lads who had accompanied their bishop on his travels, but a sonorous, well-dis-
ciplined choir whose volume seemed to shake the foundations
of the massive building. Nor was there a group of Aleuts or
Tlingits, Yakuts or Gilyaks in filthy rags, oblivious to the
cold in rapt attention to see and hear and understand each
word and movement, but senators and cabinet ministers,
royalty in their finest clothes and jewels—even one of the

[3] Canonized metropolitans of Moscow.

mightiest emperors upon earth—who attended the service. But Innocent and his prayers remained the same.

This was amply clear from the very outset of his ministry in Moscow. One of the Metropolitan's first duties was to visit the Holy Trinity-St. Sergius Lavra of which, by virtue of his office, he was now the rector or "Sacred Archimandrite" (as his title officially read). And so, on May 31, he boarded the special train which ran from Moscow to the historic cloister. In the Holy Trinity Cathedral he greeted the monastic brotherhood and humbly confessed to them that although for a quarter of a century he had borne the name of monk, he could stand to learn true monasticism from even the least of those who inhabited St. Sergius' house. In the seminary, also housed there, the pupils were introduced to their new rector, and Innocent made a point of seeing everything and visiting everyone. Despite his years he climbed the ladders into the lofts which served the pupils as livng quarters, and during oral examinations which he attended, he put the youngsters at ease by the simplicity and gentleness with which he corrected their mistakes. Perhaps he still remembered "Larva".

CHAPTER 3

DESCENT OF DARKNESS

Metr. Innocent was already over seventy years old when he arrived in Moscow, but the active life he had always led stood him in good stead. He still stood impressively erect (although he was beginning to grow a bit stout), and with strength and vigor largely intact he endeavored to maintain the same busy schedule he always had.

He awoke every morning at four o'clock, attended an early Liturgy and was at work by nine. With the exception of several hours rest in the afternoon which he now required each day, he was available for consultation until nine o'clock each night, at which time he began his prayers in order to be in bed promptly at ten. Whenever possible he found time in his schedule to attend sessions with his grandchildren's tutors (who never ceased to be amazed at his grasp of the natural sciences) and to listen to the newspapers being read by them or Fr. Gabriel in the evening. Otherwise, his time belonged to his flock.

To allow the metropolitan to keep abreast of matters in the diocese without overtaxing his strength, every week each of the vicars was to present a report to him. This proved efficient for Innocent but could by no means substitute for personal contact with the flock. His doors were never closed to persons of any station in life, and in time, as Muscovites came to realize that their new archpastor was readily approachable, cordial and compassionate, they began to flock to him with their problems in numbers exceeding 300 a week, and none of them went away unconsoled, empty-handed or unaided, regardless of the magnitude of their want. Each year he distributed over 10,000 rubles of his own money to aid them, and when a worthwhile project was brought to his attention he never for a moment hesitated to make use of cathedral funds to further it.

Never did Metropolitan Innocent allow his new office to change him. When he laughed, it was—as always—loud and sincere. He never feigned importance, reserve or severity. His face reflected an inner serenity. His speech and manners were as unaffected, as simple and as affable as ever—or at least to the extent that protocol could endure. Perhaps in the long run this more than anything else provided the surest measure of his worth, for even Moscow, with all its cosmopolitan sophistication, was captivated by him. From the day of his arrival the people were amazed by his "patriarchal simplicity" and responded with simple-hearted affection, love and trust—feelings which grew with every passing year.

The only serious sign of advancing age—and the only thing really capable of changing the metropolitan—was his vision. Cataracts had for several years been forming in both eyes, and medical science offered little hope of treating them. The doctors would have to let the cataracts gradually "ripen," until all he would be able to distinguish would be light and dark.[4] Then they could think of surgery. One eye had almost reached this stage, and the other was not far behind. This caused Innocent, virtually from the day of his arrival in Moscow, to contemplate retirement should total blindness overtake him.

By 1869 his vision had declined so drastically that the doctors warned him that unless he abandoned paper work altogether he would soon find himself totally blind. The patient proved unable (and unwilling) to obey, and by 1872 it was decided to attempt surgical repair of his eyes.

A springtime trip to St. Petersburg was therefore cancelled, and on the eve of his operation, in order to prepare

---

[4] On April 27, 1867, he wrote poignantly, "... my back does not yet ache; my voice has not yet changed. Even my legs serve me well. It's only my eyesight, my eyesight! What will happen with it? I don't know. The doctors say I won't be in total darkness—I'll see doors and windows! If only the Lord may let it be so!"

himself spiritually, the metropolitan summoned a flattered Bp. Leonid to visit him in his room. On the morning of May 10 the patient was hastily anesthetized and in fifteen minutes the clouded lens was cut out of his right eye. He awoke calm and feeling rather well. There was no pain, and the first night he slept peacefully. By the fourth day, however, the first note of gloom was sounded by the metropolitan's son, Fr. Gabriel, who wrote in the first of a series of agonizing communiques to a family friend: "There is little comforting I can tell you. The condition of his eye has worsened, but the Metropolitan's general health remains good." Three days later, chronic rheumatism flared up in the old man's legs, causing him constant pain, which in turn prevented his getting the sleep which he so desperately needed. He weakened. The doctors began expressing fears that infection would necessitate complete removal of the eye. "It is very painful," Fr. Gabriel writes, "very sad—even devastating—that dear papa will never again see with the eye which had the cataract removed . . ." Quickly, however, he adds, "This is simply human conviction, though. The Lord can yet manifest His mercy to the Metropolitan. Let us run to the Lord with all our soul and heart. There is no longer any hope in the doctors . . ." [5]

In time the crisis passed. The eye was saved but no longer served its purpose. The blindness was permanent. As he contemplated the fact that the only hope for his other severely weakened eye was an identical operation, Innocent fell into depression. As he marked the fiftieth anniversary of his ordination to the priesthood—in his hospital bed—the Metropolitan reflected sadly, "my song is sung. It is time—long since time—that I rest." He wished to retire from his high office and move into the Bethany Skete which his predecessor Metr. Platon had built for himself. "Why, Your Eminence?" he was asked. "Is your sight totally gone?" "Almost," he replied. "There are some good days when I can see some things, but it never lasts long, and mostly I see everything in a fog."

[5] Later it was learned that Metr. Innocent was not himself totally without blame in this turn for the worse. Unable to endure lying still in bed for several days, as the doctors ordered, he arose to say his prayers as is fitting on his feet. This aggravated his condition at a crucial stage.

This depression was destined to be no longer than any other he had felt in the past, and Innocent surrendered himself as always to the will of God, fully accepting his condition. His recovery then proceeded rapidly, and he was able to return to work, as full of faith and energy as ever. Now when he celebrated the Liturgy, it was almost entirely by memory. He was able even to recite whole lections from the Gospels so flawlessly that those who knew no better would never believe that he was virtually sightless. His deacons, too, became adept at leading him about in such a way as to call no special attention to his condition. Whenever he was required to recite a prayer which he did not know by heart, he simply handed it to one of the vicars to read.

It was inevitable, however, that this condition would make Metr. Innocent the butt of tasteless jokes. The personal pain these caused him could be forgiven and overlooked, but the possibility that they might contain a grain of truth could not. Could he, by remaining helplessly in office, be harming the Church? Increasingly he found time to contemplate such things as these, for often he had to content himself with spending long hours alone if his devoted aids were themselves to attend to their normal duties. As he sat, made comfortable, yet abandoned on a thickly-cushioned sofa in the middle of a room whose darkness he no longer noticed, he found that visitors no longer flocked to see him. (They were afraid, so he was told, of "disturbing" him.) And of those who did venture in to find this lonely, morose figure seated on his sofa, only a very few actually stepped inside to find him—much to their surprise, delight and profit—as full as ever of life and interest in the outside world. As days and weeks thus passed, his mind increasingly turned to retirement, and while "rest" for him was still synonymous with death, he reasoned that in the monastery "there are at least continuous services; I'll be less idle."

Twice, therefore, Innocent begged permission to retire from his office, but Tsar Alexander II, valuing his services highly and knowing that to find a worthy successor for him would be no mean task, refused the requests and besought the old hierarch to finish out his days in the See of Moscow.

"But wouldn't total blindness *necessitate* my retiring?" Innocent objected. No, the tsar replied, it would only make personal supervision of the diocese more problematic, but this could still be done by assigning greater responsibilities to his two able vicars. Such arrangements were made, and at long last, Metr. Innocent's pastoral travels were at an end. He was able, however, to draw considerable comfort from the knowledge that not everyone shared his feeling of uselessness.

Even in these bleak days we see that Innocent's sense of humor concerning himself was not extinguished with the light of his eyes. In 1876 he marked his name's day in St. Petersburg by celebrating the Divine Liturgy. After the service the choirmembers were brought to his apartment to congratulate him and receive his blessing. Each was introduced in turn. As Viktor Sokolov, the metropolitan's favorite bass, approached, Innocent told his steward loudly enough for everyone in the room to hear, "Father, don't give the basses any bread today." "But, why not, Your Eminence?" the steward puzzled. "Because in church today during the *Our Father* they didn't sing, 'give us this day our daily bread.' They haven't asked God for it." Indeed, that morning the choir had sung a composition in which the tenors alone sing these words; the basses have a rest.

CHAPTER 4

"LET YOUR LIGHT SO SHINE"

Despite the tragedy which threatened to bring them to an end almost before they began, Innocent's Moscow years proved abundantly fruitful. He arrived in 1869 already armed with some idea of the problems he would face in his new diocese, and in the months which followed he allowed his vicars and his many visitors to teach him a good deal more. By September he was ready, characteristically enough, to begin a first visitation of his entire flock.

This journey differed vastly from any other he had taken during his long pastoral career. No kayaks or dogsleds, reindeer or bull backs—and certainly not his own two feet—carried him through the territory of the Diocese of Moscow, but a horse-drawn coach whose comfort and ease he frankly found difficult to grow accustomed to. The luxury was fine, but it made him bored and left him feeling listless. For all the pain and trouble which travel in America and Asia caused, he rather preferred it. "Somehow I felt healthy there," he remarks, adding, "fresh air is a great thing."

No sooner was he back in Moscow than it was time to go—by rail—to St. Petersburg for the first time as a member of the Holy Synod.

The solemn send-off he received in Moscow—a delegation of ecclesiastical and civic dignitaries headed by not just one, but both of his vicar bishops, all praying anxiously for his safe arrival—no longer after six months in office brought him any great surprise. Amazing and truly delightful, however, was the reception that he was accorded at the other end where, beginning with the traditional Slavic greeting of bread and salt, the citizens of St. Petersburg more than made up for the poor treatment they had offered during his last visit to their city. And Innocent, feeling himself now free as an official member of the Synod to express openly all of his opinions on a wide variety of questions of life, religion, morality and even politics, produced there no less a stir than he had in his own diocese. Even the normally indolent bishops seemed, at first, to catch his energetic spirit, and he happily declared that "we keep interrupting one another like children!" In an audience with the man who as a child had thrilled to his stories of wilderness Alaska and the sea, Innocent now outlined his many simple and eminently reasonable ideas for solving some of the problems which he observed in Moscow and the church at large.

In particular, he wished to see new statutes written for the seminaries to stem the growing tide of secularism and modernism, changes made in the monasteries to restore them to vitality, improvements in financial support of the parish clergy, and new initiatives both to promote missionary work and effectively to combat the agonizing growth of sectarianism in the country. He even looked beyond the horizons of the Russian Church to the possibility of convening an Ecumenical Council [*] to bring all heresy and schism to an end.

With evident support and promises of further study of all these matters by both Tsar Alexander II and the Ober-Procurator, Metr. Innocent set about the task of initiating needed programs. Very soon, however, he found that the Synod's initial enthusiasm cooled, and as the session's work bogged down, in the end only one major project was acted upon. This one was, however, very close to Innocent's heart, and he happily accepted the assignment of preparing draft statutes for an Orthodox Missionary Society.

By the sixth week of Lent, as he prepared to return to Moscow for the holy days, Innocent completed this task. In spite of many obstacles and misunderstandings, he succeeded in presenting and defending before the Synod his draft text, which with its approval was delivered to the Empress, the

[*] A like project was being independently considered at about this same time by the Patriarchate of Constantinople.

Society's proposed sponsor. With his ideas now committed
to writing, Innocent returned home by rail.

During the two weeks which were his to spend in Moscow with his flock, Innocent devoted himself wholly to the
central mystery of the Christian faith. He personally celebrated
every solemn service of Holy Week in the city's great cathedrals. His few free hours outside of church he utilized profit-
ably by listening to the Gospels or Lives of the Saints read to
him by his grandchildren. Not only did he himself make the
most of this spiritual food by keeping a strict ascetical fast
and giving generous alms to the poor, but by so doing with
great fervor he provided an excellent example to his entire
flock. The glorious days of the paschal week passed too quickly
and duty once more beckoned. On Thomas Sunday he returned,
refreshed, to the bureaucratic tedium of the Synod's spring
meetings.

This became the pattern of his life for as long as health
permitted him to travel: winter and spring working in St. Petersburg with a break provided by Holy Week and Bright
Week; summer and fall in and around Moscow in contact
with his people. Gradually he saw the fruits of his labors as
one by one his projects were realized.

One of his earliest concerns was the healing of the "Old
Believer" schism. In his old diocese, especially in the newly-
populated region between Yakutsk and Ayan, he had seen
the tragic fruits of this two-century-old rift in the Russian
Church. Unable to learn what was officially to be done with
the schismatics, he had tried to talk to the least stubborn of
them and to bring them back to the Church. In Moscow he
learned that since the turn of the century the "old rituals"
were permitted if performed by valid clergy. In the so-called
"United Believers"[7] the greatest dangers of sectarian rejection
of the priesthood, marriage and civil authority were overcome,
and the oneness of the Church was preserved—at least on
paper. Yet extensive travels in Asia and throughout the Russian Empire had taught Innocent that "our sectarians are an
unhealed wound infecting the parts of the Church which we
consider healthy; the so-called 'United-Belief' is fruitless."

[7] *Edinovertsy.*

Therefore, finding no difference whatsoever between the Old Ritualists and the Orthodox in their essential "confession of the Christian truths," Innocent sought boldly to deepen the ties which Metropolitans Platon and Philaret before him had sought to forge.

One way of doing this, he felt, was to invite their clergy to concelebrate with him, using the "old books." (For a long time the reverse had been done: Orthodox bishops had served in "United Believers" churches; Innocent notes, however, that so unsuccessful was this program that often after the prelate left, the people would "purify" the church with holy water!) His first year in Moscow, therefore, he invited two of their monastic priests to concelebrate the Divine Liturgy with him at the Lavra on the patronal feast of St. Sergius.[*]

A second of the metropolitan's deep concerns stemmed perhaps from his own earliest years: the pitiful plight of clerical widows and orphans. Again, during his first year, as he began the tour of the diocese, Innocent stopped at a monastery in Ugresh where, after Liturgy and a meal, he took a stroll in the square behind the rector's cell. His vision that day was unusually clear, and, though dimly, he could make out the faint outlines of some buildings beyond the Moscow River. "What is it?" he asked Fr. Pimen. "The village of Ostrov," replied the rector and went on to relate all that he knew about it. Ostrov consisted of several fine stone buildings which now unfortunately lay abandoned in the early stages of decomposition. An almshouse! A perfect addition to the Diocese of Moscow, the metropolitan immediately thought, if only somehow it could be procured! Fr. Pimen gladly volunteered to approach a personal friend in the Hall of State Properties, which had jurisdiction over such things, and to enquire into the matter. "Why *not* find out?" asked Innocent. "Go ahead and ask him about it, and God bless you!"

Several days later Fr. Pimen carried out his mission, spoke with his friend (the director himself) and obtained provisional agreement to the plan, subject only to the usual bureaucratic procedures. And so, through a casual conversation in

---

[*] Previously their participation in this great festival of all the Russian people had been limited to offering their own prayer-service at his relics.

a monastery garden, the Diocese of Moscow obtained (nine months later) 106 acres of manorial lands for use as a badly-needed almshouse. Metr. Innocent's second year on the Holy Synod was perhaps the most fruitful he ever spent. It began with the establishment of a Department of Iconography devoted to collecting books and manuals on the subject, copies of miraculous icons from throughout Russia and other Orthodox lands, as well as other ancient artifacts: carvings, murals, illuminated manuscripts, etc. In addition, it was charged with studying the various painter's guides in use to determine which of them were theologically and historically adequate to aid present-day iconographers in their work. Finally, the department was empowered to gather in the Monastery of the Miracle the surplus icons from all the monasteries and churches in European Russia, where a commission would select those worthy of preservation in museums and release the rest for distribution to churches wherever needed. Under Innocent's supervision this brought great relief and profit to the struggling congregations of his former diocese.[9]

All these achievements paled, however, before the announcement that on November 21, 1869, Tsar Alexander had approved Metr. Innocent's draft statutes and established the Orthodox Missionary Society.

[9] A related project, again Innocent's creation, was the practical School of Iconography established in 1873. Its task was to train clerical orphans from the Diocese of Moscow as iconographers. This proved not only of help in improving the quality of ecclesiastical art but provided a worthy occupation within the Church for those young men unable to pursue the scholarly studies requisite for entering the pastoral ministry.

CHAPTER 5

"NO STRANGER TO MISSIONARY WORK"

"It has pleased the Lord," a very happy old man declared,

> that even here, at the center of Russia and in my
> declining years, I have not become a stranger to the
> missionary work to which, by the will of Divine
> Providence, nearly my entire life since my early years
> has been devoted in the far-off reaches of our country.

According to the statutes which the tsar ratified, the
Metropolitan of Moscow by virtue of his office was to sit as
president of the new organization with the right to name one
of the two vice-presidents and a third of the twelve members
of the Board of Directors. Innocent therefore became not only
the inspirer and founder but the first leader of the Russian
Missionary Society, and as Prof. N. A. Sergeevskii remarked,
"the great apostle brought to the whole city a real apostolate
of its own."

From its beginnings in Moscow, the society would become
a nationwide effort, as Innocent himself envisaged:

> In comparison with the number [of unchurched
> people] we have very few missions, and the ones
> which have already been established need funds in
> order to maintain and expand their activities. The
> holiness of this work and its great importance . . .
> are obvious, and our chief source of funds for this
> development must be the concern and zeal of all
> Orthodox Christians. The Missionary Society is open

to all—rich and poor alike. The comfort of service this great work provides is given to anyone who wishes and is able to do so according to his abilities.

The inaugural meeting of the Society was set for December of 1869, but as Metr. Innocent prepared anxiously to return to Moscow to preside over it, the caught cold. The illness refused to respond to treatment and as the time drew near Innocent painfully wrote Bp. Leonid (his vice presidential designate) suggesting that they proceed without him. "No matter what sadness I may feel," he writes

at not being able to be present at the opening, I can do nothing about it. Evidently this is the Lord's will . . . The speech which I had intended to deliver at the opening I will correct a bit and send to you for consideration. If you find it appropriate, use it. If not, deliver one of your own.

The Bishop of Dmitrovskii, however, was in no hurry to carry out this order, hoping that at length the metropolitan would regain his strength and be able to be present. Indeed, by January 13, 1870, Innocent's health was returning, but the doctor was not keen on his traveling yet, since almost three weeks in bed without solid food had left him rather weak. A further complication was the fact that major track repairs along the route rendered one bridge unserviceable, causing all passengers to cross the river on a foot bridge to transfer to a second train.

Despite his frustration Innocent now ordered that no more postponements be allowed. Mail was daily pouring in and lay unanswered since no staff could be created until the first meeting. Furthermore, the long delays were fueling the senseless rumors which always seemed to center on the aging hierarch. Pointedly Innocent commanded: proceed.

Ultimately it was the will of God, however, that Russia's foremost living missionary be present on this momentous day. The doctors finally relented, and on January 23 their happy patient left the northern capital. That same day personal invitations were issued in his name to all the leading citizens of Moscow asking that they not absent themselves from this crucial meeting. The next day's newspapers extended the same call to all the people of the ancient city.

On January 25, Metr. Innocent was the chief celebrant at a Divine Liturgy in the Kremlin's Dormition Cathedral. On hand was a great multitude of people, one of whom left these observations:

> This [occasion] produced a profound and joyous impression upon all who watched attentively. Thank God! we thought, it's long since been time for our laity as a whole . . . all to unite fraternally with Church authorities in common projects for the good of the Orthodox Faith and of the Church. Time it is that in such projects we abandon all foreign concepts of the Church (e.g., that the clergy alone comprise her) and adopt instead the truly Orthodox point of view—that the Church is to be seen in the Orthodox people as a whole, the clergy being only her ministers. Therefore, matters of faith and of the Church must be considered equally important and necessary for the laity as for the clergy. In this unity of the spirit consists the true power of the Orthodox Church and our hope for success in all she undertakes for her own good and honor.

After Liturgy, over 150 charter members of the Society— clergy, soldiers, government officials, senators, municipal authorities, members of the Duma, the judiciary, the university and various other organizations—reassembled in the home of the Governor-General. More than twice this number, including many common folk, were unable to find room at this first meeting, so massive was the response. Subsequent meetings, therefore, were held in larger quarters to accommodate everyone. From this first meeting, however, it was clear that the Orthodox Missionary Society was destined to be a popular and fully democratic organization.

The first meeting began appropriately with hymns from

the feast of Pentecost, after which a member of the Board of Directors read the text of the statutes. Then the Metropolitan arose to speak.

Brethren, you have heard that the goal of our Society is to advance the conversion of those who do not yet believe in Christ our Savior. That is, we accept, each according to his abilities and the measure of his zeal, to further the conversion to the Orthodox Faith and the Truth of those among our fellow countrymen who still wander in the darkness of unbelief. As you can see, the work we hope to advance is great and holy and truly apostolic.

In order to obtain the success one desires, even in ordinary tasks and undertakings, it is necessary to muster (independently of financial means) intelligence, knowledge, experience, ability, activity and energy. When with all of this the circumstances are *just* right, one has reason to hope for success.

Now, in the work which *we* wish to advance, this does not in the main apply. To be sure, we too will need (in addition to financial means) intelligence, knowledge, experience, ability and so on, but we cannot—and must not, even under the best of circumstances—count upon these factors as a sure means to attaining our goal. And why not? Because man's conversion to the path of faith and truth depends entirely upon God. "No one can come to Me," said the Savior, "unless the Father Who sent Me draws him to Me" [Jn. 6:44]. Therefore if, according to His inscrutable judgments, the Lord does not wish for a given person or nation to be converted to Jesus Christ, even the most capable, most gifted, most zealous of workers will not succeed in his task. We need not offer even the Apostles as examples here. We can point directly to Jesus Christ Himself Who, being Himself the Word and Love Itself, was (and is) better able than anyone else to proclaim the Truth and convince people to accept it. Yet how many of those who heard and listened to Him remained unconverted?

What then shall we do? How ought we to proceed when, in the words of the Gospel, the harvest is great in our country (*i.e.*, many remain unconverted to Jesus Christ)? "Pray to the Lord of the harvest," Jesus Himself teaches us [Mt. 9:38]. Thus, first and foremost, *we must pray.* If even in everyday matters people fall back upon prayer, asking God's blessing at the beginning of some task and then throughout asking for renewal and strength (where prayer means nothing more than *help*), here, in the matter of conversion, prayer becomes the *means* itself—and a most effectual of means, for without prayer one cannot expect success even under the most perfect of circumstances. Thus it is not our missionaries alone who must pray. No, we their brethren must further their work by our own prayers. And what ought we to pray for? First, that the Lord will send workers into His harvest; second, that He will open the hearts of those who listen to the Word of the Gospel; third, that He will increase our Society's numbers more and more; and finally, that He will strengthen and confirm in us the desire we all now feel to further this work to the attaining of our goal.

Let us further it also by our good desire, our good word, and whatsoever sacrifices of which we may be capable. And these—no matter how small—will be, we can state, acceptable to Him Who has said, "Truly, I say to you, whoever gives a drink of cold water to one of the least of my followers because he *is* My follower, will certainly receive a reward" [Mt. 10:42]. (Here we can understand as the "follower" our present missionaries.)

The Orthodox Missionary Society was then declared officially opened. The president announced his choices for vice-president and board members, and indicated that the next meeting to select the remaining officials by secret ballot

would be held on February 2. As the Metropolitan made his
way out of the room the clergy rose to sing an enthusiastic
"eis polla eti, despota!"

The second meeting was held as scheduled with 470
members casting their ballots.

We cannot here trace the full history of the Orthodox
Missionary Society, which flourished until the second decade
of the twentieth century, but can simply note that already by
the time it gathered to celebrate its first anniversary (five
days after a hospitalized and blinded Metr. Innocent marked
the completion of his first half-century in priestly orders) it
had expanded to include chapters in seventeen dioceses
throughout Russia. The bishops were enthusiastic, the people
responding generously, and enough contributions had come
in for a first dispersal of funds to be made to missionaries in
the field.

When the spring session of the Holy Synod began that
same year, a major topic on the agenda was related to the work
just done: the elevation of Metr. Innocent's former missionary
vicariates in Yakutsk and Sitka to the status of independent
dioceses. With Yakutia there were no problems. It already
possessed a competent bishop in Dionysius, and on March 29
the decree was signed. Innocent immediately wired his hearty
congratulations to his old friend and sent as a momento to
his flock an icon of the Holy Trinity containing a fragment
of the Holy Cross.

The problem with America was more complex. Alaska
had been sold to the United States, and most Russian subjects
were fleeing home in droves. The Ober-Procurator favored
simply declaring the See vacant, removing the bishop and his
staff to Amuria, and administering the remaining native
parishes through a priest resident in San Francisco.

Bp. Leonid, whose advice the Metropolitan greatly
valued and supported, pointed out that the bishops first had
to clarify the very purpose of the mission in America. If the

prime thrust was to be a general missionary effort among American citizens at large (as Innocent himself had envisaged and described in 1867) New York was clearly the best location for the See. If Alaska, however, was to remain the primary focus, then San Francisco would be better.

More important, however, was the man who would be chosen to live in one of these two locations and be called upon to head the Church in the continental United States for the first time. He should be, Bp. Leonid again reasoned, either a stable monk or a seasoned missionary, for American public opinion of Russia (generally hostile) and the tradition of complete freedom of religion there would place the candidate under pressures and scrutiny completely unlike those in Alaska. "In part," Leonid observed, "the Bishop of California would be in the basic sense of the term *episcopus in partibus infidelium*, despite the fact that he has a See."

From a field of six, three candidates were presented to the tsar for final selection, and chosen as first ruling bishop of the "Diocese of the Aleutian Islands and Alaska" was 34-year-old Archimandrite John, Dean of the Moscow Theological Academy, a pious, humble and kindly man, perhaps a little less experienced than the others, but possessing a knowledge of German and French which gave hopes that he would pick up English in San Francisco. (None of the candidates spoke English.)

CHAPTER 6

MEMORY ETERNAL

Eight years after this long-awaited victory, Innocent set off on January 8, 1878, for St. Petersburg to attend what was destined to be his last session of the Holy Synod. His senior vicar, Bp. Leonid, had died the year before, and now Bp. Ignatius was being transferred on an important mission to reconcile sectarians in Kostroma. To replace them the Metropolitan had convinced two high-quality men to accept monastic tonsure and this new ministry. On January 13, in Innocent's presence, Fr. Alexis Kliucharev, long editor of a spiritual journal,[10] was tonsured and given the name Ambrose. Two days later he became Bishop of Mozhaisk, senior vicar of the Diocese of Moscow. In March, Fr. Alexander Lavrov, a renowned canon lawyer and author was tonsured with the name Alexis. It was the metropolitan's intention to return to St. Petersburg after Pascha for his consecration, but the heavy schedule of Holy Week services weakened the aging hierarch, and he was unable to leave Moscow again that year.

During the summer he briefly regained his strength. A cottage in the countryside outside of Moscow had been completed for him, and with his family he enjoyed the peace and quiet of strolling in the woods. Every Sunday and feastday they went into the city for services, and he kept his usual work schedule even in seclusion. Fr. Gabriel, observing the effect this place had upon his father observed, "Oh! If only it were not for his eyes—which now see almost nothing—he'd be like an eagle! (But, may God's will be done.)"

Nine years before the same had occurred with Innocent's

[10] *Dushespasitel'noe chtenie* [Soul-Saving Readings] 1860-1867.

predecessor. 'We are told," he wrote from Blagoveshchensk on January 11, 1867, "concerning the Metropolitan of Moscow, that he is now particularly healthy, and that this amazes many. In my opinion—if this is indeed true—it is just a last burst of life in him, and if afterwards he again falls sick, surely this will be for the last time! How sad! Yet, thank God that he managed to live until a time when good sense is beginning to work even in the most foolish." As the leaves began to fall in 1878, the same process began in Metr. Innocent.

Death had never been a preoccupation of Metr. Innocent. He asked only that when the time came ("should the Lord have me die on land") a cheap set of vestments ("but not black") be ready in which to lay his body in the grave. He had no particular desire to live on and on until infirmity had made of him a burden upon those around him, but neither was he unwilling to bear that painful cross. It seems clear that living never far from sudden death most of his adult life had given him the kind of serenity and insight which he ascribed to the saints when talking about the Tlingits many years before:

> They [the Tlingits] do not fear death. Why? Because they *don't know* what will come after death. Likewise, the Christian martyrs did not fear death. And why? Because they *sensed* — they felt — what would come after death. Thus, only those who don't know or who *do* know *actively* (i.e., who *sense*) what will come after death can be unafraid of it. All of us who only know but are not inwardly convinced of the things we hope for—we cannot help but fear death.

In October Metr. Innocent still felt strong enough to take part in a strenuous procession around the Kremlin walls. Next month however, he was too weak to go as scheduled to St. Petersburg. By January he was forced to concede that the whole year's work there would have to be conducted without him. As the winter passed, his strength steadily decreased. He could no longer stand for any length of time without his knees beginning to wobble and dizziness quickly forcing him to a chair. He began preparing for his death. He donated some 6500 rubles to the Church of St. Elijah in his native village of Anga; it would help repair the building, provide some needed articles for the sanctuary and ease the plight of the clergy there. Although unable himself to serve, he made a point of attending services daily and received Holy Communion every Sunday. He still felt the drive to work, but it was only reluctantly that Bp. Ambrose would bring him regular reports on the state of the diocese. "Business," the metropolitan declared, "takes my mind off my sickness." Just four days before his death, and no longer able to raise himself from his armchair, Innocent continued to ask his vicar, "Any new business?" "Master, don't even think about business," Ambrose hurried to advise. "Take it easy." "But I'm bored," was the grim reply.

The triumphal entry of the Lord into Jerusalem was celebrated with great splendor in the cathedrals of Moscow, and as the branches were being removed and the darkness of Holy Week's tragedy fell upon the faithful, they were unaware of a second passage to be accomplished that very week.

On Holy Monday, March 26, Metr. Innocent asked that the Iberian icon of the Theotokos, the one given him by the clergy of Moscow upon his arrival in the diocese, be brought to his apartment. Aides helped the old man to his knees, where he prayed with great fervor and kissed the image which his eyes could no longer see. This seemed to help. His spirits rose as the tears dried on his withered cheeks. In the evening he called for Hieromonk Savva to hear his last confession. A subdeacon fetched his *Euchologion* and an epitrachelion, and the *Canon for the Departure of the Soul* was read over him for a first time.

Holy Tuesday, March 27. Innocent asks to receive the Sacrament of Healing. At 6 P.M. Bishops Ambrose and Alexis together with four priests and a choir of six gather around the metropolitan's armchair and the service begins. Some thirty other persons are privileged to be present. After the last prayer and anointing, all file up to congratulate him. Of each he first asks forgiveness, then bestows his blessing.

Holy Wednesday, March 28. As evening falls and Matins of Holy Thursday are being read, commemorating Christ's betrayal at the hands of the lawless Judas, Innocent asks his steward, Fr. Arsenius, to celebrate the next day's Liturgy very early—at 2 A.M.—and then to bring him Holy Communion. Dutifully the priest obeys, omitting all the special features which make that commemoration of the Last Supper unique, and by 3 A.M. he appears in the dying hierarch's chambers. In his joy, Metr. Innocent arises from his chair without aid and stands to be vested in mantle, epitrachelion, cuffs and omophorion. In a firm, clear voice filled with fervor he recites the prayer before Communion: "I believe, O Lord, and I confess that Thou art the Christ, the Son of the living God . . ." Fr. Arsenius places on the spoon a portion of the precious Body and Blood of Christ and imparts them to the hierarch. Emotionally Innocent thanks the Lord for these Gifts, and adds enigmatically: "Now no one can say that they gave me Communion after I was already dead!" The meaning of these words was lost upon everyone present.

March 30, Great and Holy Friday, the beginning of the three-day Passover. The Holy Shroud lies in the center of the church, and the mournful troparion *The Noble Joseph* has been sung. The clergy are gathered reading the *Lamentations of the Theotokos* over the bier when word comes to Fr. Alexis that the metropolitan wishes to hear once more the *Canon for the Departure of the Soul.* Again that evening he asks his deacon for a third reading of it, but this is postponed until Bp. Alexis can come and read it personally. The vicar's concern brings great comfort to the dying man. After the canon Innocent asks to hear the morning prayers and to receive again the Sacrament of Healing. He then bids farewell to all his servants.

In the early-morning hours of the "Great and Holy Sab-

bath," during which the Church sings of how "the only-be-
gotten Son of God rested from all His works through the
dispensation of death," Metr. Innocent entered into his
eternal rest. He was eighty-two years of age. Long before his
fellow ministers would put off the mournful black vestments
of Holy Week, he was vested for a last time in the white
paschal raiment which would soon herald the victorious
resurrection to all. His body was laid on a table in the reception
hall of his apartments, and Bp. Ambrose offered the first
prayers for the repose of his soul.

It was 2:45 when the metropolitan died, but the stillness
of that day when "all mortal flesh keeps silence" was not
broken until eleven o'clock, when the doleful sounds of the
great Ivan the Terrible bell in the Kremlin notified the faithful of their profound loss. For two days pious Muscovites
flocked to the Trinity Apartments to bid farewell to their
beloved archpastor, and to entreat the Lord to grant him rest.

Death in the paschal season always brings with it a uni-
quely forceful realization that in Christ death is no more,
that He is risen and "with Himself He has raised up all the
dead." And so it was on Bright Tuesday, April 4, when again
the great bell tolled to announce the transfer of the late
Metropolitan's body from his home to the Monastery of the
Miracle. The streets were already filled with waves of mourners. Banners from the various cathedrals and monasteries of
the city rose above the throngs who awaited the procession.
Abp. Macarius of Lithuania and Vilna [11] who had come from
St. Petersburg to officiate at the funeral joined bishops Ambrose, Alexis and John (formerly of the Aleutian Islands)
and a great number of priests to celebrate the Divine Liturgy
and a requiem service in the fallen hierarch's private chapel.
Outside at the forefront of a massive crowd were gathered
almost all of the remaining clergy of the city—ten archimandrites, 200 priests, 120 deacons—to take part in the procession. When the services were ended, the coffin was raised
and brought out to a waiting cart. "Christ is risen from the

[11] He was destined to succeed Innocent as Metropolitan of Moscow.

dead, trampling down death by death, and upon those in the
tombs bestowing life!" These words, the "song of victory,"
and not a funeral dirge sounded through the crowded streets.

Abp. Macarius, who had hurried ahead, met the procession at the gates of the monastery and accompanied the body
to its appointed place near the relics of St. Alexis of Moscow.
That night streams of mourners filled the Annunciation
Cathedral until all hours, paying their last respects.

Bright Wednesday, April 5. Thousands overflowed the
cathedral and the monastery grounds to be present for the
funeral. Abp. Macarius was the chief celebrant at the Paschal
Liturgy, assisted by Bishops Ambrose and Alexis and the
senior clergy of the diocese. Bp. John then joined them for
the funeral service, during which Bp. Ambrose spoke of the
deceased:

> Once, as he was leaving for St. Petersburg to attend
> the Holy Synod, our Archpastor now fallen asleep
> in God bade me farewell with the following expres-
> sion whose originality is so typical of him: "I am
> leaving. Perhaps I shall ride back again— but perhaps
> they will carry me. In the latter event, do not allow
> any speeches at my burial; there is too much praise
> in these. Instead, preach a sermon over me, for this
> can give instruction to people. Here is the text for
> you to use, 'The Lord guides a man safely in the way
> he should go' [Ps. 37:23]." This same thing he con-
> firmed to me just several days before his death.
>
> Thus, by the will and testament of the deceased
> himself, we have indicated for us both the subject
> and the goal of our words. Our *subject* is to reveal
> the special ways of God's Providence for him, mani-
> fest over the many years of his life. Our *goal* is—
> from his example—to learn to have faith in that great
> truth of the Christian life, that "the Lord guides a
> man safely in the way he should go," and to be un-
> conditionally obedient to His holy will in every in-
> cident in our life . . .

The bishop then outlined the three major unexpected turns which had occurred in the Metropolitan's life: his going to Alaska after first dismissing the very idea, his election to the episcopacy after losing his wife, and his elevation to the See of Moscow, "as unexpected to him as it was to all of us." "How beyond human comprehension this was," Ambrose continued,

is shown by the following event. Not long before the death of Metr. Philaret of blessed memory, Abp. Innocent wrote from Blagoveshchensk-on-Amur asking that he provide him refuge in his old age in one of Moscow's monasteries—probably in order to pass the final years of his life retired among educated society and scholarly people. Philaret turned down this request on the grounds that as the founder of new churches, Innocent ought to place his bones atop the field of his activity. But then, some years later, Innocent appeared in Moscow, not in retirement, but as Philaret's successor. This reminiscence will not be offensive to the great memory of Metr. Philaret if we recall the Lord's words: "As high as the heavens are above the earth, so high are My ways and thoughts above yours" (Is. 55:9).

The bishop then continued:

But what connection can we find between his earlier missionary activity and his service in the See of Moscow? Simply recall the establishment soon after his arrival here of the Orthodox Missionary Society in Moscow. This Society as it developed over nine years under this great missionary's presidency is utterly unlike any other organization bearing similar name. This is what has marked its existence: the Orthodox people of Russia have understood what mission is, where it is to be found among us, what inhibits its activities and how it can be enlivened. Mission sites have multiplied. Missionaries are

better provided for. Besides over 2,000 natives being
baptized every year now, others are arriving, 3,000
at a time, in order to prepare for baptism. The power
and tide of Islamic propaganda has been swept aside.
Missionaries now have at their disposal sums which
previously were unimaginable. Most important of
all, however, the *people* are becoming accustomed to
consider it their *sacred duty* to aid in the work of
spreading and establishing the Orthodox Faith. Thus
Metr. Innocent, led by the Providence of God, has
accomplished here things which in his former activities he was unable even to imagine—and things
which no one but he would have been capable of
doing. This work, whose true value we do not yet
understand, is a worthy crown upon his missionary
activities.

The preacher summarized Innocent's other achievements in Moscow with which we are already familiar, and
then concluded with these words:

Metr. Innocent's labors and services belong to
history. They cannot be described as fully as they
should be in a short sermon.

Farewell, our kind, gentle, loving Archpastor
and Father. We thank the Lord for the mercy and
care which He has manifested through your life and
which you, of course, wished us to proclaim to all
when you commanded us to tell how He found you
in the depths of obscurity and poverty, how He gave
you your gifts, how by labors He strengthened and
elevated your soul, how He blessed you to do great
works, how along ineffable paths He led you from
the distant regions of our country to the throne of
the See of Moscow. The Church will honor your
memory. Your country will not forget your services.
And may the Judge on high award you the prize of
victory (2 Tim. 4:8) as a pastor who has fought the
good fight. We pray to the Lord for the repose of

your soul: pray, too, *for us*, since you have boldness before Him, that He will confirm and expand the Orthodox Church which you have served so zealously, that He will preserve from misfortune our country which you loved so warmly, and will multiply in our nation pastors and citizens such as you. Amen.

As the funeral drew to an end, the banners emerged from every cathedral in the Kremlin to form an alley along which Innocent would make his final way upon the earth. When the line was completed, the city shook to the ringing of every bell in the Kremlin, and the hearse set out on its way. People perched in windows, on balconies and on rooftops to catch a glimpse of the coffin as it passed. Men bared their heads in reverence. Outside every church along the way, the clergy came out with icons and candles to bid farewell to their spiritual father. Abp. Macarius met the casket at the railway station, and after a brief requiem Innocent's remains were loaded aboard for the slow trip to the Lavra.

At four o'clock the bells of St. Sergius' house welcomed home the fallen rector of the monastery. At the station in white vestments stood all the clergy, headed by bishops Ambrose and John. The route to the Trinity Cathedral was already lined with monks and other worshipers. A triumphal paschal requiem followed in the cathedral, and once again the church was filled far into the night by lines of the faithful.

Bright Thursday, April 6. The paschal Divine Liturgy was served, and then, the funeral having already been conducted in Moscow, there was nothing more to do than consign Metr. Innocent's holy relics to their final resting place in a tomb prepared in the Church of St. Philaret the Merciful beside that of his beloved predecessor.

Over his simple tomb was raised a crucifix and two inscriptions, one above, the other below:

MAY THE LORD GOD REMEMBER YOUR EPISCOPACY IN HIS KINGDOM, NOW AND EVER AND UNTO AGES OF AGES.

THROUGH THE PRAYERS OF BP. INNOCENT,
O LORD JESUS CHRIST OUR GOD, HAVE
MERCY ON US. AMEN.

EPILOGUE

EPILOGUE

It was inevitable that a man of St. Innocent's breadth of character should be remembered by his contemporaries not in eulogies and speeches alone, but in anecdotes and fond reflections as well. And indeed there are enough of these, and of sufficient variety that to have included them in the chronological narrative would have obscured unnecessarily the essential continuity of his life. In addition, so consistent was the man himself that some stories fit equally well at almost any point during his career. Therefore they have been gathered into a final chapter.

We will begin where we left off, with the remaining excerpts from Bp. Ambrose's funeral sermon quoted above. Having given a history of St. Innocent's life, the speaker went on:

Preserving the direction which he himself indicated for us, we will turn now to the inward side of his life, in order to clarify for ourselves just how his spiritual image was formed along the ways and in the labors which God's Providence indicated to him.

Our late Archpastor was richly gifted by nature. He had a clear, perceptive and versatile mind, despite the fact that his training failed to give him that special propensity and ability for abstract thought and systematization which is gained through higher education (and which, one might note in passing, often robs minds of fruitfulness and sometimes even brings harm to them in real life). Given the work which was his to do, his mind acquired a practical bent with a particular shade of practical creativity and ingenuity. To understand the demands of times

and circumstances, to seek out the means required
to satisfy these, to complete decisively and rapidly
that which he had contemplated, to surmount difficulties, resolve contradictions, mitigate extremes —
all of these together comprised that rare capacity
and uniqueness of mind which expressed itself in
the institutions that he established both in Siberia
and here [i.e., in Moscow].

With such a bent of mind, his views on the
Church and her needs were naturally particular. We
dare say his was an *apostolic* view: He knew what
is required of one who would shepherd the Christian
people, how to approach those in need of spiritual
enlightenment, how to help and comfort people,
how to direct a Christian life according to the canons
of the Church in education, in home life, in society
and in those spiritual exercises which the Church
presents to us for moral success. But when he saw
attempts being made at putting "systematic order"
(so-called) into the Church's life, he was always
struck with fear for her good. He understood pro-
foundly that any human system which with inexor-
able consistency tries to develop some preconceived
principles of ecclesiastical administration will inevitably threaten with extinction all free manifestations
of the human spirit within Christian society, and will
hamper the approach to believing souls of that spirit
of grace which "blows wherever it wishes" (Jn.
3:18).

This explains in our late Archpastor the simplicity of manner which so amazed us—especially in
the beginning. This was not the simplicity of a stupid
man incapable of offering any more than one finds in
him initially. Metr. Innocent's speech was marked
by wit and playfulness for the simple reason that,
with his liveliness of mind, his natural ability forced
its way to the surface and made it unnecessary for
him to restrain himself or to speak with that metho-
dical severity which, in order to achieve, demands

that a person listen to himself and keep himself in
check. Never, in the spacious lands where he spent
the greater and better part of his life, did he grow
accustomed to this. His speech, therefore, breathed a
certain truthfulness and drew you immediately to
him. It gave you a certain boldness and secured your
trust. One had only to touch upon a subject of special
interest to him—particularly one concerning the
Church—and our Archpastor's face and speech (indeed, his every means of communication) were in
a flash transformed. In him one immediately perceived a pastor with a mighty spirit of zeal. His judgments amazed you by the power of his spiritual experience. His word was *powerful.* The make-up of
Metr. Innocent's spiritual personality transcended
the conditions and terms of life in our society: his
heart was pure, his intentions always good; neither
pride nor conceit could master him. He had no use
for seeking praise from people, no reason or object
for pretense before others. He appeared outwardly
exactly what he was within—a direct, and honest,
and sincere, and loving, and well-wishing pastor . . .

Another extensive memoir of St. Innocent (particularly
of his Asian years) was left to us by one Fr. Athanasius Vino-
gradov, who writes:

As a missionary, as a builder of several new dioceses, and finally as a man, Abp. Innocent must
without a doubt be numbered among the most remarkable hierarchs of the Russian Church . . . In all those
who were close to him he left the fondest of memories
and in his subordinates, most sincere feelings of
filial love.

His Eminence was an excellent carpenter. All
the furniture in the priest's house on Kodiak was built
by him. Nor did he abandon his carpentry after
his consecration to the episcopate. As in Sitka, so
too in Yakutsk and Blagoveshchensk (in Amuria)

he maintained in his residence a small carpenter's shop, and every day after dinner he would work for a while with a saw or plane, more it would seem for the exercise than with any particular goal in mind.

Abp. Innocent also loved intellectual work, as is shown by his publications. Scientific abstractions, however, were foreign to his purely practical mind. He was drawn more to practical knowledge. He never let pass an opportunity to enrich his mind with some bit of information. Sailors were his favorites to speak with, for he considered them the most highly educated people of all (being widely traveled and experienced). Because his failing eyes were a source of worry to him, he avoided reading at night by artificial light. And as his days were completely taken up with diocesan responsibilities, he was able to read only little, just the most outstanding articles in theology and secular literature. But the little bit he did read, he read with keen attention, and not as a simple pastime. He liked to talk with others about the contents of the articles or books which he himself had especially enjoyed. He did this, it would seem, in order to improve his grasp of their contents, to understand whatever things in them seemed obscure or doubtful. During his voyages at sea to inspect his island diocese he participated personally in taking observations and watched as the navigator measured the ship's progress. Without his help the sails were neither hoisted nor run down, nor indeed was the ship's course altered. Thus, the archbishop succeeded in acquiring a basic practical knowledge of how to sail.[1] "Give him command of a ship," one

---

[1] This is all the more remarkable considering how elitist Russian seamen were about their trade, as we see from some remarks by St. Innocent himself:

... in general they are honest in their work—when compared with others; industrious, even to the point of pedantry. This is widely known. But this very honesty and precision in their work makes them so arrogant (this is the case—and inevitably so—in unenlightened people) that they consider themselves better than and above everyone

navigator in Sitka once told me, "and he would make an excellent skipper." Once, as told by N. F. Vereshchagin, a former member of the bishop's choir who more than once accompanied him on his voyages at sea, he was even able to save a ship from sinking. The ship, it seems, left the harbor of Gikhnish and had to pass through one of the Kurile straits. They traveled all night, and at dawn found themselves in dense fog. The bishop awoke and asked immediately, "What's our speed and heading?" The captain informed him of these. "Can you see the rocks surrounding the Kurile Islands yet?" asked Innocent. "We should just about be upon them, you know. The current is strong here, or hadn't you noticed?" The captain was preparing to offer an objection, but the bishop hurriedly dressed and went up on deck. He looked around and asked the captain to change course. No sooner was this done than the fog lifted just enough to see in the distance the very rocks which the bishop had feared. The ship had been on a direct course for them and would surely have been broken to bits had the captain hesitated even a few minutes in changing course.

With his diligence and inquisitiveness, all His Eminence did was marked by extreme neatness—some would say bordering on pettiness. As he received papers and letters through the mail, he always opened them personally and with extreme care so as to avoid ruining the envelope. These in turn were not thrown away but placed on his writing desk

---

else. Furthermore, by reason of their education and the type of work they do, they grow accustomed to commanding everyone and everything by the highest forms of despotism. Indeed, a ship at sea is their city, their kingdom, their world. And the captain is king. Therefore, subordination—even a shadow of subordination—to anyone in another sector is unbearable to them. Having lived away from society and moving for the most part in the circle of those trained as they have been, they become extremely one-sided, and their views—no matter what they might be—become axioms for them (especially if approved by the Nakhimovs and Rikords [famous Russian navigators]).

where, if still in good condition, they were turned inside out and reused in place of a new one when he
sent out his own papers and letters. He would simply
write the address on the clean side of the envelope.
But if an envelope had been ruined, he used it for
making rough notes. Likewise, he always sealed his
own letters, and in order that the seal not break
in the mail, he always shielded it with a specially-
cut slip of paper.

Even more amazing was his care of writing pens.
To prevent rust he always wiped them carefully
clean on a cloth—but this was the least of it. When,
after long use, a pen had grown dull, he never threw
it away, but tried to sharpen it on the whetstone
which was included for this purpose in his writing
set. One steel nib could thus serve him an entire
month. Such care shown his writing materials was
not at all the result of stinginess—one could hardly
suspect His Eminence of this. It was, in fact, the result of accuracy: and why waste even the most incon-
sequential item if it can still be of service?

Needless to say, in the administration of his diocese, he manifested the same tireless activity com-
bined with extreme accuracy and prudence. To
characterize him in this respect, I shall relate a
single incident from my own ministry.

In 1859 a new rector was appointed to Yakutsk
who lacked experience in seminary matters (and of
accounting in particular). The dean, too, was a young
man, utterly unfamiliar with how to manage the
books. The year passed uneventfully, 1860 arrived,
and a financial report was compiled and submitted
to the archbishop. He, knowing the administration's
inexperience, informed the rector that he had decided
to give it a preliminary checking of his own. He
asked for all the ledgers and documentation and
found a good number of errors and irregularities.
So, wishing to teach the rector correct accounting
procedures, the archbishop ordered him to come

daily to his residence where in front of him he personally checked the documents, books and accounts, pointing out all the errors and making him correct them. Under the archbishop's direction the entire report was recompiled. This practical course in bookkeeping lasted a full month, and to be sure, it was no easy time for the rector. Often as he left the archbishop he was covered with perspiration and his face was drained of color. Admittedly, as a teacher, the archbishop was not entirely composed. The rector had to endure numerous reproaches and remarks, but the lessons were not in vain. The next year's books and accounts were faultlessly compiled, and the archbishop was unable to find even the slightest mistake. Turning to the rector with a smile he said, "With all my stern comments you were probably angry with me often enough last year, but now you see for yourself that they weren't unprofitable to you. If I hadn't checked your accounts, you would probably have commited the same errors and irregularities again this year, and the Auditing Committee would have been all over you with inquiries and remarks. You might even have gotten yourself into serious trouble."

In writing his own important papers, the archbishop employed special, and rather original methods. First, he would jot down his thoughts in pencil on scraps of paper, envelopes etc., without any particular plan or order. These scattered thoughts he would then transfer, so to speak, onto a clean sheet of paper in ink, again with no real, serious reworking. Rarely at this stage did he include marks of punctuation. A final editing was made as he rewrote it for a third time, adding punctuation where appropriate. (Occasionally he remained unsatisfied even with this third editing and then reworked and wrote it a fourth time. A threefold editing was, however, his customary procedure.) This is why all of Abp. Innocent's papers — while not distin-

guished by any particular eloquence — still bear in
them the stamp of deliberate choice in every word
and phrase.

More than once was I amazed by Abp. Innocent's
prudence in making decisions. With great insight was
he able to forsee even the most remote consequences
of his every action. The salaries he set, for instance,
were small, but for this very reason he enjoyed
giving out bonuses from time to time. He reasoned
thus: give a large salary and most people will spend
the very last cent, setting nothing aside for a rainy
day. Thus, there is little sense in raising salaries.
Occasional bonuses are an entirely different matter,
however. Should someone have accummulated debts
over two or three years, he will then pay them off,
while should he have managed to live within his
salary, he will lay his bonus money away for a rainy
day. Bonuses were normally distributed on the fifteenth of November, the date of his consecration to
the episcopate. This was usually a day of impatience
for those who served in the seminary: Would there
be an envelope for them this morning from the archbishop with a bonus?

Another incident: in 1842 some 10,000 rubles
was put at His Eminence's disposal for the construction of a wooden building to house the seminary
in New Archangel. His Eminence turned to the Russian-American Company with the proposal that it
undertake construction of the building under the
following conditions: he would give the Company
4000 rubles as soon as the building was founded,
and the remaining 6000 a year later (i.e. at its completion, during final touches and painting of the
floors). Should the seminary be transferred elsewhere, the Company would then be obliged to take
the building at a price 5% per annum less than the
original, counting from the date of first repairs. The
Company agreed.

Twelve years passed and an ukase came transferring the seminary to Yakutsk, and what happened? This: the New Archangel Seminary's money was routinely on deposit with the management of the Russian-American Company in St. Petersburg, earnings 5% compound interest per annum from the date of deposit. Thus, while negotiations over the building of a seminary dragged on, a year passed and 500 rubles was earned. The building itself took three years 'til payment was finally settled, and at the time of settlement with the Company for the seminary building there had been 1500 rubles in interest accrued on the building funds. Twelve years later, at his [Innocent's] request, the seminary was allowed to move to Yakutsk, and according to the agreement the Company paid 7000 rubles for the building, upon which interest of 2800 rubles had built up. In all, some 10,000 rubles was received from the Company, and so the seminary's twelve years in that building were spent gratis. Had someone else been in charge of the seminary, there would probably have remained nothing of the construction funds (or an utterly insignificant amount of money).

In general the archbishop enjoyed the ability to obtain money almost out of nowhere for various diocesan needs. One particular concern of his was the plight of clerical orphans. At his enthronement in the See of New Archangel the local trust fund had no reserves at all. What did he do? In addition to the normal collections for the fund he tried other means as well. For instance, having no chapel in his own home he had to go to the cathedral every day for liturgy. On a given weekday when it was appointed that a prayer be offered for the tsar, the archbishop watched attentively to see if the celebrating priest would forget it. If he did forget, no sooner had the altar curtain been pulled shut at the Liturgy's conclusion than the bishop from his own pocket pulled five rubles for the trust fund and penalized each member of the cathedral staff a like amount to benefit the same fund. By such methods he mangaged quickly, and despite a poverty of sources, to amass capital in the New Archangel trust fund sufficient to ease considerably the plight of orphans throughout the Diocese of Kamchatka.

He did the same—but better and more quickly—in Yakutsk. In the early 1860's he requested permission to collect from the Yakuts monetary support for the clergy. In the year it took to secure this, some 20,000 rubles was collected from them, and when final permission came for the collection, the archbishop gathered the clergy all together and said, "You know, Fathers, last year passed with no real difficulties, so wouldn't you like to offer your own support for the past year to aid the trust fund? It's *your* orphans, after all, who'll be thankful in the future!" The clergy agreed and adequate capital was thus accrued in the Yakutsk trust fund. The bishop allowed the clergy themselves to disperse the funds through special delegates and in accordance with rules compiled by him and confirmed by the Holy Synod. Thanks to this the widows and orphans in the Diocese of Yakutsk receive aid unsurpassed in any other diocese—and aid given not only to those who remain within Yakutia, but to those who move to other dioceses as well. I am amazed at his foresight and resourcefulness in financial matters and frequently have said that under different circumstances he would probably have made an excellent Minister of Finances.

The archbishop's relations with subordinate clergy were permeated by a spirit of love and paternal condescension, and often with a hint of his own brand of humor, one which was not only unoffensive but which indeed lent a certain charm to his speech. I think that to characterize him satisfactorily in this area I need but relate several incidents from my own ministry under his direction.

Soon after my marriage and ordination to the

priesthood, I was serving as inspector of the seminary. I went to him one Saturday with my weekly
status report on the seminary, which he read through
and then turned to me with his usual kind smile.
"Well, Father *In*-spector," he said, "I hear you used
up all your money on your wedding and got yourself
into debt as well."

"Yes, Your Eminence."

"OK. I'd like to give you a bonus, but only
under certain conditions. Will you meet them?"

"Why not, if they're easily met?"

"Don't worry. My conditions are very light.
First, your hair doesn't look right. Buy yourself a
comb and some hair tonic."

"I have a comb—here it is. But to tell the truth,
I don't like using hair tonic at all. It gets your hair
all greasy and stains your clothes—especially a
priest's."

"OK. I'll show you what you do. When you take
a bath, wash your head and slick it down good with
plain butter. Then just lie for a while somewhere
warm. The butter will evaporate, there'll be no odor,
and your hair will be as soft as silk."

I promised that I would heed his advice.

"Now here's my second condition. You're near-
sighted. You've got to wear glasses or you'll lose
your eyesight."

"I tried that, Your Eminence, while I was still
a student, but I quit. They just weren't right for my
eyes, and after wearing them a week I felt a pain
in my eyes that I'd never had before. And after all,
I'm not all *that* near-sighted that I can't read a book.
True, at a distance, I see poorly, but as I see it, that's
good—there's less temptation!"

"No. You're still young. What will old age say?
Take care of your eyes now. Don't read so much by
artificial light, and I still say—get yourself some
glasses."

"Yes, Your Eminence. I'll give them another try."

"Fine. Now, here's the third condition. When you serve the Liturgy, your phelonion is always slipping to one side. That doesn't look very nice."

"What can I do, Your Eminence? I don't own any that were sewn to my measurements, and you can see for yourself my size and build."

"You know, son, I was lean and slender once, too. But my phelonion never slipped off my shoulders."

"You've forgotten one detail, Your Eminence. In your youth you probably didn't have my narrow shoulders."

"Okay. Tell the sacristan to sew a phelonion to fit your size and 'portliness.' "

"Yes, Your Eminence."

Such was the archbishop's fatherly tone whenever he spoke with his subordinates. He loved a joke, and to laugh wholeheartedly over a funny story or astute reply. In his letters from Amuria to one of our archpriests in Yakutsk, he would discuss all diocesan matters meticulously and then send greetings and his blessing to the "*In*-spector" and to "Gabby." He explained to me this strange spelling of inspector in the following way.

"What does 'inspector' mean?" he asked once.

"Supervisor, overseer," I replied.

"No. That's incorrect," the archbishop laughed. " '*Dignus*' means 'worthy,' '*indignus*'—'unworthy;' '*specto*' means 'look,' 'see'; so '*in*-spector' means 'un-seer.' " Right?" Thus, through a philological explanation [2] of the meaning of the word "inspector," he was making a joke about my near-sightedness—and, perhaps, was hinting at some things which I had overlooked during my inspections.

The archbishop loved Fr. Paul ("Gabby") for his intelligence, his humility and his other good

---

[2] A deliberately erroneous one, however.

qualities, but he joked about his extreme reticence to speak. Thus he was always called "Gabby," while the seminary doctor in Sitka who could never keep silent in company became "Mum." This kind of nickname given in jest and causing no one to take offense lent special charm to the archbishop's relations with subordinates.

"Just how many children do you have, Mr. Over-Secretary of the Chancery?" he once inquired of a department chief known for the large size of his family. The chief was hard-pressed to say offhand. It had never occurred to him to count his children—and indeed, why should he? He saw them every day and knew them all by name. He didn't wish to get it wrong, so he started counting them on his fingers behind his back. The archbishop saw what he was up to and pressured him to hurry. "Don't count 'em on your fingers. Just tell me straight out."

The chief replied, "Ummmm. . . . eight."

"You've probably mixed them up. Now count them on your fingers." They began the count and sure enough it turned out there were nine.

"See? Right, wasn't I? Ha! Ha! Ha!"

The chief began to blush, but the archbishop smiled and said, "No need to blush. I know from experience that fathers of large families never know how many children they have. That's why I asked you how many children you had."

I recall that once in 1858 the inspector was invited to the home of an archpriest (now deceased) for a stroganin dinner.[*] The archpriest was a very good host, and always located the best and tastiest fish for this dish. The inspector accepted the invitation and was with great relish looking forward to the stroganin, when at two P.M. he received word from the archbishop that he, the rector and all members of the chancery were to come to his house that evening at six o'clock. Nothing could be done about

[*] A Siberian fish specialty.

it; he had to go. Neither, however, did he wish to
forego his stroganin dinner, so he arranged with the
archpriest (a member of the chancery) that at the
first opportunity they would slip away from the archbishop and rush home for dinner.

In the bishop's living room the samovar stood
on a table and he invited them to be seated. Tea was
brought in and they chatted about this and that as
they drank. The archbishop ordered the tea service
removed and then brought out a book.

"Fathers," he said, "this book—it's . . . *a secret.*
I want to familiarize you with its contents and to
get from you your opinions on it. It describes the
deeds of our good-for-nothing chanceries and consistories. Listen."

("Oh well, so much for our stroganin!" we
thought.)

He began to read, and the more he did the more
and more engrossed we became, until finally we for-
got completely about our stroganin. It seems this
was a book about the white and black clergy in Russia, and quite naturally leveled the widest possible
range of accusations against consistory life. The archbishop smiled as he listened to the most contra-
dictory opinions which we offered concerning the
contents of the book. Then, when he arrived at a
characterization of episcopal government, he turned
to us and said, "So far, Fathers, the author has been
describing *your* doings. Now let's hear what he has
to say about *us.* Doesn't spare us a bit; seems he dres-
ses us down with even greater relish than he did you.
Let's listen." Our attention redoubled and our ex-
clamations and amazement were endless. We had
never heard the likes of this. The archbishop was
exultant, and a kind smile covered his face the whole
time he was reading.

The reading concluded at midnight. We were
about to leave, but the archbishop invited us to dine
with him. During dinner the conversation never

flagged for a moment, and we left content, having forgotten altogether about our stroganin. And we rejoiced that the author of this book would not be able to find much material here in Yakutsk. There had been no such administrative abuses or abnormalities in relations between diocesan authorities and subordinate clergy during the archbishop's tenure. (I speak from my conscience, as one not privy to diocesan affairs.)

The archbishop was not so much a boss as a father who loved his children and took an active interest in all their problems, including family matters. He took a particularly lively interest in widowed priests. As soon as he heard that this grief had overtaken a priest — especially if he was still young — Innocent would hurry to write and comfort him like a father. If he heard of behavior unbefitting the priestly calling, he always tried by word or letter to reason before resorting to administrative penalties. He did not enjoy formal inquests and trials, nor did he like it when the clergy denounced one another to him. Under previous administrations Yakutia was renowned for intrigue, but under Abp. Innocent this became unheard of. All deans of clergy were directed that in resolving quarrels and enmity among the clergy they were to proceed as though they were all one family—rather than resorting to formal complaints. In punishing the guilty the archbishop's primary concern was always to bring them to their senses rather than to satisfy some cold, dry justice. Then, if all other measures aimed at reforming a priest failed, the following approach was often taken:

Seeing that a significant number of clergy in the region were natives of Irkutsk—since in times past, when Yakutia had been part of that diocese, the bishops of Irkutsk had punished offending priests by banishing them there—Abp. Innocent routinely summoned offenders in and suggested that they re-

turn home to Irkutsk. "*I* don't want to be your un-
doing," he would say. "So go home. Here's some
traveling money. Maybe at home you'll straighten
out, but if you don't, you'll only have yourself to
blame. I warn you, though, the Bishop of Irkutsk is
a strict one. He won't let you go on acting like this
without punishment."

A single example will suffice to illustrate Abp.
Innocent's leniency. A priest serving in Okhotsk
surrendered to his weakness for alcohol. The archbishop knew him well. He was a former director of
his choir and the husband, moreover, of his own
god-daughter. He was, therefore, for a long time
unwilling to believe him guilty of this. Finally he
was convinced of the priest's vice and summoned
him to Yakutsk, where he settled him in the same
monastery in which he himself lived. Even there,
however, the priest did not foresake his weakness,
and finally it came to the point that he once drank
so heavily that it caused a high fever. A doctor was
summoned and succeeded in restoring him to life.
"I think this should bring Fr. M. to his senses," said
the archbishop. "If not, I'm afraid there's just no
hope of correcting him." A week had not yet passed
before he was drunk again. The archbishop felt
sorry for the priest's large family— and especially
for his own god-daughter—and so, in order to spare
them he assigned the priest to a tiny village far from
the city where it would be extremely difficult for
him to obtain vodka. But the priest had grown accustomed to city life and did not find this place to
his tastes. He requested, therefore, that Abp. Innocent transfer him to Irkutsk. His first request was
turned down, so the priest sent his wife into town
to make this same request of her godfather. "Okay,"
he replied, "if *you* want to go to Irkutsk, go ahead.
I won't stop you. Just remember, though, you'll no
sooner arrive there than your husband will be de-
frocked." And indeed, this is precisely what hap-

pened. For the whole time he worked in the Diocese of Irkutsk to the day he died, he was forbidden to serve as a priest.

In order to end in Yakutia the corruption so common in all chanceries as a result of the miserable salaries which were paid, Abp. Innocent from the very day he took over the diocese decided to make use of diocesan funds to ease the financial burden of those who served in the chancery and consistories. He summoned the chief of the chancery in Yakutsk and asked him, "What's your salary?"

"Five rubles a month," he replied.

"Do you have a large family?"

"There are ten of us."

"And with a family like *that* you can survive on a salary of five rubles?"

"We get along, somehow, Your Eminence."

"No. No matter how cheap it might be to live in Yakutsk, I cannot believe that with your family you can live on just five rubles. You probably receive the customary 'offerings' from the clergy, right? I don't like it, and I won't permit it! So, to deliver you from the temptation of extorting money, I'm setting your salary at 25 rubles a month. Just make sure you drop your old habits. Okay?"

"Yes, Your Eminence. And thank you!"

With a bishop so concerned over the needs of his staff, is it any wonder that they did not dare turn to the abuses normal in other dioceses?[4]

Two examples from his Moscow years illustrate further St. Innocent's humility and pastoral love.

A young seminary graduate came to see him concerning his petition to enter the Academy. He stood before the metropolitan, coat unbuttoned and fidgeting with his watch chain. Innocent with surprise considered the young man's flippant

[4] Once he proposed (or at least mused about) giving bishops ("and especially archimandrites") less money in order better to finance married priests who have large families, and to multiply the number of dioceses. "But if I weren't already in this order," he quips, "I'd likely change my song!"

behavior for a while and then said, "I've sent your petition and my decision on to Bp. Leonid. You can find out the results from him. But I must forewarn you: I have no right to contend with you, since like you I'm only a seminary graduate —we're equals, as it were. But your *next* stop about your petition, don't forget, won't be to just a *seminary* graduate but to an *academy* graduate— a Master of Theology. So when you go, I'd advise you to button up your coat!"

The metropolitan once received a written complaint from a provincial priest against his son-in-law (who was also a priest) claiming that the latter, in agreeing to marry his daughter in exchange for obtaining the parish, had also agreed to give him a room in the parish house. The younger priest then grew disrespectful, and as a result a conflict developed between him and his wife, for she was split in her loyalties between the two. The metropolitan instructed the local dean to investigate the matter and report his findings. It turned out that the older priest was at fault. He had tried actively to turn his daughter against her husband. Innocent summoned all three parties in and dressed down the old priest soundly, ordering him to move out and leave his son-in-law in peace. He then addressed the woman in a fatherly tone, begging her to ask her husband's forgiveness. He then made them kiss three times in his presence before blessing their future life together.

Another characterization of the saint, one quite different in its emphases from the others yet agreeing with them concerning Innocent's great humility, is provided by Bernard Struve.[5] It deals with a meeting with Nicholas Muravev in Petropavlovsk in 1849. He writes:

> It is not for me to describe the lofty mind and Christian virtues of the "Apostle of the North" as he was already then being called in the foreign press. His unusual labors and feats are universally known. During Muravev's stay in Petropavlovsk he held long discussions and consultations with him every eve-

ning, and one of the most immediate results of these was the joining of Yakutia to the Aleutian episcopal see . . . and the appointment of V. S. Zavoiko as military governor of Kamchatka.

Someone familiar with local conditions had to be chosen for this position (not to speak of all the other qualities and conditions needed) and Muravev wavered in his choice between I. V. Vonliar-Liazarskii and V. S. Zavoiko. Bp. Innocent knew them both well, but this archpastor did not like to express his opinions about others. He carefully avoided this, not out of reticence or fear of some unfortunate consequences, but as a result of his natural humility. He did not trust his own judgment and was afraid of making a mistake.

For a long time Muravev endeavored to learn his opinion of the two candidates that he had in mind . . . Finally Bp. Innocent leaped out of his armchair, stood up to his full height and with impatience evident in his tone said, "Why are you provoking me? I'll not hold up my hand for Liazarskii, but Zavoiko I'll defend with both hands—and my whole body, and my soul." This decisive opinion, from such a generally evasive but doubtlessly highly-experienced person, showed Muravev immediately to whom his decision must go.

Another aspect of this same humility and simplicity we see in an incident which occurred in Amuria, as the archbishop was on his way once to visit his family in Nikolaevsk. He was traveling quietly down the shore when he reached the town of De-Kastri. Suddenly word went out that he was there. The people flocked to him with shouts of joy, seeking to receive his blessing. Patiently he stood there and gave it to each and everyone who came but forbade them to pay any special attention to him personally. Although he was in a hurry, at their request he spent three days with them, visiting with everyone in the village. Each evening he would sit in a tent on the shore, and with wind and waves providing a

ST. INNOCENT

natural background for his material, he told them fascinating stories about his many years of travels. On the third day, just as he was about to leave, the weather suddenly turned foul, and the commander's wife, Praskovia Sleptsova, hurriedly fashioned for him a makeshift oil-cloth raincoat—patterned after the cassock he was wearing—to serve him on the way. Such was the love which he inspired that it was only with great reluctance and sorrow that the people of De-Kastri gave up their archpastor.

We end this series of reminiscences with tales by two men who describe St. Innocent's knowledge of the sciences. The first, Fr. Simeon Kazanskii, a cleric who served with St. Innocent in Amuria, describes him first as very much a real monk, simple in his daily life, casual about how he dressed, eating just enough to sustain his enormous labors. He then records:

> The archbishop was very kind—and even more *reasonable*. Rarely did he laugh, but even more rarely did he raise his voice at his subordinates. He never leaped for joy, considering unhappiness to be an inevitable manifestation of the [fallen] human condition. The profundity of his mind was equalled by his industriousness, and there was scarcely a trade of which he did not have at least a basic knowledge. He was good enough in mathematics, astronomy, physics, chemistry and the natural sciences to make one wonder involuntarily how he might have managed to acquire such an extensive and versatile knowledge and to have put it to work.

The priest then offers an example of this. Once, aboard the clippership *Gaidamak* an officer was determined to confound the archbishop by showing him a photograph, something which in those parts was still quite a rarity. Innocent took the photograph in his hand, looked it over carefully, and then proceeded to explain to the amazed seaman the precise chemical processes involved in producing such an image, listed off several of Europe's leading photographers, and outlined in brief the history of the art. One would have thought that he had dedicated his whole life to nothing else.

Another naval officer, Alexis Rydalev, who had spent a good deal of time traveling with the archbishop, tells a story which shows just how large St. Innocent's reputation had grown among men of the sea. He once complained to Fr. Gromov that his pocket watch had stopped and as there was no one in Petropavlovsk capable of fixing it, asked if it would be appropriate to turn the matter over to the bishop.

"I don't know," answered Fr. Gromov, "whether it would be fitting to remind a bishop that he's a master watchmaker. Plus, he probably lacks the tools with him to fix it."

Rydalev, thus discouraged, decided to use his wits. He invited the bishop to his home for dinner and left the watch prominently displayed on a chest of drawers where Innocent could hardly fail to see it. Sure enough, the bishop came up and looked at the watch, allowing his host subtly to make his request.

Innocent spent a few short minutes examining the timepiece more closely, then turned around and held it up, now ticking, by its chain. "Alexis Nikiforovich," he laughed, "you must know—and tell everyone else as well—that a watch will never work unless you wind it!"